BREAK-UP BREAKTHROUGH

& LEARNING TO LOVE AGAIN

Jo-Anne Weiler, M.A., R.M.F.T., R.C.C.

Dear Linda
With so much gratitude
for the love you share
in the community.
love JoAnne

Published by FastPencil

Published by FastPencil
307 Orchard City Drive
Suite 210
Campbell CA 95008 USA
info@fastpencil.com
(408) 540-7571
(408) 540-7572 (Fax)
http://www.fastpencil.com

The anecdotes in this book are based on a compilation of client stories in Jo-Anne Weiler's clinical practise. These are compilations of characters and any resemblance to true people is purely coincidental. In all cases, actual client stories are held for a lifetime of confidentiality. The names of clients mentioned in this book are all fictitious. The insights and information from the composite or compilation of stories will help you have a better experience of loving your future partner. These insights will provide a useful road map to better understand ways you can choose, develop, and grow true love consciously.

Printed in the United States of America.

First Edition

For my husband Joe,
you are the love of my life.

~

For my children Justin and Ashley,
you are the joys of my life.

~

For my parents,
I wish you had read this book.

~

For everyone who has had their heart broken,
you can breakthrough and learn to love again
…Life is counting on you!

Contents

FOREWORD

I've always believed we are stronger in our world the more we count on each other. Our connections help us move through tough times and be healthy human beings. Let there be ease in our connections because there are times life challenges. I have been in clinical practice working with individuals and couples for 14 years and what I do best is help people rediscover their own joy through this core belief in relationships and the value of a positive psychology. I have a Masters in Clinical Psychology. My training has been eclectic through Family Systems, Gestalt, Cognitive Behavioral, and Emotionally Focused relational models of treatment. I am a Registered Clinical Counselor, Registered Marriage & Family Therapist, and Professional Life Coach.

I believe that just like the many hundreds of clients I have worked with over the years, you are already whole, complete and have everything you need within you to live your best life. You just may not feel that way right now because you are enduring a really tough time. I love working with people like you who are moving through change, striving for ease, searching for a fresh perspective that will give you a return of calm and personal control— key feeling states that will lead you back into love again. The impact of reading this book and in discovering you are already whole, healthy, loveable and powerful is that when you feel better, you will be able to help others feel better too. And according to 2013 United Nations World Happiness Report, you may even live longer if you are happy. The World needs you and all the ways you contribute when you are in your most caring powerful loving version of yourself.

I know sometimes life takes unpredictable turns and it doesn't always evolve in ways we expect. I have been through tough challenges and discovered pathways to resiliency, support, and found ways you can integrate meaning from deep loss. Relationship endings can feel, in varying degrees, like a death of a dear friend or the collapse of a whole city. For a while you may feel sucked into a nightmare you can't wake up from. Like Dorothy in the Wizard of Oz, you may feel vacuumed into a tornedo, which lifts every predictable part of your life as you know it and sweeps your universe into a funnel you think you have no control in. The thing about tornedos is they have unpredictable twists and turns and they can turn anything into deadly projectiles.

Though many chase these storm systems, I suspect you would like to feel your feet back on the ground again. Don't lose your ruby shoes or your rose colored glasses. You are going through a normal process in life and many others like you have gone through it too! Has anyone not gone through a breakup at some point in his or her life? It will get a whole lot better. You may even discover that when the dust settles and you regain your footing, your life will become more enriched than you ever thought possible. This book will be your call to action. Its purpose is to help your life get better faster. You don't need to live a life in any more pain than you have already experienced. You deserve to be happy. Through the pain, believe it or not, there will be great gain.

If you are struggling with the anguish and devastation of a relationship ending, this book will give you a chance to regain a more empowered way out of the storm and unbearable sadness. If someone you have loved has suddenly quit on your shared dream, or if you yourself have left your relationship because the shared dream has become more of a nightmare, this book will help you shift perspectives. This book is your breakup breakthrough guide.

It is so challenging when you have built your life on the dream of - 'sharing the rest of your days together' and then everything falls apart. You can easily lose your center and feel lost in the intensity of emotions – fear of being on your own, fear that you will never find another love, fear that you will never again be at home in your heart. Your head may be spinning with anger because you resent, regret, and can't change the past. In relationship endings, your desperate inner self can take over to the extent that you are no longer free to make your own choices, much less maintain your own identity. You may notice yourself grabbing for answers, and even seeking rescue, while you inhabit your own dark steps through fear, anger, regret, sadness, and anxiety. This is a horrible life experience. I know this all too well because I have worked with hundreds of clients just like you, over thousands of hours strategically moving them through this pain. The major breakthrough is discovering freedom when you gain a deeper understanding of who you are at your core. Love expands when you invite your 'whole self' back into the light. You aren't broken, flawed or unlovable. There may be things you wish you had done differently in your past relationship. The more you can curiously discuss and learn from your past relationship, the less your own bad habits will repeat in your future. The less you feel victimized by your past, the more empowered you will be in your future. The better you feel about who you are, the more capacity you will have to love again.

Elementary and high school curriculums do not include enough learning about emotional health, and matters of the heart. Yet, later in life, we come to know that learning how to love well is a critically important life skill. Choosing your life partner wisely may be the most important exercise of your judgment in your lifetime.

The experience of a healthy love is a lynchpin in the evolution of your soul. To reach a point of being able to fully trust the way that your light leads you on the path of true love, takes more than a little practice. But, over time, if you know what you are doing, you can make your way with ever-increasing confidence and self-assurance. I don't claim to be some kind of Delphic Oracle of Love, with knowledge of all of the secrets of how to love your partner well. But I do have some useful strategies and decision-making tools about how to manage the experience of going through the passages of love in your life. The thing about tornados is that at the center of them, there is so much calm you can apparently hear a pin drop. At the eye (center) of a tornedo you can observe the World changing and yet powerfully you can remain safe and curious while you let the pieces fall where they will. In fact, you can even click your heals three times and know you are at home with yourself after all.

I will refer to 'client stories' in this book from time to time. These are compilations of characters and any resemblance to true people is purely coincidental. Actual client stories are always held in the 'vault' for a lifetime of confidentiality. The names of clients mentioned in this book are all fictitious. I think the insights and information from the composite or compilation of stories will help you have a better experience of loving your future partner. I am convinced that these insights will provide a useful road map to better understand ways you can choose, develop, and grow true love consciously.

I am so glad you have picked up this book. I am excited for you that you will be able to finally close the door on your past relationship. It's a brave first step you are making towards a new life that can fulfill your dreams. At this point, you probably can't see yourself ever being happy again. And yet you are curious to discover ways you can gain a fresh perspective. It's hard to believe you have everything you need already. Think of this book as a map to access all the wisdom, strength and potential within you. You have had it all this time.

There are three parts to this book. In Part One, I will discuss how you can examine some of the common patterns that you may recognize in your earlier partner relationships. You will discover step-by-step ways that will help you move through your grief process, re-frame, re-story and re-build your life towards an experience of better love. In Part Two, you will begin to understand yourself in your own emotional style. You will discover how your spiritual learning through family, friends and significant relationships shows up in patterns of engagement. Part Three leads you into romance, sex and love again. This of course, starts with you! We all know something about how to love. But do we know enough to navigate through and out of not-quite-right relationships towards one that is just right for us?

The goal of this book is simply to help you love better. If you are able to love better, your life will have more joy, happiness, and fulfillment. And surely the world will be a better place if that happens. So let's change our world, one better love at a time! The final chapters of this book are designed to help you set up your own mission statement and your own vision for what you will recognize as your "true love"— your One.

My girl friend suggested that this book should come complete with a soothing tea and a bottle of wine. Love that! Her email this morning reminds me of my deep gratitude in friends who have continued to show up in the process of 'Breakup Breakthrough' coming together through title changes, chapter movement, and topics needing inclusion. I really can't begin to express how thankful I am for the gracious inputs from first readers Maria Le Rose, Stacey Brown, Julie Bernard, and Melanie Graham. All of who provided key edits in the shaping and the flow of 'Breakup Breakthrough'. Additionally, I contacted every client whose story is woven into the content and 'compilation' of clinical examples in this book. Their permission was always at the ready over and over again. Every client responded with some form of "I'm so happy to think that my experience will help someone else", "Please go ahead and use my story," "I love to think my story might help someone else going through what I went through!" My clients' generosity of spirit in contributing their life experiences and learning has been so meaningful to me. As my clients continued to get behind this book and its intention to help people like them avoid the post breakup pitfalls they experienced, I felt inspired to the end. Finally I want to thank my family: my two children Justin and Ashley, my two-step children Berkley and Patrick, and especially my husband Joe. Joe offered many helpful suggestions for improvement at various stages of the writing of this book as well as consistent support and encouragement along the way. This book has definitely been the beneficiary of many generous hearts.

PART 1

CLOSING THE DOOR

CHAPTER 1

PUT YOUR BREAK-UP BEHIND YOU

Part One of this book is all about you closing the door from your past relationship. Its time to move on as a whole person and open a new door towards a life you will love. In this section you are guided through ways you can better focus on what you can learn from your past about yourself and about your loved one in order for you to better apply this learning to a future relationship with the right one for you.

In my clinical practice, I have worked with a lot of people who have felt degrees of desperation, aloneness, lovability and loss. I'd risk saying it is by design that break ups hurt so much. If they didn't, you wouldn't be motivated to develop yourself and not repeat the same painful patterns in the future. We are all creatures of habit and this first chapter is to help you be honest with yourself and who you are when it comes to loving relationships. I know you don't want to feel like crap any longer. That's why you are reading this!

There are three reasons it's hard to move forward from a painful ending:

1. It's painful and pain takes time to heal,
2. We are creatures of habit and we tend to choose the same partner over and over again,
3. Sadly, its human nature to blame others for our pain.

And when you blame others for your experience in life, you make yourself a victim or at a least passive participant your life. Have you ever noticed a friend who has gone through a breakup, start a new relationship with someone who is just like his or her previous partner? To gain insight about how to set yourself up for love consciously is actually quite easy. If you follow some of the ideas in here you will create a new improved version of you. With your own upgrade, you can choose a new upgrade in partnership too! Yes, living your best life in love always starts with you. And of course there is the part about moving through grief, so you can truly let the past go and avoid carrying a lot of negative energy into your new life to come. No matter who you are with, you will always need to know who you are and how you can improve your body, mind and spirit. If you felt bullied, lonely or caught off guard in your past relationship, you will need to discover how to stand up for yourself, take care of your needs, and be more intentional about relationships your next time around. In the same way that bullies set up political allies to gain social power in communities, beware of unwittingly setting up shame satellites within yourself because you won't let go of a story of failure.

One of my clients 'Buffy' who I recently saw in my practice, left her former husband three years ago because "he was such a bully". 'Buffy' was referred to me from her physician for the treatment of anxiety and to help her overcome burn out at work. What we discovered in our work was that 'Buffy' had ended up in the same position she was in with her marriage. When her marriage ended three years ago, 'Buffy' explained, she had felt so liberated, finally free from the controlling experience of her former husband. 'Buffy' had thought leaving him was her answer to be happy again in her life. This may have been true and it was a brave step she took three years prior, but in fact until 'Buffy' fully understands herself as more confident and deserving, she is prime grade 'A' meat for the next aggressive person who comes along (in this case at her workplace), because deep down she might still hold on to the story that she is a victim. You can't fully close the door to a misfit partnership until you fully integrate your own learning. Even if you are not in contact with the stressful person who was in your life, there are plenty more of the same style of men and women who will naturally fit into the complimentary spaces you haven't filled yourself. 'Buffy' needed to learn about how to set clearer boundaries, and how to feel more empowered with the emotion of anger. She needed to learn how to communicate without being defensive so that she could develop more empathy and insight. Today you can spot 'Buffy' in a room. She is the one who isn't afraid to let her voice be heard. 'Buffy' stands an inch taller and yet she walks with more ease than she has ever known. You are going to become an expert on boundaries, and ways you can name and be curious about all your emotions as you move chapter by chapter through this book.

Experiencing a break up is like getting blistering sunburn and then committing to the need to wear sunscreen. You never intend to get burned when you spend too long in the sun. As your skin blisters and peels, you know you will prepare next time. You know next time to set up properly and get out when you've had enough exposure. Without the pain associated with relationship loss, you wouldn't pay attention to the ways you need to get better at balancing life and love. Without attending to new learning you will get burned over and over again every time you expose yourself to the elements of love and loss. With repeated sunburns you will eventually end up with skin cancer. To not prepare better for love, is to risk developing a type of cancer of the heart. You have a long life ahead of you and lots of love learning to do!

You will be guided to look reflectively at who you have been in your relationships with others in the past. I'll share some of my own experience of the ending of my marriage, as well as my observations of the lives and loves of my siblings, children, friends, and in particular through my observations of clients' experience during my years of professional practice in counseling psychology. They all have provided me with some valuable insights about how to follow a constructive strategy of new self-management before you press your reset.

When your breakup happened, you may have told yourself stories about who you were and who your former partner was in the ending of your relationship. Have you noticed that you generally tend to be a little negative in this painful early stage of your break up? Everyone is. That's normal and it's a good idea to do a lot of journaling to let those negative thoughts go. Let your negative feelings tumble out on the page, no judgment. To close the door to your past relationship, you will need to spend some time in the angst, frustration and grief that surrounds the ending.

It's Time to Start a Journal

Here's how to do that: journal these thoughts on one side of the page, leave the other side of the page blank. Then you can come back to what you wrote a few days later. A few days later, write whatever your perspective is then on the blank page. You'll start to notice the catastrophic thought, "He/she was 'never' there for me", may shift into "Some of the times he/she was missing in action".

You may also notice that your thoughts about yourself may shift too. You may start with writing "I was a really negative partner...no wonder he/she hates me". And then a few days later on the blank side of the page you may find a new softer perspective "I was a little negative some of the time...I can understand how that might have been hard for him/her".

Your psyche wants you to be happy and you will naturally develop a kinder perspective of both you and your former partner with the passage of some time. This journal writing is a great way to start to redirect your thinking towards insights about yourself that you can grow from. It also grows your flexible thinking. It's going to be important to realize that you are choosing your perspectives, your thinking, and therefore your feelings that result.

When you are ready, you may want to ask yourself questions such as:

- What did my past relationship(s) teach me about myself?
- What do I wish I had done differently?

Good questions for a trusted friend might be:

- What do you (my good friend) see as my blind spots?
- What do you (my good friend) hope I will get better at?

And don't forget to balance these inquiries with what you did right:

- What does your friend most admire about who you were in that past relationship?
- What is the most surprising strength you discovered in yourself through your former partner?

These are just some of the questions to start being curious about. Reframing your past negative stories into new learning curves about yourself will help you gain a fresh perspective of how you can get better in your next relationship starting with your relationship with yourself. 'Closing the Door' is designed to help you grieve and release yourself from the tornado entirely. These types of inquiries are the start to you understanding and appreciating your 'whole' self—the good, the bad, the reactive, the needy, the controlling, the martyred, the pleaser, the gentle, the passive, the aggressive, the inspired, the powerful, and the amazing you within. Become friends with 'all' of you. This type of self reflective honesty is kind of like… well you decide what its kind of like. The bottom line is that this time of self-reflection is essential to being able to truly close the door. Focus on who you were, not the deficits of your partner. It's a big mistake to stay in a blame game too long.

Divorce, especially when you have children, is particularly difficult to move forward from. It can feel very overwhelming when you have children because the process of change conflicts with the solid framework of core values you may hold dearly like family and constancy. You can still be a family if you move through the grief process and rise above the politics as much as possible. This transformation of your family will require a healthy dose of mindfulness and patience to get over the moving parts of 'overwhelm'. And if you have children who are counting on your stability, you will need to make sure you are processing the full extent of your regrets, resentments and recollections with someone outside your family who you have high trust and confidence with. This may be a professional. Regrets and resentments are where you may get snagged in the past. You may feel the sense of remorse that percolates from the hunch that you or your partner really blew it in the course of that relationship; that it was just one big mistake you long to correct. The trap that you must avoid in going through a breakup is that you might get stuck in your own dark and anxious fears that tell you that you are not good enough. You may obsess and blame yourself that your failed relationship was 'all' your fault; or even worse, that it was "all" your partner's fault. You may tell yourself that the ending was the result of a clash of cultures with your partner, that difficult economic circumstances or some other projected object of blame caused the breakup. Does that sound like you?

Don't worry. It's natural to go through such a stage. Just don't stay there. In 'Feeling Guilty', you will learn that the longer you stay in this painful state of guilt, remorse, or self-loathing, the more likely this stasis may cause serious damage to your spirit and physical health. In this toxic state, your anxious brain then sends messages that can spread like a virus within your social circles, at your workplace and to your loved ones. There is an anxious energy that others will actually feel coming off you. Our brain is electric and you'll be zapping those around you before you even say hello! That is why it is important for you to do this work. It will be of critical advantage not only for you, but also for those you love.

I once worked with a client 'Abigail' who left her husband 'Ed' because their lifestyles became misfit. This story about them is actually a composite of a host of clients. It's remarkable how commonly these dynamics have shown up in my practice with clients in their mid life, time and time again with family after family! After 'Abigail' and 'Ed's' daughter and, two years later their son, was born and as their two children reached adolescence, 'Ed' became more and more of a homebody and 'Abigail' became more and more of a social butterfly. The tensions between them showed up in bouts of passive aggressive behaviors where 'Ed' would refuse to join 'Abigail' in social events, sometimes refusing to attend things with her at the very last minute. 'Abigail' was angered by her husband's lack of participation in her life. In reaction, 'Abigail' became even more social. Their emotional distance resulted in a massive gap in lifestyle. The bottom line was that they were misfit in their styles of living. As time had gone by, 'Abigail' said she had felt more and more resentful going out to social events on her own. She confessed that 'Ed' had told her he felt lonely spending his evenings at home. Their differences showed up especially when their children reached adolescence, differentiating from the family rituals that once anchored 'Abigail' and 'Ed'. The marriage ended as the ever-mounting pressures sucked the life out of the fabric of their marriage partnership. 'Abigail' reported she and her husband never argued. They just stopped talking all together. The tensions between them became unbearable and to their relief, they made the decision to separate.

When 'Abigail' came to see me for therapy, she was in the process of morphing her family and processing the unresolved frustrations and disappointments of her fifteen-year marriage. At the initial stages of therapy, we explored her grief and loss through the marriage itself. She felt angry and bitter for how difficult her former husband had been and she came (as we all do at the early stages) complete with a laundry list of 'his' deficits. "I never want to go through that again!" she claimed. Little did she realize all the deficits she described in him were to become explorations of her own dark side of herself.

Byron Katie has such a great exercise for anger and resentments where she suggests you write out a list of all the deficits of the other person and then take his/her name out of the statements so that they read "I am so___, ___, ___". In fact the negative traits we identify in others are usually yet to be discovered dark traits of our own needing re-discovery. In 'Abigail's' counseling with me, she came to understand that her perception that her husband was: thoughtless, detached, and mean spirited, were all traits she could actually recognize in herself over their fifteen-years of marriage and baby making.

Write out your own list of resentments about your former partner. Then take his/her name out of the statement and put your own in. Try reading these statements and consider the ways these insights reflect in you. This isn't to make you feel crappier than you already do! It's actually a helpful exercise because it gives you the power to change and develop. You have some constructive things to work on.

As we moved through 'Abigail's' process, she recalled that her attraction to her husband in the initial stages of their relationship had been driven by her longing to have a child at the time. They had met when she was sensing her 'ovaries call to action'. 'Abigail and her ovaries' had been 40-years-old when she and 'Ed' met, and she longed to be a mother. At 40, she felt her window of opportunity was rapidly closing. 'Abigail' realized that she fell in love with the idea of creating a family, more than actually falling in love with 'Ed'. She wasn't actually thinking about 'Ed's' feelings or how she didn't truly love him. In reality, other than their mutual vision as parents, their personalities were distinctly different from their start. 'Abigail' described 'Ed' as an **introvert** who liked his solitary time reading, watching sports, and mountain climbing. 'Abigail' described herself as an **extrovert** who loved being with lots of people at social events.

In the beginning, 'Abigail' overlooked 'Ed's' reclusiveness. She had hoped she could influence him to be more like her over time. He was such a nice guy that she thought time and her buoyant energy would shift his stubborn resolve to solitary life. She knew she could count on him and that they would make beautiful babies together. He may have thought she mirrored the things he wanted to grow into – an ability to be more outgoing like 'Abigail'. Did you celebrate your partner or did you secretly want to change him or her? There are so many positive attributions about introverts. Introverts love for 'time in' makes them very creative, innovative, thoughtful, and grounded partners. These traits however were not in 'Abigail's values for living. She just tried to make the best of what she felt were his deficits.

As an extrovert, 'Abigail' feels energized in contact with people. Were you truly yourself from the start of your previous relationship? 'Abigail' tried to be the quiet stay at home partner with 'Ed' at the beginning of the relationship. She thought she could develop more balance in becoming more home centered. However, truly 'Abigail' is an **external processor** and sharing ideas with others is how she feels inspired and alive. Additionally, from what 'Abigail' shared, 'Ed' is an **internal processor**. My hunch is that 'Ed' may have withdrawn from 'Abigail' because he felt guilty that he could not keep up to his energizer bunny.

'Abigail' reported she felt frustrated and even abandoned by 'Ed' with his increasingly stubborn resistance to engage in the social activities she loved most. The polarity of these two personality types resulted in their lonely unsatisfied life together. While 'Ed' would process his thoughts in his head, 'Abigail' was an external processor hungry to connect in 'Ed's private emotional escape. As you think about this story, you may identify yourself as someone who tends to please your partner instead of truly being yourself. Your grief may need to focus on the lost parts of you over the time you were in your past relationship.

'Abigail' and 'Ed' had functioned well as parents, but as their children became more and more independent as adolescence arrived, the gaps in their marriage partnership began to show. 'Abigail' came to resent her husband and they fell into a relationship pattern of **withdraw-withdraw**. This is when couples stop resourcing in each other and withhold intimacy and communication. The more 'Ed' refused to join 'Abigail' in social events, the more 'Abigail' spent time away from 'Ed'. In the final years of their relationship, 'Abigail' reported that when they were in each other's company, they barely had eye contact. 'Abigail' felt 'Ed' was a "big disappointment" and "completely self-absorbed". She felt 'Ed' had betrayed her by becoming so socially withdrawn as the years had gone by.

Without considering her own part in how this marriage had set itself up, 'Abigail' felt she had been living in a prison of loneliness caused by 'Ed'. She was completely stuck in her angry story of how he had failed her. Stuck in this resentment rehearsal, 'Abigail' was crippled from moving forward from their breakup. You can't change your former partner. Resenting him or her for the ways you felt let down is a loss of your time and energy. 'Abigail's' anger towards 'Ed' blinded her from considering any of her own learning.

As we explored her family of origin and her relationship with her original man—her father, 'Abigail' shared stories about her father leaving her mother when she was a teenager. There is no coincidence that she also left 'Ed' when her two children were the same age as she was. Clients often unconsciously re-experience old wounds when their children are the same age as their emotional traumas have occurred. Because 'Abigail' had not resolved the painful feelings of abandonment and loss from her childhood, she may have unconsciously sought out a distant relationship with someone like 'Ed'. Attraction happens for a multitude of conscious and unconscious reasons. In choosing 'Ed' she unconsciously recreated the story that men betray women and that she was not worth loving. This irrational belief resulted in a **projected** resentment which 'Ed' may have worn for the fifteen years of their marriage. The more he may have sensed her distance and lack of intimate connection, the more she may have sensed his withdrawal and felt abandoned.

'Abigail' benefited in understanding and by taking responsibility for her own distance in her relationship with 'Ed'. Without understanding how she actively participated in the ending of their relationship, she would continue to see herself as a victim in the future. From this perspective, 'Abigail' would then set herself up to repeat the same attraction over an over again —the choice of an unavailable man. She would then be at risk with all men, and therefore bound to repeat continued disappointments and breakups in the future. Also, staying in this idea that 'he' caused the dissolution of their marriage turns her into a victim or a martyr. Do you know any martyrs who live fulfilled lives? Do you tend to compromise and please others more than take the risk to bravely say what you want or need? Are you as honest with others as you could be?

'Abigail' also needed to gain insight into her own accountability that in some ways she had actually used 'Ed'. If she hadn't wanted to have children so badly, she might not have married him at all. For many women and men, the driving need to have a baby no matter what it takes, is larger than life. It's not difficult to understand how overwhelming these feelings were. Would she have done anything differently? Maybe not, because in the results were their beautiful children. However, the more she could take hold of her own commitment to live more honestly, the more empowered she became in moving out of chronic loneliness in her future.

To be empowered in her future, 'Abigail' needed to understand what she had done in betraying herself and 'Ed' by marrying someone she didn't truly love. Though the benefits outweighed the loss, at least she could claim her own gratitude that she was to become a mother, no matter what. The gratitude was that she found a beautiful partner to share this purpose. 'Abigail' will gain greater freedom and happiness by being more honest in her future. Without understanding this concept, there is no way she will ever truly be able to close the door on her attachment to the past. Guilt is a dark anchor. There is an entire chapter on the topic coming up later!

The bottom line is that without discovering the courage to stand in her truth, 'Abigail' would have continued to entrench herself in the irrational belief that she wasn't worth loving. The saboteur voice of negative beliefs would have perpetuated a chronic anxious need to fill a gap in her heart that only she held the key to.

To move forward, you will need to do some soul searching of your own, to bravely look at your own deficit behaviors. If a relationship fails, there are always two parts to its denouement. The longer 'Abigail' would have rehearsed her former husband's failings, the less relationship ready she would have become.

When you wake up tomorrow morning, say to yourself "I stand in my light, my truth and no one can hurt me there". You don't have to impress anyone. Everyone has their own learning, their own flaws, and their own growth points. It's your vulnerability that is most loveable to others! *In your truth, you are love.*

'Abigail's' breakthrough was to really metabolize her own adolescent losses when her father left her mother. As she came to a fresh perspective that her parents were also misfit in misaligned personalities and lifestyle desires, she forgave herself and understood her parents through an adult lens. As she integrated compassion for her 40-year-old self and her call to motherhood, she developed the capacity to truly close the door to her past. No more chronic resentments and regrets, 'Abigail' learned to trust and value her commitment as a mother and open herself to a perspective that she could be grateful for her marriage to 'Ed' who was also a good father. She developed compassion and a deep acceptance for who he was. After all, her children embodied all those same traits!

Give some space for your grief and resentments too. No doubt there are ways your former partner let you down. In the next chapter, you will find a tool to guide you through your loss, including a hands on 3 R's exercise. Continuing into the following chapter you will see that as you sit back and begin to see your life in an insightful perspective, over time, you won't be running away from your feelings anymore, tempted to the 'rebound' relationship. If 'Abigail' had not been motivated to understand herself, she would have fallen into the trap of a desperate search to fill her loneliness. You may see yourself trying to escape your feelings by finding someone to fill the gap in your heart as soon as possible. The fear of being on your own and that you will never find love again, along with the self-judgment that there may be something fundamentally flawed or broken about you, can propel you into anxious determination to actively 'hunt' for a new mate ASAP! As human beings, we are designed to be in pairs. So if we are not in a pair, we must be abnormal! How about those thoughts to get your anxiety going?

Upcoming I share some of my own experiences in the ending of my marriage with two children and my own experience of learning to love again. Apart from helping clients in my clinical practice, I have been through this process myself and know some of the feelings of dread, angst, grief and loss you are having right now. My story is simplified. I could have been more candid in the depth of what I have shared. But this book is about you. I just want you to know that I've been through this too!

Moving forward through Part One, you will learn how to deal with anxiety, the common tormentor of body and brain when moving through a significant loss or change. There are some helpful tools at the end of chapter five that really work to overcome anxiety symptoms. Take your time with each chapter of this book. Be curious about each stage of grief and your re-discovery of YOU! There are no fast fixes. And what about affairs? Whether someone betrayed you or you betrayed someone else, a cold turkey attitude will save your life and soul. At the same time, if an affair expedited the denouement of your relationship, you will learn what the emotional drivers are when it comes to affairs. Regrets and resentments in a kind of agonizing, hand ringing, and second-guessing reminiscence can freeze you in the epicenter of your wounded heart. This stuck rumination prevents you from moving on to a healthy next life. The 'Boundaries' chapter teaches you how to be clearer in your communications and less overwhelmed generally so that the best version of you can show up more often. Chapter thirteen helps you finally swing out to get 'unstuck'. You have made it through grief and its time to let go of him or her once and for all. By the end of Part One, you may find yourself starting to realize that the ending of your relationship has actually set you free. You can access more gratitude in your life as you see your break-up with the perspective of learning and personal evolution.

✦✦✦✦✦✦✦✦✦✦✦

Give yourself a subjective rating of how you feel now at the beginning of this book. At the end, I will ask you to rate your feelings or state of being again. So go ahead and give yourself a number right now between 1–10:

1 means:
'I feel bleak and stuck in the pain of what has happened in my life'.

10 means:
'I feel positive and free. I've closed the door to my past relationship'.

-1——-2——-3——-4——-5——-6——-7——-8——-9——-10-

****

****

How happy are you today? Write that number on this page here. I'll remind you at the end of this book to write a new number. You may be surprised at how much capacity you have to truly shift your outlook on life and yourself in it. You are about to discover an amazing YOU!

****

Learn to take your time and enjoy being on your own for a while. Rebounding, the quicker you mate up again, the more likely that you will set yourself up with a new partner who is also a little anxious about being on his/her own, just like you. The more needy you are, the more you will attract someone with that same state of low **differentiation** and high reactivity. What other kind of person would ignore that kind of 'locked on' type of anxious attachment vibe that calls "save me, save me, save me"? This kind of intense **fusion** in a relationship will often lead to high volatility, roller coaster exhaustion and quite possibly… another sad ending. Your heart shouldn't have to take this kind of beating, so pay attention!

There are tool kits at the end of each chapter so you can create proactive change, step by step of the way through this book.

In Part Two you will start to understand how and why you were attracted to previous relationships because of your early relationships with your parents, siblings, and first love. In Part Two, you will also learn ways to regain a solid state of peace within YOU, so that you feel 'at home' in your own skin again. This state of internal resonance (resonance or dissonance is usually referred to as the open connection or disturbance between two people) or coming alive is you being fully in the present moment. Harold Whitman once said *"Don't ask yourself what the World needs, ask yourself what you need to come alive. And then go do that. Because what the World needs are people who have come alive"*. The better you trust and feel about you, the more you will be ready to form a secure attachment with a new partner in the future. Instead of saying 'save me', you will be saying things such as "I don't want you saving me; I don't want to save you; what are we learning together; how can I get better at love?"

To get better at love, you need to know every working part of your learning to love in the histories of your family, culture, and first love experiences. Time to get into your own personal health and style boot camp in Part Two. This is a fun part of this book where you get to treat yourself as well or better than you ever thought possible. You will learn to love your body, mind and spirit. Its time to start dating you! You will also find out who impacted your story of love through understanding how your caregivers showed love. You will learn how your first love experience can form the script for all your relationships going forward. You'll understand the impact your birth order may have had on you.

In Part Three you are called into action as you move towards opening a new door to dating, sex and intimacy…and your next experience of love. Imagine what your life will be like when you let go of your fear and trust yourself to dream again! In my opinion, one of the key quests through this whole rebuild challenge that you are on is that you are able to regain trust. You will dance into love once more when you regain solid, unconditional trust in YOU.

'Opening a New Door' is a guide to help you feel transformation: whole, solid and anchored in yourself. Part Three guides you through your re-entry to dating, intimacy, and sex, and how to plan a life you will love. Your transformation comes with a regained perception of control in your life and future. You are powerful. When you are feeling empowered and free, you will also notice a rise in your capacity to connect with others. The more you feel truly emotionally healthy, the more others will be drawn to you.

You can have confidence in your commitment to close the door to the past when you can see on the other side of the closed door is a world you can love. Current brain research about our nervous system reveals how important it is to feel in connection to others, whether this connection is with a significant partner, our families, our social groups, our athletic clubs, or fellow workers, etc. This theory of stability, the 'open limbic system' of emotional health, mood and personality is what Dan Goleman explains in his book "Emotional Intelligence" where he describes how emotional disease is contagious. Dan Seigal in his book "Mindsight" speaks to the value of "time in", which involves having a practice of meditation, and self-reflection for limbic revision. The fracture of a significant relationship can feel like a tearing apart of your emotional ground floor… with all your insides being strewn across your universe.

However, if you have the benefit of a map through this free fall, there is an opportunity for you to gain a new, fresh, more complete you who you yourself can love. This solid reworking of you as a person can provide you with a new a core strength that you can truly count on in the future, no matter what difficult circumstances you might face.

Take a moment right now to close your eyes and imagine there is a bright light shining inside you. Breathe in and as you breathe out, imagine turning your light up even more. With every breath, turn your light up brighter and brighter as you imagine you can fill a room with your light. This mini meditation integrates a new harmony that love and light exist within YOU. The more you have the ability to turn up love within you, the more capacity you will have to love others.

There is little doubt the connections that we have with our loved ones in our tribe, in our social group, can provide us with the core ingredients for our security, safety and survival. Going through a breakup is not the right time to isolate yourself and if at any stage you are tending to do that, go back to Chapter Four 'Establishing a Support System You Can Count On' which reminds you of the value of friendships and having a support system you can count on. In the wake of a breakup, the aforementioned key ingredients of connection can feel scattered, shaken, and reassessed. But the process of your rebuilding, while this may feel unnerving, also brings a great opportunity to look at strategic ways in which you can choose to participate more in relationships that support you and less with those that stress. You will also learn how to build strong internal supports in finding out how to **self-regulate** better when you are anxious or angry.

You will gain more inner confidence as you hone in on stronger inter-personal skills, and thereby live less at risk in your future socially. The more depth and confidence you discover as you skillfully navigate through the shifting and strengthening of old and new relationships, the greater chances you will have of attracting a mate who will surely be an upgrade when it comes to forming a new life partnership. The more **differentiated** and evolved you and your new partner become, the greater your freedom to loving. The more you can communicate your own vulnerabilities, the more capacity you will have to hear the vulnerabilities of others.

So begin looking back into your life experience in a constructive way. Start looking forward with hopeful, confident anticipation one chapter at a time.

As you imagine yourself three years from now, embrace the sense of elation of your future relationship with a renewed openness and a stronger potential for deep caring. Statistics are witness to the fact that on average, within three years you will likely be in another committed relationship. The key is how well you are going to do in that relationship. What will your healthy and fulfilling relationship feel like to you in the future?

You can experience the magic of what love entails if you can stay open to love. If you remain Sir Mick Jagger confident, *you might just get what you need; you might just get what you want.* The capacity to love is totally within you. You loved before. You will love again. Your capacity is massive. What's not to love about that? Love attracts. You can enrich your life if you can gain a more nuanced understanding of what loving well is all about. Connect back in with your own inner visionary— the you who has known you all your life. Stop worrying about how others feel about the end of your relationship. For example, you may have been in the most horrible relationship situation and held on just because you dreaded the thought of failing. Or as mentioned earlier, you may have been fearful that there wouldn't be anyone else out there for you. You may worry about what your friends and family might say. Get out of that trap: you know you are a conscientious, caring person who does your best. Those who love you know that too.

You need to stay aligned with your own values and core integrity to be peaceful in your future life. Consider the impacts you have on others, so that you can do your best to do no harm in your future dating life. Keep in mind that if your future relationship(s) become constrictive or emotionally toxic, you will know the ways you can gain mastery over your own relationship behaviors. The more you know yourself and what you have the capacity to change, the more you will know you have done everything you can to be different in it. It's with that knowing you can release yourself to just move on. The Serenity Prayer comes to mind:

"God grant me the serenity
To accept the things I cannot change, the
Courage to change the things I can;
And wisdom to know the difference"
—*Reinhold Niebuhr*

Try on an idea that you can think more expansively about "God" as defined by any particular religion. Consider that our loving experiences may contribute to a web of positive energetic connection in our World. Whether each loving experience you have lasts a lifetime or a month, each time you love, you contribute to our bank of global caring in our Universe. The universal threads of care and safe attachment are strengthened therefore by your capacity to love. If you see each of your love experiences in this way, you may release yourself from any sense of failure or success. In other words, let your ego go and get on with love again. Anxiety floats right past you in this new stream of consciousness. Close your eyes right now. Take a breath. Reconnect to that bright light within you. Brighten the light within you and now imagine you can radiate your light to fill your room, your office, your building, your city, your country, our universe. Just imagine. Breathe in…and breathe out… breathe in…shine out. Thank you. I felt that!

As you let go of the prior 'object' of your love (former partner) and now as you think of your capacity to live in a loving way, you change everything for you. When you refuse to let go, you choose to live in a world of fear. You fabricate your reality based on negative assumptions—your own Rocky Mountain Horror Show. Anxiety spreads out and the world around you constricts in reaction to your fears that you are not enough. You are enough. You were born enough. You and your former partner have simply outgrown another love relationship. The downward life spiral that comes from fear is that the more you spend your life in a world of resentment and regret about your failed relationship, the more negativity will consume you. This will make you absolutely unappealing to others, at home, at work, to your friends, and of course, to any future romantic partner. When you cling so desperately to all the details of the past that you remain stuck in, the anguish of your life will seem out of your control. Enter Anxiety stage left.

Please take a breath! You can control your life right now in this admittedly difficult context of your breakup if you adopt an attitude that looks to the past for hints about how to conduct yourself in the future. When you look back at your former relationship, try to take a more balanced perspective about what happened, about you and your former partner. Look up at the blue-sky moments, and not just at the dirt on the ground. In that way, you will be surprised at the gratitude that develops that you had the benefit of spending time with your former boyfriend, girlfriend, husband, wife, siblings, parents and people in general.

The trap that you can fall into during a breakup involves telling yourself a lot of stories, and creating excuses about what happened when you are hurt. I visited Beijing in 2007 and saw, among so many other amazing things, the Whispering Wall at the Temple of Heaven Park (Tian Tan). The Whispering Wall surrounds a circular courtyard. If you whisper to the wall, the message travels all around this famous wall and then comes back to you. Our lives are like that. When confusion happens in our life with regards to love, we whisper stories about what happened into our own whispering wall. Through life, these stories constrict or expand our potential to love and be loved.

When you are overcome by painful endings, you will naturally want to protect yourself... add another few feet to the height of your wall! The higher your wall, the less chance there is for the light of life to get in. In the darkness, you can become a myth-making machine and struggle to climb out of this courtyard of sadness. So, step away from your wall. Change the messages you whisper about yourself and your former partner. Rebuild yourself, not your wall.

Turn off the heat and stop putting so much pressure on yourself. Learn to enjoy and grow from many relationships. The experiences you gain from the past relationships will provide you insights about yourself and how you function in a relationship so that you can better equip yourself to choose the one big love of your life. Every relationship you experience allows you to develop, to become better, to become more evolved, and to be savvier about others and yourself. If and when you decide to marry or re-marry you will then be able to contribute more to the new partnership, so that it will be more dynamic and expansive. Relationships provide opportunities to experience other family cultures, and other styles of living. When you meet and engage with new people, you experience each other's interests, ideas and opinions. This will provide stimulating information about spirituality, philosophy, sports, music, science or the arts as experienced by others. These earlier relationships also help you grow from the experience of being held accountable for your own feelings and needs, while being open to those of others.

As you move away from your wall, and as you look at all the relationships you have had with men over time, what did you learn about yourself? Are you an **internal or external processor**? Do you tend to say the first thing that comes to your mind and end up hurting those around you? Do you need to take more time to communicate with more compassion and more accountability?

****

Difficult conversations have a better outcome if you can remember this formula:

1. Start by expressing some kind of appreciation for the other person. This lets him/her know you value him/her as creative, healthy and whole. It allows him/ to let their own wall down so that they can actually hear what you need from them, without being defensive.
2. Say what you are feeling. "I felt hurt when you (did whatever happened/the story)". There is a great YouTube video out right now called the "Girl with the Nail in her Head". It's a funny video that drives home the notion that we don't need to fix each other. We just need to be empathic listeners. You are already creative, healthy and whole. You will discover your own best solutions to any difficult situation. In this safe holding, your brain is less stressed and more able to problem solve. As you share your feelings, your partner is allowed 'in' and your attachment grows stronger.

****

In the same way, when someone you value has been critical of you, try to take a breath and listen deeply. If you have a big reaction to what he or she is saying, he or she is probably hit on something you need to learn from. The only way you can grow is by getting feedback from others. So why be defensive? Ask yourself "am I defending or defining myself"? If you are defending yourself, you are stuck at your wall. You are fearful of judgment and likely not to develop from what could be a valuable learning opportunity for you. So take a big breath. Imagine the light within you and turn it up so you can shed some light on the upsetting criticism the other person is trying to share with you. I know this takes a healthy dose of ego strength sometimes. Tuning in supportively towards your partner when he or she is upset with you is not easy. You are not perfect. You are learning to love better. In the active experience of shared discovery, you will learn how to love through difficult dialogues. If the person is yelling, slamming something, or making you feel unsafe, you will need to reconvene when he or she has calmed down enough to talk to you in a voice you feel safe with. There is a chapter ahead, which focuses on anger and its pathway to intimacy. Anger is a stage of grief and both you and your former partner are bound to experience it. It helps to have some tools so that you can experience it safely.

In closing the door to your past relationship, it can be helpful to think about the context of life at the time. For example, if you or your partner have had health problems, career changes, family deaths or any other significant life stage change, you may consider these events as cause and effect. If you have been left, this can be a helpful way to make sense of your loss. Significant life events often trigger people to end relationships. Sometimes like an untimely death, a partner can 'out of the blue' call an end to life with you. If he or she does not have the capacity to have closure with you, it can help to consider the context of change happening around the two of you. A subtle example may be, if your boyfriend/girlfriend has lost his/her job. He/she may be preoccupied and irritable with the stress of finding new employment. He/she may feel unvalued and betrayed by his/her former employer and then choose to dump you in reaction to that loss. And if for example he/she may say "I don't want to see you anymore because you are so thoughtless.. You don't understand what I'm going through. I've lost my job". You might respond empathically "You've been let go from your job and you are panicked that you can't trust me either" focusing on his/her loss.

And you also need to reflect the insult (thoughtless you) "It hurts to think you feel I'm thoughtless… now you are ending our relationship out of the blue…do you worry about your own thoughtlessness?" If the conversation continued you might say "what would feel thoughtful right now?" But the end game will be out of your control. And if you really sit back in this exchange, you will start to realize that if he can end your relationship when he's under stress, he is probably not the right person to build a lifetime relationship with. Maybe it's a good thing to find this out now.

If your relationship ended with high conflict, you may want to avoid contact with your former partner entirely. If he or she is in grief and storming in a way that is unhealthy or bullying of you, you are best to wish him or her well, but let go. Breathe in and breathe out into that universal spirit of love. Just let it go.

You will have a difficult time closing your door to the past until you fully understand your love relationships in a context of your lifetime. It can be so helpful to write a lifeline of every man (or woman) you have had a deep connection with starting with your parents. On one side write what felt good about the relationship (in one sentence) and on the other side write the things you struggled with (in one sentence). On a fresh page write out a list of all the things you have learned about yourself and ways you can grow from each person. Keep the 'stories' to one-sentence bullets to prevent your ego from developing stories that distract you from metabolizing the simple truths about yourself. Be reflective on the misunderstandings and points of confusion.

What will you learn about yourself from each significant relationship from your past? Think of my client 'Abigail', who learned to appreciate her own good qualities and be grateful for the gifts of her past: that she has two beautiful children, she has supportive friendships, she is creative, and she has an amazing zeal for life. She identifies with the warm charisma of her father, and the enduring loyalty of her mother. She sees her lifeline and realizes that she was choosing unavailable men, a story line, which may have started with her Father leaving her Mother. As 'Abigail' grieved and processed her childhood experience when her parents divorced, she integrated new meaning into living solidly in her own values, needs, and core beliefs. The more she gained insight about her 'whole' self and valued 'all' of who she is – her dark and her light, the more freedom and spaciousness she has with men in her future. In slowing down through a practice of meditation and in a practice of simply walking slower, she is finding more self-confidence. The more other focused she has trained herself to be, the more other-focused type of partner she is attracting.

It can be agonizing to sit back and trust that you are enough, truly loveable, and that you will be (as the stats suggest) in another committed relationship within three years. This is the only time in your life you will get to enjoy your own company with all the freedom and joy that you can imagine. Joy is doubled in the company of someone you love, but see how much you can create within yourself first. EnJOY learning to love being you.

I am so convinced that even the best relationships can fall apart if there isn't a solid commitment to tune in and 'tune up' every day. Note to self for future relationships: if you want a healthy growing relationship, you should commit to the practice of communicating body, mind and spirit, at least one hour with your significant other every day. When you do this practice you build **limbic resonance**, a kind of 'being in the zone' where you will know you have unconditional love for and from your other, and a secure emotional landing no matter what. You can feel love simply being in each other's presence, without words through any stress or big life change in the future. Your true partner will 'get you' and you will get him or her. You will feel consistently validated and acknowledged to the extent that the wounds of you and your partner's whispering walls are heard, held and healed.

As you look back at your relationship lifeline, consider how you have understood the language of love through time. We know from research, children as young as two years old learn how to give and receive love through interactions modeled by caregivers. For example you may have had parents who did acts of service for each other, and your partner may have had parents who wrote love letters. You may be washing your partner's car in an expression of love that your partner totally misses. He/she is waiting for love letters! What this means is that we can easily miss each other's messages having grown up in different families, exposed to different styles of loving. The way that you express love to another may go completely un-noticed because he/she doesn't understand love in the same way as you do. Gary Chapman discusses this idea in his book "The Five Love Languages". Are you someone who expresses love with acts of kindness, gifts, physical touch, quality time, or words of affirmation? Be curious about your style of expressing love and find out what his or hers is too. If you speak Italian and he or she speaks French, you may have a new discovery and learning curve to work through. But in order to benefit from this work, you need to approach it with the perspective of a child's mind – open and curious to grow.

As children we dance into contact with others. We relate with the 'whole' of our personalities because we have not yet been impacted by the negative judgments and fears of others. The open playful ways a child faces the world, shows up in an attitude of curiosity and fearlessness. As a child, you asked why and how? Sadly as life happens and when the messages you get from others is confusing, fear and judgments start to limit your emotional capacity. In discerning the reactions of others, you shrink spiritually. We all do. Fight back on shrinkage! Keep your inner curiosity alive and stimulated by asking open questions such as "What did you mean when you said this..? What is important about that?"

I worked with 'Shane' a man in his mid-life, parenting years, who came to see me because he had started to experience anxiety symptoms—racing heart, dizziness, shortness of breath, and excessive worry. As we moved through the process of his treatment, he realized that these symptoms had begun since his two boys had started elementary school. Insightfully 'Shane' realized, witness to his two boys, he was re-experiencing himself at nine and twelve. He recalled his childhood and a particular time when one of his teachers had embarrassed him in front of his peers. As 'Shane' described his experience, he recalled he had been singing (in his teacher's opinion) out of alignment with the school choir. In his childhood experience, 'Shane's' teacher had stopped the choir practice. She pointed to 'Shane' and abruptly, in front of the whole class, scolded him to stop singing. Understandably this became a turning point in 'Shane's' discovery of music and the tuning of his voice. This shaming experience not only blocked him from ever risking public vulnerability in the future, but also caused a wounding of trust for all learning in the academic environment. He reported that he continued to love music but only in the privacy of his own space. Though he would listen to music, he never sang again (which by the way, is a fabulous way to exercise your right hemisphere and stay brain healthy).

'Shane' began to feel he was unattractive to women in general. 'Shane's' teacher had been a woman and he described his mother and his sister as "critical and judgmental" too. His belief system that women were not safe resulted in a turbulent marriage with his wife. Certainly 'Shane's' negative belief of himself and fear of 'all' women swamped his experience of all women going forward. This landed him a life in which he felt somewhat invisible to others. With practice of deep breathing and holding his space, 'Shane' learned to ask his Wife open ended questions, such as "Why were you upset when…what does that tell you when I…?" These types of questions helped 'Shane' rewrite the stories of his childhood that women are critical and unsafe. If 'Shane' didn't check his experience out by asking those types of questions, his childhood feelings of pain would have continued. Today 'Shane' feels like he is married to a completely different woman, even though his wife never came to therapy. The more 'Shane' gained the emotional freedom to just say when his feelings were hurt, the more his wife became acknowledging, respectful and loving. Never underestimate the impact you can have in a single moment in time (both on yourself and on others). We shape each other. The stories you believe to be true will become your life. You have the capacity to heal yourself and those you are in contact with. We ARE stronger together.

If you have ended your relationship because you felt your partner was critical and judgmental, you may want to reflect on your own confusing childhood messages. To close the door on your past relationship, think about the ways you may have projected past hurts on your former partners. It's so empowering when you realize you can experience off put comments with freedom and curiosity. Never under-estimate the power of asking great open questions. Here are some you can squirrel away:

- How does this affect you?
- What elsc is there to learn here?
- What other perspectives are there on this?
- How can I be a better partner for you?
- What can I learn from this?

Do your best to find common ground. Seek to understand. You don't need to spend your precious life in the purgatory of total compromise or in the confusion of predictable power struggles. Love relationships are not prison sentences. It's not to anyone's benefit to live your life with an ill-suited partner. Hone in on your own sensitivities so you develop stronger emotional curiosity and resiliency. In the end, if your choice is to move forward, it will be a good one. Rather than be stuck in an emotional jail, go through the Khyber Pass to a successful fulfilling relationship.

Learning to love well is I guess, a little like boot camp at times. As you work out through this book, you will be breaking down old muscle fiber and rebuilding new muscle memory in the most important part of your body – your heart. Your heart is a muscle and your heart is actually the most vital part of your whole body function. It is not your brain. Your brain counts on your heart for blood supply. Without caring well for your heart, you can't think, feel, move, play, learn, grow, or adapt. If your heart stops you die! If your brain shuts down, you can still live. In fact, I bet if you think a little less and focus on your feelings, your life will open in ways you've never imagined.

Take a moment right now. Breathe in… breathe out…Feel your feet…your feet…Feel your calves…your calves. Feel your thighs…your thighs. Feel your stomach…your stomach. Feel your heart…your heart… Feel your arms…your arms. Feel your neck…your neck. Feel your face…your face… Feel the tip of your nose…your nose. Feel the top of your head…your head. As you move through each of your body parts, they just are. You don't judge them as good, bad or indifferent. They just hang there in the way they do without your judgment.

Did you notice the calm and clarity you felt after that brief mindful exercise? You are going through a process of shutting one door so that another door can open. Just walk through the process. The past is just what it was and everyone is doing just what he or she tends to do. If you just breathe into the present moment without judgment, imagine the freedom you will have to walk through this process of transition you are in? Thinking is important because you are called upon in this process to think differently. New thinking will support your heart, but mission control always resides in your heart.

****

According to the World Health Organization, if you live to the current average life expectancy of 82, your heart will beat on average, more than three billion times. Considering every part of your healthy function starts with your healthy heart, my favorite activities for heart care, heart appreciation, and heart health are as follows:

1. Every morning check in with your heart: how do you feel when you first wake up?
2. Drink a big glass of water, which will increase your blood volume.
3. Take your heart out for a brisk walk, jog, or some type of 20-minute cardiovascular exercise. Keep your heart in training. Your heart is a muscle and it needs to work out.
4. How do you feel now? Share your feelings with someone.
5. Exercise your right brain by singing, dancing, listening to music, playing a board game, or musical instrument, laughing or being mindful in nature.

****

Learning to love is like getting in physical shape. Using the cyclist meta-phor, it requires you to show up, start your wheels moving, feel the exhila-ration and the sweat, and know when it's time to work harder. You should also know when you should take a break, or get off the bike! There has to be an emotional trust you can draw from when confusion within your future partner relationships happens. You are called to learn how to expand your ability to love generously, to receive feedback with optimism, be a good citizen, and to the best of your ability, do no harm. If you can do these things, you will be happy. Build within yourself and you will make your world better and stronger.

As my trainer at spin class says to me with a grin, "You are here to work Jo-Anne." While the sweat is just pouring off me I wonder, 'can't he see I'm working hard?' I think his direction applies to our lives and loves gen-erally. I appreciate that my instructor is motivating me to push harder and I receive his coaching in kind. I assume he is coming from a trainer per-spective and that he has my best interest in mind. I always set my own pace, but I'm buoyed up by his unrelenting attention to my workout.

Healthy relationships are also like this when we are open and curious about our 'other' and ourselves. Someone without a fitness background might be insulted or put off by the directive style of my trainer. It takes a common language, lubricated by open communication and constructive feedback to be able to work in sync with someone whether within an inti-mate partnering relationship or a professional working relationship (with either a work associate or a fitness trainer). Three times a week in spin class I choose to be in sync with my trainer. I trust him, and as a result I'm getting fitter each week. In the context of an intimate relationship, you need to choose to be in sync emotionally, to speak and hear with the same language if you want that relationship to work. The gain, however, has to be worth the pain.

Wouldn't it be great if everyone did their own personal work to under-stand themselves better? It would be so helpful if there was an emotional 'Projectormeter App' with which we could scan moments of conflict. Is this how I felt when that (moment in time) happened? Is this feeling pro-jected from an old wound? Am I now wounding my beloved, bonking him or her with a hypersensitivity drawn from my past? We could preload this emotional tool with firewalls that prevent defensive reactions, and with storage of powerful questions we could have at the ready. "What can I do to adapt?" "What do I need more of right now?" "How will that change things for the better for me?" "What is happening in my partner's world?" What does he or she need more of right now?" "How will that change things for the better for him or her?"

Just imagine if there was an App like this? This App could scan all conflicts for projections that come from us, or our significant other. We wouldn't load up negative energy to build cases against each other. We could stay in the present dealing with the one issue that has the potential to help us to develop. We would be guided towards more intimacy and integrate more caring behaviors, rather than defensive behaviors that frustrate or exhaust, lead us to ridicule or otherwise diminish our partner. Imagine, no more bonk! Honk if you agree. This would be another way to move our world from Me to We! The world could use a little more trust. Trust in self. Trust that others are doing their best, even when it hurts.

Be yourself and trust your instincts in all relationships. Relax, pay attention to this moment right now as children do. Gravitate to friendships that make you feel happy and grateful. Loving well may be life's greatest achievement. In the right significant relationship, your body, mind, and spirit will grow. Love is an action and a state. Love is a way of being that never stays still, it dances and discovers. This practice of being in love involves accessing your emotional intelligence in order to be present in the moment. Loving starts with you before it involves another. You are one hundred percent free to be yourself in love. This may be the only time in the rest of your life you will get to enjoy choosing everything. As you begin to integrate the possibilities that come from that realization, don't you feel a little curious and excited?

When you think back to the relationship that just ended in your life, do you notice that your body, mind and spirit had become a little dormant, contracted? As you think back, can you recall the experience of symptoms such as anxiety, depression, weight gain or loss, or maybe an overall fatigue? You can probably think of all kinds of ways that you let yourself down in the time you stayed stuck in the wrong match. Your body knows and tells you when you are not in resonance with yourself. That is when your daily stresses start to overwhelm you and your thinking becomes brittle, reactive and confused. Things just start going more and more wrong for you, until one day you wonder "How did this happen? What has happened to me? Who am I?" Close that door!

Fidelitas Veritas Integritas!
Live with wholeness, integrity and health.

CHAPTER 2

HAVE YOU BEEN IDEALIZING THE PAST?

Do you find yourself longing for the chance to go back to the past? Have you found yourself thinking if only I had done this one thing better, we'd still be together? He/she was actually not that bad? Maybe he/she was actually pretty good? If you have fallen into a pattern of regret, this Chapter will help you overcome what can be a long slow spiritual madness. A client 'Alice in Wonderland' came to see me after her two-year relationship with her boyfriend had ended. Sadly he had called it quits and moved abroad from Canada. She still missed him one year later, and on an impulse, invited him to come to Vancouver to spend a week with her. She paid for his flight and set up a romantic weekend get-away at a resort. Unfortunately (and predictably) when he arrived, his intentions were simply to have a free holiday. The relationship had ended previously because she felt frustrated with his unavailability both physically (because of all the travel he did with his job) and emotionally (because he wasn't willing to talk about things that were upsetting to her when he was in town). Nothing had changed.

Despite their history, 'Alice' had hoped they might rekindle their flame. She had idealized the past and projected her loving intentions into a new future with someone who was a poor fit for her in the past. Sadly, her idea was scorched in an emotional plane crash when she realized that their two intentions were painfully at odds. As a couple, they were misfit; their intentions, miss intended. In the heat of an angry exchange in their hotel room, he reportedly threw something at 'Alice'. She returned with a physical push back. She then called the front desk of the hotel for help. All of which landed 'Alice' in a local jail.

'Alice' came to see me when she was facing assault charges; wondering how this could possibly have happened. Based on the information in the initial complaint, as filed by the estranged boyfriend, the police made a judgment call to lay a criminal charge on 'Alice'!

> *"But I don't want to go among mad people," Alice remarked.*
> *"Oh, you can't help that," said the Cat: "we're all mad here. I'm mad. You're*
> *mad."*
> *"How do you know I'm mad?" said Alice.*
> *"You must be." Said the Cat, or you wouldn't have come here."*
> *—Lewis Carroll, Alice in Wonderland*

All this confusion was the result of the projected anxieties of both parties of a misfit union, past and present. Going back to an old relationship to try to re-kindle the past is like getting stuck on an impossible exam question. Have you ever done that? "I should be able to figure this out". I can recall many of those during my time as a student in university. With the pressure of limited time, and the examiner's clock ticking, I'd dwell on and rack my brain to figure out the answer to that one challenging question… and then run out of time to complete other questions that I could have handled easily. If I had simply moved on, I could have easily answered the rest of the questions on the exam and passed with flying colors. I might even have found the time and insights to return to successfully complete the difficult question that I had been stuck on.

You may have fallen down your own rabbit hole thinking "if only I could have been a little more (this or that)". It's natural to go down this dark hole in your tunnel where you may beat yourself up so much and idealize your former partners as the perfect fit for you, in spite of all the evidence to the contrary. You might be thinking that it's your entire fault, and imagine that you alone can shift the dynamics of the past. This would be a big mistake on your part. Even if you have changed since your break-up, make sure your former partner has done his or her own personal work too. Otherwise you will be, like 'Alice', drinking old poison and going back into the same dynamics that ended the relationship the first time around.

The end of the wrong relationship does not constitute failure on your part. Failure is not dreaming big for YOU. 'Alice's former boyfriend ended up dropping the charges, and 'Alice' has finally moved through her grief. She also came to understand that the allure of this boyfriend was her own need to control outcomes. And his worldliness was like catnip to her because when they spent time together he would wow her about global adventures he had had. She has learned to accept his inability to love her and recognizes that she wants much more connection with her true love. Today 'Alice' discovered the romance she truly wanted was to travel the world her self having adapted her career to fit her own longing. She is happy not to take any more rabbit holes. You are the one you sleep with every night and wake up to every morning. Don't let a lost relationship swamp the possibilities of romance defined by you or with ten other wonderful partners you are still yet to meet!

Honestly, if a relationship didn't work in the past, there is probably a good chance it won't work in the future. We can't make anyone love us (or make ourselves love anyone else), nor should we. It's an insult to our self-worth. 'Alice' learned the poignant lesson of acceptance and the un-realities of living in Wonderland.

> *"You used to be so much more..."muchier. You've lost your muchness."*
> *—Lewis Carroll, Alice in Wonderland*

It takes two to choose love in order for love to happen. Never try to convince someone to love you or you to love someone else. You just might end up, like 'Alice', asking yourself, "How did I wind up in this (emotional or veritable) jail?"

My client 'Alice's' breakthrough came about when she was able to recognize how important it is to have closure when a relationship ends and in the clarity that she wanted to become worldlier herself. Closure gives you clarity about why the relationship has ended, what you have learned from the precious time investment you have made in that relationship, and what you can do differently in the future. Closure is different from grief. It's hard to move forward in a grief process without clarity. You need to understand what you are grieving about yourself as well as what you are grieving about your other.

The way that I encourage my clients to engage in the three R exercise, is for each person to write out a list of 10 items in each "R" (described at the end of this chapter). This is best done privately and over a period of time, such as a week or a month depending how long the relationship was. If you were to go through this exercise, the two of you would get together in a neutral location that feels safe for both, and you take turns talking through each of your 3 "R's". You may also want to talk through the lists together over a period of a few days or weeks depending how attached you both had been and depending on how long the two of you were together.

In achieving closure, you will find the end of the relationship is cleaner and leaves you with a clearer sense of what you need to work on through your healing process. Sharing a mutual process in this way can also take much of the drama out of a break up. It's a useful breakthrough process that helps bring you a peaceful release. Better still, you won't find yourself stuck in an idealized picture of the past relationship such as the one experienced by 'Alice'.

An interesting phenomenon in the experience of grief is that as human beings, we often recall a lost loved one in an idealized positive light that might bare little resemblance to the reality of them as a whole, perfectly imperfect person. If you were the one who left the relationship, or if you are the one who is left, this phenomenon can show up at various stages of your letting go. Clients I have worked with express feelings of resentment and anger one week and the next week they express feelings of deep sorrow and longing. This 'snakes and ladders' experience of grief is normal, although not productive if that party cannot emerge from this spiral of vacillating emotions. If you identify with this pattern, you may need to open that 'heart-head box' that your feelings are stuck in.

Open your 'box' and express your feelings to a trusted friend, or by writing these down in your journal or by talking about these with a therapist. Don't be overwhelmed by your feelings to the extent that they can ferment inside you and keep you stuck longing for an idealized past. This human phenomenon is especially true when it comes to processing the death of a loved one. The loss of an intimate relationship can feel just as powerful as a death of a loved one, with all the same impacts to you and your whole family and social system. Idealizing your former partner as a 'saint', you will set yourself up to be unsuccessful in love again because you will create an unreachable expectation of what kind of person you should look for as your love interest.

This is another reason it's important that you write your lists of the three "R's". Balance your recollections of the good, the bad and the ugly qualities of your former partner, so that you can better fortify your focus towards a healthy new path (with room for fresh possibilities). Moving to a stage of acceptance and reintegration takes a process of communication, clarity and letting go. Know the reasons why you and your former outgrew each other so you can move on with both enhanced knowledge and confidence that next time you will hit the bulls eye of a better love. And don't forget to write down all the things you have learned about you!

The clarity of your homework will release you from imagining all the 'if only's and 'why didn't I's'. This is especially true for those of you who have children because your children remind you forever of the best part of your former partner. For those of you who have shared social circles that you continue to mix with, you may see your former partner in the company of new partners and wonder why he or she wasn't that way with you. The very reasons that the relationship ends may form new beginnings in the future. Its remarkable how different parts of your personality and your former partner's personality behaviors can shift depending on whom you, he or she is with? Don't drive yourself crazy by solving that Rubik's cube of 'why not with me'.

I recall a twenty-something client of mine 'Cheryl' who absolutely could not understand why her boyfriend 'Aspen' would refuse to join her family events. This was so upsetting for 'Cheryl' that she eventually ended the relationship. The stress of explaining her boyfriend's absence and his inability to 'stretch' himself to join her in family dinners and outings was crushing to her spirit. She came to see me because two years after, 'Aspen' who continued to play in their shared social group, was dating someone new and would proudly talk about how much fun his new girlfriend's family is and how much he loved having a bigger family now that 'Jolene' was in his life. This was so triggering for 'Cheryl' who was crushed in the knowledge that 'Aspen' would stretch for someone else, but hadn't for her.

What 'Cheryl' came to understand through a new perspective was that her values of family were core and she learned to forgive 'Aspen' because she realized that possibly in the sad ending of their own relationship, 'Aspen' finally learned the value of stretching himself (even if his more grown up love capacity did finally come late in the day). Love is seen in other focused behaviors and 'Aspen' had learned how to love because of the pain in losing his relationship with 'Cheryl'. Relationships may not be 'forever' but the ripples of change that comes from love lost and love found are 'forever'. Is there a new perspective on your loss that you may consider? What are the ways you have helped yourpartner grow?

****

Many clients who successfully navigate through the grief process find it helpful to go through a process with the departing partner, in which you both ask yourselves three "R's":

1. **Remembrances**: What are the best memories of our shared time together? This is a great place to start as it reminds you of all the positive take-away memories that will always be yours. This gives you a sense of inner peace in knowing that your time together has been meaningful and worthwhile, and the memories within are enduring. For some, this will be special occasions, shared holidays, shared contributions, the birth of children, support you may have given each other through parents, family, friends, or pet passing.

2. **Resentments**: What do you resent about the other? This is a really important inquiry because it allows you to let go of the frustrations and fury of the ways you feel you were let down. It also allows you to process information that your partner may choose to grow from. It is hard to forgive someone if you have not gone through this stage of

inquiry. Many clients find that they experience a massive release in listing all the deficits they have experienced with their significant other. Later in this book you will discover that these negative traits of the other party to a relationship are often lost parts of your own personality. One step at a time though.

3. **Regrets:** What would you have done differently? This reflection helps so much in the rebuilding of self. By listing out the ways you feel you failed and the ways you wish you had behaved differently, you can heal from the pain of failure and integrate new ways of being more solidly present in the future. For you and your partner, this step is an act of kindness in that both of you can acknowledge that no one person is at fault for the end of the relationship. In this way, it sets up both of you for a healthier and less dramatic end to the relationship.

****

CHAPTER 3

CLOSING THE DOOR MAY TAKE SOME TIME

Are you feeling impatient with yourself and frustrated being alone… again? One of the hardest things in the wake of a breakup is remembering you are 'whole', that you are 'enough', and remembering that you are 'loved'…especially when you are laying in bed by yourself, looking at the ceiling and feeling the cold spaces beside you. You may find yourself aching to feel the comfort of having a new partner again. This Chapter is to help you gain the value of patience and the appreciation of taking the time you need to fully heal before you get ready to 'dance' with someone new. Remember that we live longer lives today, decades longer than our great grandparents. This longer life span has implications on the way we commit to key relationships in our lives. The longer you wait, the more developed you will be. While you are on your own developing, your potential 'other' will be learning about him or herself too.

Statistics Canada released findings that couples are marrying later, having children later and living longer (1). This is also true in the U.S., with similar trends as the Census Bureau from 1890 through to 2012 shows. These findings are showing up more specifically with long-term outcomes in marriage eighty percent of the time for women who have university degrees and marry later than twenty-five years old (2). This chapter is designed to help you understand the benefits of taking your time before you commit to 'love and hold' for your lifetime. I believe that the statistics of marrying later is a positive development leading to you to make better choices in relationships because marrying later will give you more time to develop and to differentiate yourself as an individual, which in turn, will provide you more stability and longevity in marriage.

The outcome of developing yourself emotionally, intellectually, and financially will be less overall stress. So even when you are in the pre-marriage stage, take your time! Enjoy dating, courting and the process of envisioning a future together. Enjoy the stage of being engaged, of bearing the title of being a 'fiancée'. Revel in each experience and stage of every relationship. Share the caring of plants, then choosing and raising a pet, before you consider the next step towards a choice of whether and when to have children. See how you and your partner function through the increasingly complex responsibilities attached to the myriad roles of forming a family. See yourself and your significant other in graduating stages of the sharing of life and love. If we all approached the process of becoming a family in a step-by-step way, I believe that there would be less incidence of divorce and far fewer subsequent disruptions in the lives of our children.

For some, the anxiety of being solo leads to a kind of anxious, desperate hunt for a new partner (with the industry of a job); which is actually self-defeating because the hunter seems far less attractive when engaged in this anxious pursuit. The sense of urgency involved in finding a new mate can drive the single to obsessively pour into on-line dating sites. Then follows the intense over-scheduling of multiple coffee shop meetings and other awkward encounters. In the very least too much of a good thing, can be a waste of time and at worse can lead to greater levels of anxiety disappointment and despair. Whether you are actually a single person available for a date or not, this type of locked-on-target practice is more of a repellent than a success strategy for success. My cat Tallulah proved my point at a Super Bowl Party that we recently hosted. We had a number of friends over for dinner, one of which was my single friend Julie. Now Tallulah, who is known to be a loving lap jumper, was disregarding Julie's efforts tapping her knees to have Tallulah leap up on her lap. I grabbed the opportunity to ask to just sit back in her chair and stop tapping her knees for Tallulah. Two minutes later, Tallulah jumped onto Julie's lap. This Tallulah Wisdom Moment is illustrative of human experiences. The more you sit back and just enjoy being you, the more you will attract all the right cats to sit on your lap!

Part of the reason that the urgent hunt for a mate can be a turn off to others is that the anxious addictive quality of finding a partner, puts your brain into a chemical state that actually distances others. Daniel Seigel, M.D. writes about the impacts of healthy brain states on human interactions (3). Anxiety is a brain state that is contagious, with the result that the more anxious you are, the less attractive you are in relationships. The life lesson here is that of you take care of yourself and your inner calm comes out, then this will enhance the chances that your dreams of enjoying a loving, contributing life will come true. When you are calm and feeling whole, your most attractive version of you shows up.

The brain has the capacity to develop through our life span and what we know from brain research is that we can actually lengthen the telomeres in our brain by meditating. Telomeres are stretches of DNA, which protect our genetic data. They make it possible for cells to divide, and this relatively new understanding of how our brain functions holds some secrets to how we age, including how we get cancer. Research in California and the Netherlands have found a direct connection between depression and accelerated cellular aging. The study, which looked at more than 2,400 Dutch participants, found that people with depression had shorter telomeres than healthy people (4). The role of telomeres has been compared with that of plastic tips on shoelaces because they prevent chromosome ends from fraying and sticking to each other. But telomeres have also been compared to a bomb fuse because each time a cell divides, the telomeres get shorter. When they get too short, the cell can no longer divide and then it dies, a process that is associated with aging, cancer and a higher risk of death.

Adults who meditate on a regular basis have significantly greater capacity to handle stress than adults who do not meditate. Our brain's plasticity in lengthening our telomeres with meditation, gives us more capacity to cope with change and stress. We now know from scientific research that we also have the ability to develop our **mirror neurons**, which help us experience each other's emotional worlds, and to be empathically connected in relationships. The simple biological fact is that the less your brain is stressed, the greater the possibility of experiencing a loving connection with another like-minded person in the future. So my advice to currently unmarried people is to sit back, meditate and enjoy every stage of your life flying solo. It's probably the last and only time you will ever get to make whatever you want for dinner, to decide which movie you want to see, or to paint your bedroom walls purple if that is a soothing color to you. Enjoy creating your new world as you evolve and integrate this new, differentiated you.

Take a moment right now. Sit back in your chair and notice the feeling of your chest rise and fall as you breathe in and breathe out. Breathe in…and let go. Breathe in…and let go. Imagine yourself as a child of six years old, and playing on an open field. Recall the smells of the grass and green space. Feel the warm breeze of summer air on your face. Imagine yourself at a time when you were joyfully playing on your own. Bring that snapshot to mind right now. Recall yourself and the feelings you had at the time. Breathe in and breathe out. Where do you recall those feelings in your body? Imagine them right now. Are you curious, joyful, happy, or playful? Does that feel bubbly in your heart, sparkly on your shoulders, warm in your stomach? Identify the freedom you felt at six years old. Open your eyes now. As you sit in your chair, how is that different for you today? As you practice bringing those feelings you had at play when you were six, you will notice a new freedom, exhilaration and actually peacefulness grow in you today. How does the recollection of you at six teach you about how to embrace the opportunity of flying solo today?

Many people have a pressing need to speed along in their stages of relationship. This is sometimes due to age and a need to have babies, or it's because your friends are all getting married or are married and you don't want to be left behind. It can also be that you have heard the stories of your parents who had quick takeoffs into marriage after brief engagements. Are you someone who can't wait for the next step? I recall my work with a young, twenty-something couple, 'Bob' and 'Mary'. This betrothed pair initiated couple's therapy one month before their wedding date, just after 'Bob's' stag night. As is the case with many grooms' stags, the boys had hit the town and let loose in a way that was reportedly "very disturbing" to 'Mary'. 'Bob' had received a lap dance from an exotic dancer during the evening and 'Mary' was so upset to find this out from her girlfriend (whose boyfriend had spilled the beans) that she wanted to call the wedding off. While tribal behaviors commonly show up at stags as ritual passages of manhood, this indiscretion was outside the bounds of 'Mary's' sense of moral propriety and for her constituted a significant fracture in trust between them. 'Mary' was vehement that 'Bob's' intoxicated participation in the lap dance was "unforgiveable". 'Bob' understandably was shaken to his core, as he expressed his devotion to 'Mary' and claimed initially that this "story" was not accurate. What was actually true, as 'Bob' gained more confidence and came clean about what had transpired at the stag, was that he was unable to share the details of his escapade because 'Mary' was so rigidly judgmental of what had happened and he did not want to upset her.

As I listened to the couple, I heard their fear of separation: (separate thoughts, feelings, values, and possibly life paths). 'Mary's' core fear was that if 'Bob' would lie about his stag, what else would he lie about? She tearfully grieved "who are you"? 'Bob's' fear was in relation to 'Mary's' rigidity and need for control. For him, this rite of passage was a once in a lifetime event, and if she had such a catastrophic reaction to a simple lap dance, was the rest of his life going to be held in an iron grip of continuous criticism from 'Mary'? Certainly this event highlighted the need for them both to understand how they could come to mutual values through an open dialogue and thereby regain trust in their relationship.

'Mary' started asking questions about why 'Bob' had started to button up his feelings, why was 'Bob' not telling 'Mary' his truths. The more attacked 'Bob' felt by 'Mary's' impatient and judgmental style of communication, the more he feared conflict between them, which in turn stopped him from telling her things that might lead to a fight. As therapy progressed, 'Bob' admitted that he loved everything about 'Mary' except her "puritan values" when it came to their communication about sex.

'Bob' and 'Mary' are an example of what is called 'an emotionally-fused relationship'. This emotional fusion is often seen in relationship commitments, which have a fast uptake (when a couple moves rapidly from infatuation to love, and life-long commitments). As a therapist, I decided that 'Bob' and 'Mary' needed to work to develop more emotional differentiation, more authentic communication, and with a wedding date pressing (only one month away), a speedy path to enlightenment! With the time pressure, this work would be intensive and short term. We met every second day for the following two weeks as I worked as their coach to realign them with those elements that made up their fabric of commitment. We looked at the length of time they had known each other. It turned out that they had met one year previous to their engagement and they had been engaged for only three months before the fateful stag party.

'Mary' admitted that she felt jealous of 'Bob' through much of the period of their relationship. Her previous boyfriend had cheated on her and she had met 'Bob' one month after their break-up. This rebound experience told me that the emotional process from her previous relationship was probably still locked up and had stated showing up in her fear 'Bob' would cheat too. 'Bob' described frustration with 'Mary's' chronic jealousy. He had never cheated in any previous relationships, nor had he experienced any previous partners cheating on him. 'Mary's' sensitivities about 'Bob's' possible disloyalty to her were so anxiety provoking for 'Bob' that he started getting rashes on his skin. He also reported trouble with his sleep and an overall pre-occupation with 'Mary's' happiness.

These multiple pressures on this couple resulted in 'Bob's' lying about what happened at the stag, which then lead to a progressive shut down between them spiritually. They reaffirmed that they both shared common core values of integrity, honesty, love, loyalty, family, friends, community, and giving back.

When 'Bob' finally had the courage to be honest about how he had participated in the stag, he described the details of that event in the way he felt was in fact consistent with all of their shared values. He did not have physical contact with the exotic dancer as others might have. She had danced above him, but without body contact. 'Bob's' version of what he had done at his stag was in his view consistent with his values of friendship, love, and loyalty, not only to his fiancé but also to his buddies who were sharing in what he described as a much-anticipated transition from his single life. He described the stories often shared in his family of origin about his father's stag before his parents married. He had viewed this event as a challenge and joyful engagement with his childhood 'Team Danger'— "The Boys".

I watched 'Mary's' demeanor shift as she witnessed 'Bob's' tearful, honest expression of love for his childhood buddies, his father, his family, and her. Thankfully we were off to a good start and headed in a positive direction towards reconciliation.

Certainly, I had to manage my own anxieties in wanting to help this couple get back in their 'love zone' within such a short time constraint. I imagined their parents standing like ghosts in the room, on guard to make sure therapy brought positive results considering the investment of time, money and family reputation in the forthcoming wedding celebrations. However, I also needed to help this couple get clarity if in fact they were misfit for marriage. Who wants their children, life's work, protégés to make the mistake of a lifetime and head into a life of marital conflict? If they wanted to put off their pending commitment, we would need to reach resolution fairly quickly. I couldn't help think of movies like "Run Away Bride" where pews full of people would be waiting in the church for this marriage ceremony to happen.

Here we see a clear example of what happens when you move too fast in the process of love... or therapy! The faster you go through the stages that lead to marriage, the more insecure will likely be your attachment. What this means is that you may get into patterns of withholding your thoughts and feelings (like 'Bob') or anxiously chronically pursuing the urge to 'bonk' your partner in order to control your partner's behavior (like 'Mary'). 'Mary's' fears that she wasn't good enough, adequate, attractive, strong enough compared to other women, took her out of her loving self, shaping her more into a jail warden rather than loving partner.

As we explored in therapy their respective family scripts, we discovered 'Bob's' parents had married right after they completed college in their early twenties and they then had children immediately. Certainly 'Bob' had this made at home script of speedy romance. His parents were still married forty-something years later, so he was encouraged to follow in his parent's footsteps.

It's remarkable how unconscious we can be in setting up our lives based on the scripts for living we have gained from our parents. In some ways and for some people these expectations and unconscious patterns are not a bad thing. Values of commitment and integrity had been clear anchors supporting marriage longevity in 'Bob's' parents' forty plus year marriage. However, keep in mind that the experience of 'Bob's' parents may not necessarily replicate in others because we are living in a different generation with different external stimulus. For so many couples, the faster they move through the stages of commitment, the more anxiety and reactions may show up in their relationship. Bouncing back from one relationship, take your time before you start back into another.

In the speedy courtship of 'Bob' and 'Mary', and because of 'Mary's' previous relationship and unprocessed grief, 'Bob' and 'Mary' had become emotionally fused. 'Mary' was unable to hear 'Bob's' pain because she was so afraid that he would cheat on her like her previous boyfriend. 'Bob' was full of shame and angst because he felt so guilty he had participated in the stag events not knowing the stories would leak out. However considering how increasingly constricted 'Bob' had become as a result of 'Mary's' chronic controlling behaviors, the stag incident eventually became a catalyst for a welcomed evolution of greater trust between them. 'Bob' had been so aware of 'Mary's' feelings that he had let her needs engulf his own. One impact of this submersion of 'Bob's' needs was that he had become hyper vigilant to 'Mary's' discord, micro-expressions, behaviors and emotional peaks and responded by withdrawing. On her part, 'Mary' had become hyper vigilant about 'Bob's' micro-expressions, behaviors and unspoken feelings and responded by pursuing her instinct to control 'Bob'. When 'Mary' got upset, 'Bob' would 'button up'. The result was that their relationship, with the added stress that came with a wedding date looming in the near future, had become a pressure cooker of unspoken trepidations. In Harville Hendrix "Receiving Love" we learn how this pursue-withdraw pattern that 'Bob' and 'Mary' had entered into can shut down intimacy in their relationship. In the Hendrix's model of Imago, it's in the space between two people where love and secure attachments form (5).

I met with the couple on an intensive schedule, three times per week, and they agreed to hold off making a decision about the wedding for three weeks. The number one goal for them was to develop more capacity to communicate their truths. The number two goal was to resource the strengths of their relationship to gain clarity in a decision to go ahead with the wedding as planned or not. We established a third goal, to focus themselves on their own personal development within a life they would love together. Their openness to seek help and develop their relationship over time was a huge asset of intention between them. With a commitment of this kind, ultimately they felt secure in their break-through decision to continue with their wedding date.

In order for couples to heal attachment wounds, rebuilding must start at trust for self. This involves embracing trust that we are enough, that we are worth it, that we are loveable, and that we can get better at communicating our thoughts and feelings in the safety of the relationship. Rebuilding a fracture in a relationship includes a regained sense that we can trust ourselves to speak up, to share our thoughts and feelings and to practice new openness to hear what our beloved also thinks and feels.

'Mary' had lost faith in her own value when her previous significant relationship had ended in betrayal. Prior to their therapy experience with me, she had never shared her story of loss from that relationship with 'Bob' because she had felt shame that somehow the betrayal had been her fault. She had held a belief that she had let her former boyfriend down sexually and that was why he had strayed in their relationship. With the help of emotionally focused therapy, 'Bob' was able to hold 'Mary's' pain from the past and help her to overcome her fear that there was something wrong with her (otherwise she had thought), "Why would my previous boyfriend have cheated on me?" 'Mary' was self-conscious about her sexuality and had not ever felt confident or nor had she fully actualized this part of her life. 70% of all women have never had an orgasm with intercourse, which impacts motivation and confidence in this aspect and expression of love.

The more self-conscious that 'Mary' was sexually, the less confident 'Bob' became in developing a more playful and frequent sex play with 'Mary'. 'Bob' grew up with a "very controlling" mother and father. He was used to holding his needs and feelings back in order to avoid conflict. He still felt a little nervous around his parent's scrutiny and judgment even today.

The couples' therapy process of 'Bob' and 'Mary' worked to deepen their attachment as their vulnerabilities were expressed, held and validated. Through the trust that 'Bob' and 'Mary' gained in sharing their histories, past wounds, thoughts, feelings about those stories, they reconfirmed their love. Their values and dreams for the future were identified and absolutely aligned in a life they would love together. In this process, they made a decision of what I term 'conscious trust'. You may consider trust as a feeling you experience in your body. Conscious trust is gained through communication of what you feel, and then are able to express; checking in (with your partner) versus totally checking out (avoiding or cutting off from the discovery). When 'Bob' and 'Mary' came to understand themselves and one another and could empathize with each other about how some of the confusing messages of their family, culture, and religion had been constricting on their relationship, they were able to flip their trust switch back on. Trust is a decision we make. I believe we make a decision to turn trust on or turn trust off. Based on information we perceive in a moment or collect over time, we decide if our 'other' is a 'safe landing' for our vulnerable precious self (our thoughts, behaviors and feelings). Then, to some extent, there needs to be a willingness and practice to share the truth of our discoveries. Primarily though, as a precondition to trust, we need to trust ourselves before we can trust anyone else. Through the deepening practice of intimate sharing and with the positive results and return of empathic caring, the turning towards your 'other' will happen more and more. Blind faith may be an instinctual process in our brain. We recognize familiar features of those in our childhood (from other members of our family), which predisposes us to trust a new potential partner with similar physical features. You may observe the phenomena in couples that look alike; or friends who seem to have similar color hair, height, and weight.

When you first meet someone, you unconsciously screen for visual cues that tell you whether this person is safe. This is why couples often resemble each other and as you reflect on your previous relationships, you may notice similar physical or emotional features of those you grew up with. You tend to trust your family members and yourself and therefore unconsciously you trust people with similar features to your own. You may also observe this dynamic with people and their pets! Have you ever noticed how much people look like their pets? Be an observer of pair bonds on your next walk and you will laugh to see how predictable we are as human beings.

You have feelings that are either positive or negative, like a type of radar that is activated, based on being in the company of another. This is when personality traits (such as sense of humor, intelligence, introversion or extroversion) come into play. From that point on, you will either maintain trust or you may re-experience life events that have cause wounds that impair the development of a secure attachment with your other. If you talk through these difficult events and come to understand and have empathy for your partner, you will feel less triggered, less reactive, forgive and move on. Actually if you communicate through the speed bumps of life, your attachments actually become more secure than ever. The more security you experience in your attachments, the less life will feel dramatic and full of speed bumps. 'Bob' and 'Mary' re-committed to their wedding date, and married on schedule. The interesting thing was that the story regarding the stag became so insignificant to both of them compared to the insights they gained about themselves and their dearly betrothed. I look forward to continuing the work with 'Bob' and 'Mary' at some time in the future.

If you need to change your own attachment patterns from moving too fast on the uptake, to a pace that feels less stressful (from anxious to secure) and are motivated to develop better pace and focus for your life generally, my next breakthrough tool is really effective. We are so stimulated by our family, friends, media, and all the moving dynamics of life that we often end up engaged before we are ready, saying yes to commitments we can't keep, or simply spreading ourselves too thin.

Have you got a worry cycle that has shown up since your breakup... right before you go to sleep?! These worry gremlins are horrible! I have known them myself!...And don't you find that the more you worry about everything, the less you actually get done?

After two days of putting this tool to practice, one of my clients recently emailed me to say, *"Okay – it (this tool) has to go in the book! I am knocking things out one at a time... and it relieves my stress too."*

The following exercise does help you let your thoughts go because you release your worries to the written page so you can sleep more peacefully at night. In the morning you get to laser in on what matters most to you of all the things that you wrote down. You will now have a system to figure out how to operationalize your next best step. As you train your brain to focus on one thing at a time, you'll notice your energy goes way up and things just start to feel easy again. In the intentional practice of this, you may also start to notice that your worries start to shape into more of what you want to happen in your life, rather than what you dread. At that point, you will have shifted yourself from scarcity thinking to abundant expectation. This is in some ways a little similar to a vision board exercise. From a cognitive perspective, you are reprogramming your brain to bring on the frontal lobe creative juice and lay off the gremlin haunted stress centers. What you can dream up, you certainly CAN do! The result of this will be that you gain a more manageable expectation and clarity for transformation. With better, more managed pace and focus, you will feel more in charge of you again.

✶✶✶✶✶✶✶✶✶✶✶✶

Here is how this Focusing Tool works:

1. Put a paper and pencil beside your bed. Before you go to sleep tonight, unload all your worries onto the page. Write one word for each thought, for example: children, money, relationship, career, health, parents, residence or community. What keeps you up at night? What are the things you need to do? Worry digs you deeper into the stuck. Action provides immediate release. If you wake up in the night, don't turn on the light. Keep your eyes closed and just add to the list on your nightstand. Believe me, even your most vague scrawl in semi-conscious state will be decipherable to you in the morning!
2. When you wake up, look at the page and circle the ONE thing that stands out to you on the page the most. Go ahead and circle that one thing. You have now chosen your focused intention. For example, today I will focus on how I can get more exercise.
3. During the day, focus just on that one thing you circled. You may do a survey of what your friends and family do for exercise. You may take the stairs instead of the elevator today.

4. That night put a new piece of paper on top of the other one, and beside your bed. Again write down that one thing from your day. (In this case 'Exercise'). Write it at the center of the page and from it, all the 'next steps' action(s) you can take. I might write down spin class, weight train, run, hike, hire a physical trainer, or dust off my tennis racquet. Then go to sleep.

5. In the morning, look at all the things you wrote on the page as your 'next steps' ideas. Again, circle one idea – the idea that stands out for you the most at first glance. Your first choice will be your best choice. So don't over think this. Just circle that one thing that pops off the page. In this case, I might circle 'tennis'.

6. Again, I'd spend that day focusing and taking some type of action on that one thing. I really love tennis. I will sign up for a tennis league today. I'll call my friend who loves to play tennis too. I may meet new fun people when I do this.

7. Before bed, put that action that you will have focused on, in the middle of another new page. In this example, I would write the word 'fun'. From that word, I would stream the thoughts that branch from that (including the fun things that already happened that day). I am there-fore rehearsing positive actions and feelings, building new 'feel good' brain pathways. I might stream new 'next steps' or I might want to just appreciate the positivity coming back in my life. It's all good grist for the brain mill. Repeat the pattern each evening and morning for the following week.

This practice gives you an amazing new capacity to focus. It is also so very energizing because you are continually completing one thing every day. You will be so surprised at how much better you sleep, the results of which give you a generally clearer mind. You also won't believe how much overall energy you begin to have because you are choosing and completing one progressive action every day. If you aren't rushing from one stage to another, what opens up for you? If you enjoyed this time flying solo, what would your life feel like?

****

CHAPTER 4

ESTABLISH A SUPPORT SYSTEM YOU CAN COUNT ON

As human beings we are tribal. When you are going through significant changes, you need to be able to count on your friends and family. Their support will make such a difference as anchors to who you have been and who you are becoming. They contribute to every aspect of your overall health. You need them and they need you. Researchers define this as 'eusociality', which suggests the innate human drive to be part of a group is genetic. Within our 'group', altruistic behaviors rise because of an unconscious need to improve our gene pool. This phenomenon is called 'eugenics'. "And the 'eusocial' group contains multiple generations whose members perform altruistic acts, sometimes against their own personal interests, to benefit their group. 'Eusociality' is an outgrowth of a new way of understanding evolution, which blends traditionally popular individual selection (based on individuals competing against each other) with group selection (based on competition among groups). Individual selection tends to favor selfish behavior. Group selection favors altruistic behavior and is responsible for the origin of the most advanced level of social behavior, that attained by ants, bees, termites and humans" (6).

The more supports you have in place, the less anxiety and anger will undermine you. The less these emotional states overwhelm you, the faster you will breakthrough your stages of grief and get to transformation. One of the first questions I ask clients who are in any process of transition is "who are your supports"? Supports secure you when anxieties undermine your stability. Your good friends will show up in good times and in bad times. Watch out for ants, bees and termites, they'll want to join you too! A key indicator of mental wellness is the established presence of three to five core friends who you are current with and can count on as your home team. If you cannot name who those people are, this chapter is to help you build or re-build that essential area of your life in re-balance.

Unexpected Changes in Your Team Line-up

And there will be surprises too. I recall with great sadness one of my closest girlfriends saying to me about a year after my former husband and I had separated, "well I guess you are going to have to start to find new friends". I was devastated. She had been my confident and closest friend for the past ten years. I had supported her through a number of life's ups and downs and she had been there for me through the initial stages of my separation. We were close. Was she saying to me that she was no longer my friend? Was she saying I was totally on my own? I was so hurt in the moment; it was difficult to express my loss at the time. Many of my clients struggle with the politics of who maintains which friendship. Sadly it can be difficult to maintain some friends when the relationship you have with one person is complicated by another.

Most of my old friends continued to be my core supports showing up in big and small ways. Part of it was just keeping some of my usual routines with girlfriends who offered their time. I was so grateful that both my former husband and myself would be invited to Christmas parties and other special celebrations. It took the drama out of the process and really helped in our first adjustment year. One big example was a friend Elaine Galt who invited me to start my therapy practice out of her medical office, sharing her secretary with me and helping me with the smallest details like how to order business cards! Another friend Debbie Williams took me on a vacation with her (flying us business class... a first for me)... and some friends drifted out of my life. These sad realities are a part of the grief. The loss of the relationship with my former husband was not isolated to just our family, but impacted on our relationships with others who we had known as a couple. I think to some extent this is normal and both of us have developed some new social circles as a result.

I know myself, as I see other friends go through transitions, that it's hard to adjust to the idea that the friend is no longer a part of the couple with whom you had a relationship. The loss of one part of the couple puts the relationship off balance and your friends may grieve not seeing you together anymore. In the case of the loss of my dearest friend, my former husband had been a companion to her husband. It's not just you that will miss the security of experiencing the intact couple relationship. There is also the dilemma about who gets to maintain which friends? If you are friends with one person and it becomes uncomfortable to see the other, your partner may resent having to make a choice and want to avoid the politics all together. Breakups come with natural complications. Walk through all the feelings and just keep talking about the adjustments, fears, grief and resentments. I believe that some people fear break ups are like a bad virus – proximity to a divorcing couple might infect your own marriage. You might catch unhappiness.

The bottom line is that as you move through grief, so do your friends. For some of them, that grief may be too triggering to deal with. I didn't understand this when my dear friend told me I would have to find new friends, but I have come to understand that she made a choice that was best for her. It was pretty difficult to deal with at the time, but when I bump into her today, I realize that our friendship had truly run its course and taken us in different directions. I will always have fond memories of polar bear swims, soccer tournaments, and birthday parties. She was a dear friend for the time we shared and maybe it's true that some friends are for a season, some for a reason but few are forever. As I accepted the loss of her friendship, my life opened up more space for new friends. Life and love are dynamic and not to be owned. And there is always a possibility that our friendship may just be on pause, to be continued at a later date. I have learned and practice the profound art of acceptance.

Consider also how much value you have put into your friendships in the past. Have you been a good friend, or a lazy friend? You need good friends and to have good friends, you need to consider how much creative time and intention you actually commit to the connections. Also, when you are with your friends, are you honest about your feelings, letting them into your emotional world? It's hard to connect to someone who lives like an island unto them self. Take a risk and be honest about how you are feeling and what you are going through. This is also a little tricky because you also don't want to flood someone with an overwhelming list of dread and grief. This is where boundaries (discussed in more depth later in this book) start to become important.

When you spend time with friends, do you worry you have said too much? If so, you probably have **diffuse boundaries** and may want to work on managing how much you share in a balance of what challenges you and what interests you. A good way of pacing yourself-disclosure is to share one thing and let the friend share one thing. This may sound absolutely basic, but many people feel so frozen with the insecurities of being on their own at first, it helps to have a way to pace yourself. It's also nice sometimes to have a fresh new friend because they may not be asking you about your former partner and therefore provide relief... a small break from grief. You know what you need.

If you are in a social setting, ask for people's phone number or email address. Taking someone's telephone number and following up on calling them, is the first step towards friendship. Make sure you follow up. Be reliable. In the process of transition, you may notice yourself becoming a little more forgetful than you've ever been before. Use the calendar on your cell phone to set reminders for any follow up needed. Also, try to remember one thing that the other person is going through and put it in the reminder too. Many clients tell me this is so helpful. Even the intention is helpful because they say "Its weird but I forget to ask about what is going on with everyone else...I'm so wrapped up in my own life right now". If that sounds like you, don't worry its about this stage of transition. It's stressful. When you are stressed, your focus is much narrower than it would be otherwise. Having said that, you still need to practice getting back to being a good friend to others. Use technology to help you remember.

Facebook or LinkedIn are helpful technologies you can search friends from school or previous employment. When you bump into old acquaintances in your day, make sure you send an invitation to join their social network. When you post on either Facebook or LinkedIn, don't be afraid to ask questions such as "Who knows a great Friday night activity?" or "Who's going to see the new movie…tonight?" These are great ways to count yourself in and develop relationships you can build from over posting frequency.

∗∗∗∗∗∗∗∗∗∗∗∗

Another great idea is to make a socio-gram. On a large piece of cardboard, write out a diagram of people in your social networks. List people who are in your work and recreation activities. Circle the people who are single and things you might have in common. Sometimes when you see a visual of your social network, it can illuminate a hopeful plan to rekindle friendships that get you back on track. One friend quite often leads to three more new friends.

Breakthrough Exercise:

1. Take a moment to reflect on your social circles right now.
2. Write a list of all the family, friends, and colleagues you have been in contact with over the past month, six months, or one year. Make three lists with these snapshots in time, because in doing so, you will be able to see who your core five is by comparing the three lists.
3. If you have trouble identifying five core friends, its time to get busy on initiating more contact in your community.
4. Start by thinking of activities you like to do. If you aren't sure what that might be, get on line and start Googling (Love that Googling is now a verb we have created!) "Things to do in your city", "hobbies to do in your city", "single in your city".

Join a running group, a yoga class, a tennis club, a wine tasting club, a cooking school, learn a new language, take up photography, join an art class, or join a meditation group!

****

CHAPTER 5

MY EXPERIENCE OF BREAK-UP BREAKTHROUGH

For tornedos to start you need two air masses – one hot and one cold. As I look back it may have been my return to university that heated up our wind system. When my twenty-year marriage ended, I felt like Dorothy in the Wizard of Oz… sucked up into a tornedo that lifted up the life I had known with every part flying in the circumference of change. With tornedos there is usually a funnel cloud that begins the weather system. In these forces of nature, the cool air goes under the hot air and if the hot air rushes up, this then produces a kind of vacuum. Michael (my former husband), myself, our children and all the parts of my life as I knew it seemed from my perspective to be unpredictably swirling in the up and down drafts of change. I have been told that if you could stand in the middle of a tornedo, there is an eerie stillness. I tried as best as I could to imagine I was able to stand in the change and be an observer rather than try to stop the things that seems to whirl around in the twister. I found myself in a numbing type of fear that we would never be a family again. I worried whether our two children whom I adored would land on their feet. The metaphor of standing in the eye of the tornedo was where I found a strength I never knew I could access. I tried my best to be able to be present for the emotions and thoughts of those I loved, and at the same time not surrender to 'Dorothy's' nightmare. I knew the twister, like all twisters, would settle and I would find new ground for myself and all those I cared so dearly for.

So here's some background of my life before the breakup. I was married to my former husband Michael for twenty years, a marriage that felt beautiful to me at the beginning, but as it evolved over time, like a roller coaster ride of highs and lows. The lows, from my perspective, resulted from my ongoing difficulty in managing interpersonal conflict with Michael and my inability to just let go. When we decided to have children thirty years ago, (I was twenty-three and my husband Michael was thirty-two at the time), I made a commitment to the members of my family that I would do whatever I could so that they would know that they could count on being loved unconditionally. I felt I could walk through fire to provide the security of an intact family in order help them to pursue their dreams.

I saw having children as both a privilege and a responsibility- an investment of time, love and money that would give us a big return of joy now and forever. But somehow Michael and I lost sight of each other in this process of having a family, and ultimately we just ceased to be a good fit as life partners. I am confident today that Michael, if asked, would be able to say he felt the same way. But when we first got together neither of us could have forecast that after twenty years of marriage during which we parented our two children well, we would break up. Neither Michael nor I are quitters, and it wasn't a question of quitting when our marriage came to an end. You can tell I held a lot of guilt around this idea of being a 'quitter'. One of the guiding principles of our marriage and in our parenting style was "You never quit anything you start. If you sign up for something, you need to see it through. If at the end of the program, you decide you have given it your all and it's not for you, you don't sign up the next season". I suppose Michael and I came to a change of seasons in our marriage. One of us simply had to call an end to the unhappy sense of being stuck in a relationship punctuated by repeated and unresolved conflict, and lack of growth dynamic both individually and collectively that our lives together had become.

My relationship with Michael of course never actually ended either. But it has gone through a fundamental re-framing of what is possible with love with a given person, in this case my husband of twenty years. One of life's big realities is that relationships change, some grow, some end. But to love well includes the ability to recognize when it's time to let go and re-define a loving relationship. Thankfully, Michael and I have been able to do this, and now twelve years after our breakup, we are both in a much better place emotionally.

I feel good about my part in our marriage breakup. I managed to move through the separation and divorce process in a way that didn't leave me stuck in a negative, blaming space trying to build a case against my former husband. Michael will always be a very important person in my life as the father of our two children. No one benefits from assigning the burden of blame when a relationship fails.

There is so much I'm grateful for in my years that I partnered with Michael. We were great parents together and like-minded in our commitment to provide unconditional love for our children, Justin and Ashley. Both children have had a pretty stellar experience of life so far, academically, athletically and musically. It takes a lot more than luck to bring up two resilient, contributing, happy human beings, who are independent and enjoy their respective professional careers. A wise person once told me that 'you have to be smart to be lucky' and I would consider Michael and I to have been smart parents.

Michael and I were big contributors to our local community. Michael coached our daughter's soccer team. I read to the children at our neighborhood elementary school, organized their school sock hops and other special events and served their school Parent Advisory Committees. I loved being a 'stay-at-home-mom', and our children's friends fondly knew me as 'Mumma Jo'. Our neighborhood community was a pretty close knit one. Some of my favorite times in that stage in my life were spent in the social networks of family engagement that soccer, tennis, and music recitals create. Michael and I were all safely wrapped in the inspired tapestry of community spirit and child rearing. It was an idyllic time in our lives. I will always be grateful for those twenty years with Michael including the privileges that his career in family medicine provided us.

I cherish so fondly my memories of that time: giving birth to two beautiful babies, coaching baseball to six year olds (not actually really knowing the game very well myself), cheerleading our children's soccer teams, traveling around Canada and the United States supporting our son's tennis career as he built his rankings in pursuit of a tier one university athletic scholarship in the United States. It makes me laugh to think of the crazy, hectic 'meals-on-wheels' life of our young family, including the children's sports apparel changes in the car while I passed them plates of pre-prepared food into the back seat. We ate a lot of pasta in those days! There were a few years when we had both our children in piano, soccer, tennis, and horseback riding. I'm surprised we got through it all with all body parts in tact! Just the same, our family stresses were high because of the lack of kick back time and the rising financial demands of our family's high do'ing lifestyle.

In the big picture and looking back, I wouldn't change a thing about how I spent those years with Michael because in the result has been two children who are now happy and successful young professionals whose lives are guided by solid community-oriented values. But I now know that my marriage to Michael might have been more successful in the longer term if I had been more proactive in keeping our overall family stresses down, and in leading our family to a place where we experienced a state of peace a lot more often. (My next book, by the way, will be called "Love Up and Stress Down").

When Justin and Ashley entered the latter stages of high school, I went back to university to upgrade my education. Looking back I now recognize this change of course was the beginning of my delayed **differentiation** as a person that I should have gone through as an adolescent.

We all go through our own stages of differentiation and integration: when we learn to walk, when we go to school, when we become teenagers, when we launch from our family homes, when we go to university, when we marry, and when our own children then follow the same life stages. In their growth and stages, we re-visit our own. We move in and out of growth, a process that can either bring us closer together in our significant partnerships or can divide us. In our case, over the course of our twenty-year marriage, Michael and I simply outgrew each other. We just didn't have the skills or the level of **differentiation** to be able to stay connected and to resist the temptation of being defensive in our interactions. As our tensions with each other increased, the attachment that brought us together in the first place frayed. And I now understand that when I went back to university and experienced again the joy and wonder of learning and satisfaction of increasing my self-development as a professional, we became more divided as a couple.

The more I grew, the more our emotional distance showed up. I discovered a differentiation that released me from the roller coaster of **emotionalfusion** to Michael but the changes in me gave me a perspective that distanced me emotionally. Differentiation, a term defined by Murray Bowen (1978) is being a unique person in emotional times, but also being connected to the feelings of the other. But rather than this being a healthy process, one that would help Michael and I grow together into the next stage of our relationship as a couple, it lead us in opposite directions. We couldn't seem to sit in each other's emotional worlds without a loss of our own. I withdrew. With differentiation, we should have a more developed self and then therefore more to share in relationship with our other. More anger, more blow ups, more tensions, more stresses, our marriage just unraveled as its earlier focus on trying to be the world's best parent dissipated as our children flew out of our nest.

Today I see anger quite differently. I am no longer retreating from the experience of anger in my life. I see it now as an intimate, two-way experience. Developing my autonomy and ability to express myself has taken time and practice. I would say that my own differentiation has, and continues to develop with practice. Anger reveals the young vulnerable self in both the receiver and giver. Whether expressed or withheld, I now see anger as part of being a healthy and whole human being. My younger me saw anger as something to avoid at all costs. Today, I know that anger teaches us how to love better, if we are not defensive in its presence. If we ask ourselves, and are curious about the other in what he or she feels and needs, in what we feel and need, anger can be a key pathway to the heart. Of course we will feel angry at times. But if we are able to understand anger and embrace anger for what it might reveal in our interactions, it will not cause fear. On the contrary, anger can help us to grow.

I still believe that in many important ways our marriage was a twenty-year success in raising two contributing children. We will always have wonderful memories about our time together as parents. And I am happy to report that today we enjoy a warm friendship with each other and a continued connection in the love our children. Better still, both of us are now in committed relationships with more aligned new loves and we have the most wonderful children and stepchildren.

My own breakup-breakthrough was to befriend patience, to proceed quietly and softly, and to rely on my inner trust that everything would all work out. It wasn't easy though. This involved experiencing a multitude of gut-wrenching feelings, as I went along a most mindful journey from past to present. I learned to love and forgive the 'whole' of imperfect me and to love and forgive the 'whole' of imperfect Michael. I learned how to nurture the part of me that plays small at times, to celebrate the part that loves to learn, to engage the playful, to mind the curious. I have learned to welcome judgment (because of the opportunity for growth that judgment invites).

It's not all rosy every day. There are times I get anxious about how our breakup changed the course of our children's lives and our own for better and for worse. Our children are generally confident, happy and resilient. I need to remember that when they go through life's bumps and natural learning curves. As I go through my own bumps and learning curves, I try to embrace being a human and do my best. I also allow space for Michael to do his best. As former partners, that best can change from time to time, and when it does, the boundaries become stronger or more dilute. What I know for sure is that I am grateful to have come through each stage of transition and know everyone is totally so much better for it.

And I believe that because of what I've been through, I am able to give back in a much greater capacity to couples and individuals in my clinical work. I have learned a lot more about my family of origin. I embrace my flaws and my strengths. I am a lot more forthcoming about what's important to me. Because of my own experience of 'the tornedo time' of change, I can be with you to walk through your grief, calm your fears, discover new confidence, and celebrate your courage. I truly believe you have to experience life to be able to truly love in the work you do, no matter what your career is. We are all in this life together. We can help each other a lot more than we do. Helping is so innate to our nature as human beings. Knowing how to ask for help and when to provide it are some of the tenants of your own breakup breakthrough.

Breaking through from a breakup, to come alive again takes time. It helps a lot to have a guide to get through your own closing of the door to your past. It takes your 'wholehearted' commitment to practice new ways of thinking and to be patient with your feelings. I know from my personal experience and from the clients I work with, that the tools in this book work! Through all the pain, you will totally experience your own gain. As the years move forward, I can see clearly that, outside of parenting, Michael and I may have just been ill matched. (Isn't hindsight wonderful?) The symptoms of our ill-suited pairing were anger, frustration, fear, and recurring unproductive conflict. Despite all the resistance to change, all the twists and turns of emotion, it always just comes down to that – two good people in a misfit pairing.

We also live longer lives today than our ancestors did. Maybe it's unrealistic to think we are necessarily going to be with one person our whole lives. Our great grandparents only lived until their sixties. With the benefits of health science and a fitness focus, at sixty, we may have another forty years to go in today's world. Either way, there is a certain point, thankfully, when clarity can emerge out of storm clouds of dissidence and conflict. The clarity for Michael and I was the realization that, although grateful for twenty years together, it was time for us to move on.

Then there is my work as a clinician working with clients who are moving through relationship change, and experience as a mother of two adult children and two adult stepchildren. I have witnessed the morphing of many hearts (including my own) and the painful suffering that comes with the territory of change.

This book is for adults of all ages. At any point in our lives, our hearts may be called upon to face adversity and the grief of loss. The beneficial experience of strength, bliss, joy and fulfillment that are possible as we face these times head-on will come from trusting that we have what it takes to move forward. This book will provide you with the insights that I have gained through my personal and professional life. My hope is that it will provide you a more solid base within yourself, and that you can build the trust and confidence to navigate through these tough times in your life. The good news is that the end of one relationship can provide the opportunity to succeed at love in a future relationship. We all know we need to close the door of a relationship to be available to open the door to another and confidently to bask in the glow of that new loving relationship forever.

My own tornedo dust settled. I spent the first few years rediscovering myself and then I met Joe. Meeting Joe was like the coming together of two light sources. When he walked up my front steps on our first date, his presence was like the first light of a sunrise. We all know that at the end of every storm, there will be light! After three years of being on my own, living with my daughter (a period that I fondly call our 'Gilmour Girls Time'), dating a little, and growing a lot, I am so grateful to have discovered Joe Weiler. Patti Bolton, a close mutual friend, introduced Joe and I three years after my separation from Michael.

Joe and I had our first date on May 4th, 2004. What a sensational experience that was! Honestly there were so many weather effects that night: hail as we headed out for dinner, rain as we talked for hours and hours in the restaurant while not even ordering food, thunder, lightning and heavy rainfall on our walk after dinner, finishing with a break in the storm clouds and a brilliant full moon. I laugh to recall that Joe had tried to protect us from the deluge under an umbrella, until we realized that we were walking under a veritable lightning rod. We stepped out of the umbrella and got soaking wet as we accepted each other's invitation to travel together two months later to Prague (Joe's idea) and Tuscany (my dream trip after having seen the film Under the Tuscan Sun). I know how corny that story sounds, but it's absolutely true!

Our first date was like a meeting with the elements, the coming together of the forces of nature. Sharing an evening with Joe felt like the Gaia winds were sweeping into my soul, calling me to share my life with this man. It honestly was falling in love at first date, which was totally contrary to what I have always advised my clients and our children. My message about the pitfalls of falling in love right off the bat was that this infatuating experience was not to be trusted, that true love takes time to develop. But my experience with Joe that night proves that like all truisms, there is an exception that proves the rule! When love happens, you know that in your body, mind and spirit – Love IS Light. I fell in love with the light that shone from Joe's spirit that very first night we were together. Right away I loved and respected what Joe stands for. Joe is a law professor and lawyer who came out of the 1960s with a career ambition to do whatever he could to change the world, to make it a better place through his teaching, writing, professional and community work. He is dedicated to being of service. He is the embodiment of caring.

Everything changed in our lives from that night of our first date when we came together, realized that we were the perfect match as a life partner that we had both been looking for all our lives. Looking back now nine years later, I believe everyone in our two families have been enriched because of their experience of Joe and I being together. We married two years after we met in August 5, 2006. I am so grateful for having Joe in my life. I feel so empowered with Joe as my partner. Every day I feel like I am sitting on the cat seat of life, smiling out at my world. But I know that the origin of that smile comes from within me. And it took awhile to get there. Let me tell you about anxiety...

CHAPTER 6

THE UNINVITED GUEST - ANXIETY

Many clients who are working through a relationship transition (in or out of connection) come to therapy because they have developed anxiety. This chapter will give you some helpful ways to deal with anxiety. Anxiety is the most common mental illness in North America, affecting 40 million people in the U.S., which is 18% of the U.S. population and 12% in Canada. If you've experienced mild, moderate, or acute anxiety with full-blown panic attacks, you are not alone! The symptoms of anxiety are: racing heart, sweaty palms, shaking, and sensations of shortness of breath or smothering, feelings of choking, nausea or stomach upset. If you have felt these symptoms, you have probably experienced anxiety or full-blown panic.

As you move through your own stages of change, your body often speak ups with physical symptoms such these to get you motivated to communicate, and reach out more to others for help. Some people are 'masters of emotional disguise', and their signs of distress are so well hidden, their family and social circles may assume they are doing a whole lot better than they truly are. I believe that our body is a fail-safe for our health and survival. For this reason, it presents physical symptoms when we don't speak up. If you are having anxiety symptoms, your symptoms may be related to your grief, the pressures of a new decision in moving forward regarding your home, friends, family, or finances. What isn't there to worry about?! You may also find you have been overwhelmed in receiving over-zealous advice from others. Has everyone become an expert on your life lately? Your anxiety may be telling you to step up your boundaries (which I will address in chapter twelve).

Think of your body as your best friend, shaking you to: speak up (let someone know you need support), slow down (you have put too much pressure on yourself in the pace of change), or to take better care of your physical health (get some exercise, eat better, sleep better). It's not a pleasant feeling when anxiety shows up. I know this because I have experienced it myself! The sensations in your body can be really overwhelming. I recall a time when I was three months post separation from my marriage to Michael. I was on a hike in a familiar trail–the Capilano Dam, when these symptoms seemed to grab hold and freeze me on a lookout point, part way up my climb. I couldn't move. I couldn't breathe. I felt so dizzy, I was afraid I might fall off the edge of the cliff. There was a wooden railing I was standing by, and I was well on the safe side of the lookout. But at that moment in time, I was completely overwhelmed. I was absolutely overcome with the sense that my heart was going to burst through my throat.

You may find that you have these 'out of the blue' nightmarish moments. In that stage of my separation I was determined to get through a massive change in my life. I wasn't as open with my girlfriends as I could have been. I needed their support, but I was so determined to keep the details of our divorce private that I had isolated myself, keeping all my worries to myself. At the time I was thinking I didn't want to say anything negative about Michael (or myself), so I just didn't say anything at all. Share your fears with someone you trust or hire a clinical counselor. As I mention in the 'guilt' chapter, when you have children there is a built in emotional bind. You don't want to vent about your resentments regarding the other person—he/she is half of who your children are! So, don't forget this idea that relationship endings can give you posttraumatic stress. You have experienced a crash of hearts. For this reason, talk to a counselor or psychologist a.s.a.p.! You can't just deny your resentments, or hold in your regrets; they become the fuel for anxiety and panic. These complex feelings can bite you in the butt the rest of your life! You will be so much better off if you go through the process of grief with a trusted guide.

I told myself, "The Capilano Dam is a somewhere I run frequently". "Why am I so overwhelmed by this hike today?" Possibly the 'hike' versus 'jog' pace slowed my experience down. At a full-out 'run' pace, I may have had more endorphin release. I had never felt these types of body sensations in my life before. Endorphin (the feel good chemistry) counteracts cortisol (stress hormone) and there is more endorphin released on a run, than is released on a mindful hike. As I reflect on that day, doing something out of my routine (such as going to the lookout) may also have triggered me. I would have normally just stayed on the trail and kept a steady pace. All of these factors may have triggered the floodgate of truth— my life path, my families' life path and all the details in it, had completely changed forever.

> "The Moving Finger Writes; and, having writ,
> Moves on: Nor all thy Piety, nor Wit,
> Shall lure it back to cancel half a Line,
> Nor all thy Tears, Wash out a word of it."
> - Omar Khayyam

The truth is you may find yourself with the unwelcome visitor of anxiety during your first adjustment year. If so, know it is a body response (your sympathetic nervous system), which is triggered by a conscious or unconscious thought to a perceived lack of control. The unwanted thought stimulates the limbic brain to release the stress hormone cortisol. This then fires up your sympathetic nervous system to release adrenaline to your heart in a fight or flight response. The physical symptoms may be experienced as mentioned above. Anxiety can feel like your heart has lifted out of your chest cavity, right up into your throat. If this happens to you, abrupt your body's cycle of anxiety with a tool you can count on. Try this trick. It will over-ride your symptoms and restore homeostasis as your parasympathetic nervous system, (which relieves your sympathetic nervous system), kicks back in to rescue you. You have an incredible body with everything you need to get through this tough phase of your own life in change. Let me explain…

Your brain has a whole neural network of connections, which stimulate physical responses in your body. For example, if I ask you to think about hot apple pie with all the smells of cinnamon, apple, fresh baked crust, your mouth waters. Right? Well that is because you have tasted apple pie and the mere suggestion of it, stimulates your salvation glands (just like Pavlov and his dog experiments). The idea of this is that we can build a cue in our brain pathways to stimulate regulation and relaxation.

****

Find a quiet space right now and try this out:

Put your thumb and index finger together and focus on your breath.

Breathe in and breathe out.

Do these breaths four or five times.

Notice the touch of your thumb and index finger.

Then hold your breath for four or five seconds, and release fully.

Repeat this sequence two more times.

****

Notice that when you hold your breath in a prolonged way, you begin to experience symptoms similar to anxiety—racing heart and sweaty palms. Your body teaches you not to hold your breath. You can also learn from your body that you should not hold on to your thoughts or feelings. When you hold your feelings in and block yourself from receiving help from others, anxiety will show up to motivate you. Communicate, share, and invite a trusted friend into your confidences. The more you feel you are safe, connected and belong, the less chance anxiety will ever return.

In the second part of this exercise, put your thumb and middle finger together and focus on an imagined walk on a favorite beach (if you prefer trails, you can go there instead). As you hold your thumb and middle finger together, imagine yourself walking on a beautiful beach. Smell the ocean air and sea kelp. (The sense of smell goes directly to the limbic system to calm you). Imagine the sound of the waves gently tumbling up on the shoreline as your breath joins the rhythm of the ocean in your mind's eye.

Breathe in, let go.

Breathe in, let go.

Imagine the sounds on the beach.

There may be some birds you hear, or some children playing in the distance.

Inhale the clean air you imagine and envision the openness of the ocean.

The air is clean, misty and calming.

Breathe in fresh perspective.

Let go of fear.

Notice the touch of your thumb and middle finger.

You are building a neural connection of relaxation response that will link your thumb and middle finger to the smells and experience of being at the beach.

This is a two-step practice that was absolutely calming for me in times when I felt a loss of my center. The trigger for anxiety may be connected to some type of loss of control. Certainly until I had a true sense that those I loved, (including myself) were going to be ok, anxiety was an unwelcomed visitor I needed to deal with from time to time. The more confidence I had that I could right my physical symptoms by doing this two finger trick, anxiety went away forever.

You may also have anxiety about decisions you are making during this transition time. If so, an effective decision making tree is to write out the pros and cons of your decision with five or ten reasons that promote yes or no. Make sure you think of the pros and cons in equal distribution for and against your decision. When you have written your two lists, give each reason a number between one and ten. Ten would mean you feel very strongly about the point. One would mean that it's not important to you. When you are done, add up your lists. Whichever list has the greater score that will be your best decision.

****

For example, if you were struggling about whether you should join some friends on a night on the town, you might write a list that looks like this:
Pros:

1. I love these friends. = 10
2. I want to get out and have some fun. = 7
3. I need to spend more time with my friends. = 8
4. The last time I went out with my friends I felt great. = 10
5. I haven't been practicing work-life balance. = 10
    Total score of reasons why I should go out = 45

Cons:

1. I shouldn't spend the money. = 6
2. I have a lot of work to do tomorrow = 7
3. I have some anxiety about going out = 5
4. I may not have a good time = 4
5. I always eat and drink a little too much = 4
    Total score (reasons why I shouldn't go out) = 26

****

As you look at the total for pros 45 versus cons 26, I would make the decision to join my friends on a night on the town. This is such a helpful and simple tool, which can be applied to big and small decisions. After you have made your decision, cognitive dissonance will dissipate and you will tend to accumulate more and more reasons to support your decision. Values and beliefs back in alignment, you will know you are doing the right thing. If you find that your decision leads you to discomfort, you can, after all, make a new decision. So, take the pressure off and watch your anxiety disappear.

I had anxiety once more about two years ago when I was travelling on a small seaplane to Vancouver from Salt Spring Island. The pilot had asked me to sit in the cockpit with him and seeing all the dials and a gas tank register at near empty, it was not exactly an irrational fear that set me off. Either way, I had to give it up to God/Spirit/Universal Goodness and trust that we wouldn't run out of gas. I had to believe that the plane would not fall from the sky. I had to believe the Pilot knew what he was doing. We would be all right. The great thing about my two-finger tool is that you can use it out of the blue (in this case, in the blue) without anyone being aware at all.

Breathe in, breathe out. Let…go…

Once my parasympathetic nervous system kicked in, I was able to ask the Pilot about the low level of gas showing on the dashboard of his plane. He assured me with a smile "There is enough gas in the tank for us to make it to Vancouver". I probed, "Are you sure? There is no rush… (breathe)… Are you sure you don't want to stop somewhere near by to fill up?" and he laughed. Somehow the exchange of words through our headsets, and his laugh was a comfort to me. My anxiety lifted.

As I looked out beyond the racket of the motor and its sputter, I started to pay attention to an incredible view of the B.C. coastline. Blue Open Ocean and a mix of curiosity took over from my fears. I started to look for whales, and my mind wandered to thoughts of my son and I fishing in a small outboard off the Coast of Hornby Island when he was six. Justin and I had been absorbed in telling stories together while we fished. We hardly noticed a pod of Killer Whales travelling right beside our small boat. There was no anxiety for my son or myself in that moment. (We learn anxiety from our parents). Seeing whales this close was a first for us both. As we pulled up our fishing lines, the beautiful dorsal fins of six Killer Whales travelled right by us. It's amazing how magnificent the World is when we are not afraid. Your brain is resilient if you can manage your own fears (whatever they are) and allow your own natural states of love and curiosity, to calm and lead you. All was ok for Justin and I then. All will be ok for you too.

Just breathe.

∗∗∗∗∗∗∗∗∗∗∗∗

Breakthrough Tools for Anxiety:

1. When you feel anxiety symptoms coming on, put a breathing technique such as the one above to practice. Breathe in BE, breathe out HERE. Breathe in BE, breathe out BE HERE NOW. Extending your outbreath, you are training yourself in a concept of letting go. Let go of the fear. Let go of the need to control. Be here now.
2. Have a bottle of cold fizzy cold water such a soda or Pellegrino on hand. Drink it slowly and notice how calming it is with the cooling to your throat. The body sensations of drinking cold fizzy water, redirects your thinking off the anxiety symptoms. It literally flushes stress and the discord the down your throat and restores your calm. Just like a toilet, you can flush your fear out!
3. Drink lots of water during your day, as cortisol is stored in the kidneys and the additional water naturally clears it out of your system.
4. Is there a trusted friend you can share your feelings or fears with?
5. Start a journal (if you haven't already). It helps to write your thoughts and feelings on a page. Write the problematic thought on one side of the page and write the positive opposite on the other. You can train your thoughts. For example "my relationship is over" (fear) and "I'm ok on my own" (positive opposite). Then during the rest of the day,

look for the evidence in moments that tell you "I'm ok on my own". Guess what, it's true!

6. The chemical release of endorphin that you get with cardiovascular exercise (twenty minutes or more) is a natural way to abate cortisol. Try jogging, swimming, bike riding, or brisk hiking. There are additional mood effect benefits if you do these activities in natural light.

7. Aromatherapy does work. Your brain processes smells in a way that bipasses the anterior lobe (where we process thoughts and feelings) and goes directly to the limbic center (where we process fight and flight) to calm you. According to research:
   - Rosemary is shown to reduce cortisol,
   - Lavender improves brain function and mood, and has some calming properties, which reduce cortisol.
   - Lavender helps to calm you before sleep (good to spritz on your pillow at night).
   - Peppermint has shown increase memory and alertness if you are fatigued.
   - Ylang-Ylang promotes calm and reduced stress.
   - Lemon has been shown to possess an anti-depressant type of effect (7).

8. If your anxiety becomes chronic, consult with your physician.

9. Don't isolate yourself. Choose group activities over solitary ones, as much as possible.

10. Understand what is going on in your body. Knowledge is power. Core triggers for anxiety can be: fear of separateness or a perceived lack of control.

11. Ask for help! Even if you don't think you need help, ask anyways. You are not alone and you have the opportunity to communicate your needs when you are in the company of others.

12. Join a group activity of choice. Some ideas might be to join in a running group, a cycling group, an exercise class, a yoga class, a meditation group, a quilting group, a photography group, a sailing class, a skiing group, a dance class…you have options. Exercise them!

13. Knitting or some other hand on activity can be a great way to reduce anxiety. It's not my first choice for you, unless you join a knitting group.

14. Try to limit your caffeine and high sugar intake as stimulants such as these can cause peaks and valleys in your energy, which can also link to anxiety response.
15. Get your sleep. Lack of sleep can contribute to anxiety. If you have been putting the sleep hygiene tools to practice and you are still not sleeping, check with your physician to see if you have sleep apnea or a need for a temporary prescription for sleeping pills.
16. Music can be a great help in overcoming anxiety if your anxiety seems to peak for you at night. Try a meditation tape before bed. Meditative music can really help to get you to sleep.
17. Anxiety may also be linked to unexpressed anger. Journal, journal, journal.

Breakthrough Tools for Social Anxiety:

1. Try to get some type of twenty-minute exercise before your social event. This gives you an endorphin boost to set you up for the occasion.
2. If the event happens every year, try Googling to see what people wore and get an idea of what you can expect. Information is power.
3. Wear something you feel confident in. You don't want to be distracted or feeling self-conscious. Rule out the things you can easily control for.
4. If you know someone else going to the event, see if you can car pool. This will reduce your stress of finding the location, parking, and arriving on your own.
5. When you first arrive at the venue, drink a cold glass of fizzy Pellegrino or soda water. Drink it slowly. It will feel soothing and works to calm your system down.
6. Stand on the outside circle of the event. Let people come to you. This gives you the chance to get used to the stimulus of everything in the room.
7. Choose one person you can talk to first.
8. When you are engaged in conversation, turn your back to the room so you can concentrate on just the two of you.
9. Switch the spotlight off you and think about the person standing in front of you. Consider what they might be feeling, what they are wearing, what they may have done before coming to the event, how are

they feeling right now? In 'switching the spotlight' your anxiety will disappear as you engage your curiosity and flow with meeting someone new.

10. If you feel overwhelmed at any point, take a moment and use the washroom to do a quick breathing meditation or try a tapping idea. Put your hands just above your knees and firmly tap alternately. Continue to tap for about one minute and then hold your hands in place on your legs. You will feel a warm sensation through your legs, which have activated the attachment hormone oxytocin. Oxytocin abrupts anxiety symptoms and gives you regained calm.

11. If you need a quick fix while you are standing, simply cross your arms with your hands midway up you side. Tap alternately with a similarly firm pressure. Do this for about a minute and then hold your hands in place. You will experience a similar rush of warmth through your core and even into your jaw. Your body has everything it needs for you to feel whole, healthy and calm.

****

CHAPTER 7

ANGER: THE GOOD, THE BAD AND THE UGLY

This chapter will help you give you some new perspectives and tools for anger – receiving and expressing it. Whether you were left or you did the leaving, anger is a soul sister to anxiety. When you can't express or tolerate anger, you will be likely to experience anxiety (back to chapter 6). And suppressed anger eventually leads to depression. (Anger is also a symptom of depression). One of the reasons anger is such a roadblock for many is that anger has a bad reputation; many would prefer to just avoid it all together! Considering we are all going to feel some level of anger every day, it makes sense to become skilled in understanding ways anger can actually serve you. Anger is just confusion in an emotional tornado of sorts. Anger can energize you to shift gears, get your point across, and be more assertive in your life. So in that way anger can be a good emotion. With the right tools and personal management, anger can lead you to deeper understanding of otherwise, hidden fears or judgments, which is also positive. Anger when its 'bad' is seen in the power struggle, where you lock into a need to be 'right' or react to someone else's need to be 'right'. When it comes to breakups, make a policy that no one gets to be right! It's painful enough without the case building, name calling, shaming and blaming game. Then there is 'ugly' anger when it is abusive, fear inducing, line crossing, physically or emotionally threatening. It's in 'ugly' anger that you need to walk away from, ask for help, or even call the police.

When all the old structures of your shared life have been knocked out with the breakup, it is going to take some time to regain your footing as a single person and you are likely to feel anger along with many other feelings through the stages of grief. Learning to cope with all the changes you are going through, you may find yourself feeling horribly angry or irritable in the most benign circumstances.

****

Here's a test: You can't find your keys to your car and you are in a rush to get to work, so you: (a, b, or c)

a. Yell a few words in a language no one understands, but so loudly you get a phone call from the apartment next door, or

b. Hate your work and decide to send an email to your boss to say you are not coming in today or any day in the near future; or

c. Sit down in on your couch for a five-minute break to do some breathing exercises until your brain regains its full capacity and you can remember where your keys are.

****

Of course, c. is always your best choice, but can you relate to a. and b. too? …well maybe not exactly, but something similar? When you are stressed and experiencing burnout, you can start to feel angry about the 'otherwise' ridiculous. In this sense, anger is a '**good**' indicator (like the canary in the coal mine) that you need to slow your life down and regain more work-life balance while going through this relationship transition time. Many clients feel a compulsive driving need to just truck through the adjustment by pouring into the distractions of work. And with this type of strategy, symptoms of burn out, irritability, and peaks of rage will only get worse.

If you act impulsively with anger, you risk doing damage to supportive members of your tribe which are otherwise valuable foundations for you moving forward. Your family, your friends, your work, and your colleagues are all important to you. Don't lose control and mess with their good natures. They are the people who matter most to you. You may think of yourself as being the most 'Zen' type of person, and while you are going through this relationship transition, sides of you show up you have never known before.

I heard a story from a client (I will call 'Sam') that he had made the effort to get to a neighborhood yoga class and when he got there the class was full. 'Sam' made a huge stink and yelled at the front desk staff. He was so enraged they wouldn't let 'just one more person' into the class. Five minutes later the police came. On revision, and after being detained by the police, 'Sam' realized that it wasn't about being blocked from going to the yoga class that was so upsetting to him. It never is actually about that one moment in time. In his case, he felt a surge of embarrassment and resentment mixed into the reality that his girlfriend had broken up with him the week prior. Here 'Sam' felt he was being rejected from yoga too! 'Sam' discovered that he had been hiding his fear of rejection for most of his life.

'Sam's' feeling of inadequacy had started showing up in childhood. He recalled, for example, a time when he was not chosen for his school basketball team. As 'Sam' considered the fact that he wasn't a very tall boy, he considered a perspective of height selection and remembered that ended up on the school swim team instead. When he reconsidered his **schema** (the personal construct) around sports "I'm not good enough", and with constant rehearsing of the **scripts,** (the stories) that fulfill that schema, deepen and entrench his trigger points to anger. No one feels happy to think they are not good enough. He started to identify his emotional cycle. The more he lived in his old internal schema of inadequacy, the more anxious and insecure he felt. The more he felt insecure and inadequate, the more he would withdraw from conflict. In this pattern, he kept deepening his sense of inadequacy. As he reconsidered a new schema about sports "I am good enough" because I was on the Swim Team" his new script developed into "I was a pretty good swimmer.. I knew I belonged there". With that new positive story, he was less avoidant and more secure in taking risks to feel competent. You pay attention to information that fits into the schemas you have developed over time. These are attachment fears and unmet needs from childhood confusion. The distress you may have felt from childhood can become the truths of your adult life unless you actively work to organize your thinking into healthier patterns. In fact research shows that you will actually not process information that is not congruent with your schemas! So the schemas you hold about 'having a date' or 'being in a relationship' are important when you are working on feeling better again after your breakup. If you carry a lot of negative schemas about relationships – which you can't trust, you are unlovable, you will collect stories, building scripts that fit into those negative thinking structures. The more negative thinking structures, the more negative feelings (sadness, anger, frustration) and the more rejection, overwhelm, abandonment, and misperceptions of your own unlovability will rock your life.

Here's how that works: If you feel you 'lost' because you were the one left, the schema of 'loser' starts to manifest in your cognitions as you internalize the negative thoughts and feelings that identify you ARE a loser! That is something to feel angry about! And guess what, as your cognitions go in this direction, you will start to pay attention to details in the day that support that negative thinking. You actually end up not noticing any positive information. That's how scripts and schemas work. Its like you are blind to positive things. When you don't share your painful feelings of loss, frustration and anger, you internalize an identity developed from the feeling itself over time. Our feelings inform our thinking. That is why it's so important to communicate and correct like 'Sam'. The more positive schemas you build about life and relationships, the more you will pay attention to positive information in your day. The more positive data you notice, the more positivity you will attract. IF you have a lot of negative schemas (thinking structures), you will naturally notice all the negative data of the day and probably be more inclined to feel angry, negative, and depressed. So here's the answer, don't shove your feelings underground because you judge them. Through communicating your anger, you give the other person a chance to correct the misunderstanding. And, no matter what the other person says to you, you have let go of the frustration. You matter. Your feelings matter. That is something to grow from.

You also want to learn to have the capacity to hear feedback so you can end up with a deeper understanding of your own impact and how to give and receive more empathy and care. The bottom line is that if you don't communicate, your feelings will go under ground. Percolating into a negative identity, you can end up in lifetime of emotional cut-offs and tumultuously **fused** relationship patterns. So here's the way out of this roadblock: If you feel you are a little like 'Sam', write a list of things that make you feel angry or frustrated in the day. Write those things down on a list on one side of your journal page. On the other side, write out a sentence with the positive opposite "what else can be true?" This is a great way to activate more positive schemas: "Many people are nice", "I can trust many people", and "I am a loveable person". This journal work will multiply your positive scripts, and you will start noticing: "He brought me coffee to my desk". "She helped me complete that project at work today", "He opened the door for me". It's the small things that really matter over time. What ever you attend to, will build your mood through the day.

Rage— 'bad' anger is generally anchored in some type of childhood emotional wounding/confusion and/or learned belief – 'not feeling good or safe enough'. When anger rages it can also relate to a conflicting core value. Again, these are some of the reasons it so important to go through the steps to understand what is boiling under your anger or someone else's anger. What just happened really? Why is this important to me? What is important about this for her or him? What value of mine is impeded here? An example of a values trigger is the following: your boss makes an inappropriate gender or racial statement and you lose it. This is when its definitely important to have skills to self soothe: breathe, take time out, a break in the washroom, collect yourself, and then return to the conversation with an adult perspective "I felt quite offended when you said...I'm trying to understand why you would have said such a thing?" This type of difficult conversation builds a bridge of learning and respect for your future work relationship. If these types of comments continued to come from your boss, you might let your anger inform you about 'next steps'; i.e. to possible change jobs so you can work in a situation that is more congruent with your core values, or talk to your HR department who may follow up for you.

What's important about this is that you pay attention to what anger will teach you. In the same way, if someone is chronically angry towards you, what is his or her anger teaching you about yourself? You shouldn't just assume the problem is their inability to self regulate. Take some time to explore anything you might learn from. If there is nothing you can change or want to change within their expectations of you, its time to exit stage left! There is nothing more hard on yourself-esteem and spirit to be in a relationship that is doomed to roller coaster rides and chronic anger. It's just unhealthy and will lead to a shortened life.

But if anger is showing up some of the time and you want to get a handle on what, how and why it's showing up, the first step is to start to be curious. Anger is intimate because it exposes vulnerability. When it's expressed it should not intimidate or feel unsafe. This chapter will help you hone new skills to be able to identify the underlying driving themes that cause anger to rise up in yourself and in others. Having said this, please note that No one gets to yell at you, slam anything in a threatening way, block you from leaving a room, or cause any type of physical harm to you. This type of 'ugly' anger is where you need to draw a line in the sand to say "NO", and possibly call the police. There are times when you will simply need to walk away from anger. So let me be clear that for all men and all women, no one should remain in shared space with someone who threatens you in any way. If you are ever in this type of risk, get yourself out of harms way. This chapter won't deal fully with 'ugly' anger and circumstances when you actually need to call the police for assistance, and/or file a restraining order to protect yourself or someone else from harm.

Feel empowered even when anger shows up in your life. Anger is one of five primary emotional experiences; happy, sad, excited, frightened, and angry you are normal. We all spend some time with these feelings every day, sometimes and especially when you are going through tough times, every hour. As Thich Nhat Hanh suggests in his book "Anger", anger is like a crying child. When a child cries you don't walk away from the infant, slam it against a wall or try to mini lecture what he or she should do, say or feel. You just hold a child until he or she is soothed. Think of anger like a crying child, to be held and soothed until it stops crying. I love this perspective of how to be curious and soothing of anger.

Anger can be your great teacher. I spent a lifetime withdrawing from it, avoiding it, and dancing around it. Finally when I started researching it, I realized good, bad, or ugly, anger is just another weather system in our emotional world. Like bad weather, we can experience it, know that it's temporary, or blow it off. It's actually very revealing though when you get curious about it. As an adult, I have come to realize that anger is actually intimacy in action because through your curiosity, anger reveals your vulnerable self. So the next time someone is angry towards you, try to consider what they are afraid of, or how they may be feeling judged. Usually anger is anchored in some type fear, shame or judgment. Think about the last time you felt angry. What were you afraid of or feeling judged about? You might even consider when you first had that insecure thought. Is this a theme of powerlessness that you have been living in since you were ten, twelve, fifteen, and twenty? Is there another perspective to consider? If not, you may be letting your ten, twelve, fifteen, or twenty-year-old wisdom run your life!

Here's what I know to be true today. Anger reveals a young vulnerable self in both the receiver and the giver. Whether expressed or withheld, anger is bound to show up from time to time. Anger teaches you how to love better if you are not defended, or avoiding it. Love the 'whole' heart, not just the pleasing parts. You do want to know yourself don't you? Aren't you curious to know what is really going on for that person who just lost it in front of you? If you ask yourself, what is 'really' going on, you will discover unmet needs. It's a fact that we all feel angry at times; even the Dalai Lama. Life is confusing, intense and in dynamic change every second of every day. When you are in a practice of living well and taking care of yourself, you will probably have better access to insight, what you are invited to learn about yourself and/or deepen compassion for the other person who's anger is coming 'at' you. Having some kind of touch stone reminder to keep you on an open and balanced path, you might post the **Dalai Lama's 18 Rules for Living** in your kitchen.

****

Dalai Lama's 18 Rules for Living

1. Take into account that great love and great achievements involve great risk
2. When you lose, don't lose the lesson.
3. Follow the 3 Rs: respect for self, respect for others, responsibility for all your actions.
4. Remember that not getting what you want is sometimes a wonderful stroke of luck.
5. Learn the rules so you know how to break them properly.
6. Don't let a little dispute injure a great friendship.
7. If you've made a mistake, take immediate steps to correct it.
8. Spend some time alone every day.
9. Open your arms to change, but don't let go of your values.
10. Remember that silence is sometimes the best answer.
11. Live a good, honorable life. Then when you get older and think back, you'll be able to enjoy it a second time.
12. A loving atmosphere in your home is the foundation for your life.
13. In disagreements with loved ones, deal only with the current situation. Don't bring up the past.
14. Share your knowledge. It's a way to achieve immortality.
15. Be gentle with the Earth.
16. Once a year. As often as possible, go someplace you have never been before.
17. Remember that the best relationship is one that your love for each other exceeds your need for each other.
18. Judge your success by what you had to give up to get it.

****

One of my jobs as a clinician is to help people gain perspective from their anger. Let me illustrate a perspective on anger with a story from my life today. My current husband Joe and I were vacationing on a medi-moon in Costa Rica a few years ago. We were walking down a very remote beach (north of Nosara where the turtles come in to lay their eggs in December) when a pack of wild dogs (complete with frothing mouths) showed up in hot pursuit of us. Joe instinctively picked up a stick to protect us. I asked him to let it go. I'm certainly no expert dog trainer, but I think I have come to know the power of a calm and steady presence. We kept our natural walking pace, eyes forward and practiced a little backward breathing. This is a useful exercise, by the way, when you are upset. To reverse your breath, push your abdomen out as you breathe out and tuck your abdomen in as you breathe in. This counter-intuitive practice focuses your attention away from the stressor and on to your breath. In this instance, the dogs chomped and snarled inches from our heels. I can still recall their breath now as I'm writing this. Fortunately without a reaction from us, the five dogs backed off our heels and left us in peace to continue our walk.

Anger is like wild dogs. When it shows up, breathe without defense. Fight and flight are natural reactions for survival. Our inner Zen, however, is our source of true power. Anger, when you access your Zen, is a powerful state from which you can strengthen and deepen your connection with others. The fear was actually in the dogs that were barking. We were travelers on their beach. In tapping into our Zen, (although I do not wish a pack of dogs on you), we were free to enjoy Costa Rica all body parts in tact! When you get past the power struggles, there is a heartfelt place where you can develop yourself and possibly, your other.

If you have the tools to experience frustration or anger, (and then the capacity and motivation to process the new thoughts they may lead you to), your feelings will become helpful information.

1. Why am I upset? Why is my partner upset?

2. What did that information say about me? What did that information say about him or her?

3. How has this story of fear, judgment or vulnerability shown up before in my life?

4. How has this story of fear, judgment or vulnerability shown up for my partner?

5. What do I need?

6. What does he or she need?

7. What can I do differently next time?

8. How can he or she express his or her needs without shouting, swearing or putting me down next time?

There needs to be a safe way you can talk the confusion through. Using these types of self-reflective questions, you can process your anger in a way that will lead to resolution and build intimacy. With emotional safety, when you take a deeper look at the data (the story) you begin to re-story the irrational negative beliefs that you may have told yourself at ten, fifteen or at any age. In having a way to talk about anger, you won't have your inner child running your life. Think about it. Do you want to rehearse "I am inadequate, not worthy, undeserving, unloved, stupid, incapable, and wrong—that's a biggy"? Or do you want to rehearse "I am adequate, worth it, deserving, loved, smart, capable and curious (don't need to be right or wrong)".

When you become curious about your anger, and your partner's anger, you are alive and growing. The need to defend yourself totally goes away. Being curious, you are alive and growing a deeper connection to yourself and with your other. When the trigger of anger shows up, you have a window of choice – defend your position or define your feelings and be curious about the other.

Am I defending or defining myself?

You have a choice to practice possibility thinking (which rehearses growth and goodness) or negative scripts (which entrench hopelessness and inadequacy) that take you deeper into your own personal hell. If you never express anger or tolerate hearing it from others, you hold yourself ransom to the power of the growl. This can have devastating results to your health and your relationships.

A lot of couples experience anger like an attack. With it, everything freezes and shuts down. I recall working with a young couple (I will refer to as 'Andrew' and 'Arlene') that had just had a baby. They struggled in a conflict over something as insignificant on its face as a choice of dishwashing detergent. Reportedly 'Arlene' had gone out to buy groceries and came back with Joy liquid soap. 'Andrew' was really angry that 'Arlene' had not come home with his favorite – Ivory Soap. Through a safe process of joint dialogue about this, it turned out 'Arlene' had bought whatever was on sale. 'Arlene's' deeper issue was her presumed need to save money because she wasn't working at the time and didn't feel as entitled to spend as she did when she worked outside of their home. Looking deeper yet, 'Arlene' had felt inadequate since she became a parent. As 'Arlene' hadn't valued mothering as a career, she hadn't felt entitled to spend money since the birth of their baby. From 'Andrew's' perspective, 'Arlene' wasn't paying 'any' attention to him. He expressed feeling jealous of their baby because it had captured "all of" her attention for the past year.

Have you ever noticed how much your experience polarizes when you are angry? Words like "always or never" come with angry territory. These types of words undermine understanding because they heighten impossibility thinking. 'Andrew' felt that if 'Arlene' had really cared about him, she would have thoughtfully bought his preferred brand of dish soap. He had always preferred Ivory and "why didn't you think of me when you were shopping?" The deeper issue for him was not feeling loved since the birth of their child. With deeper understanding and enhanced communication skills, anger can be helpful in revealing ways we can care better for each other rather than be positional in a power struggle and possessed of a need to convince each other out of an emotional experience. Anger can lead us closer to our hearts and into what is often termed "agape love"— the kind of love that is "other focused" and spiritually enriching.

Too often anger shows up as road rage, sharp words, aggressive and sometimes devastating flare-ups at home and at work. These symptoms fester like a contagion through workplaces and through families. If you don't talk about your hurt feelings and misunderstanding, these themes continue to present themselves in 300 different ways like tsunamis on a beach. To avoid stepping on catastrophe, you may navigate gingerly through your home or work life and over time, we lose what you want most – to feel valued, to feel loved, to matter, to feel safe. I loved the movie "The Good, The Bad and the Ugly" and I've come to think of anger as the smoking gun in town. When it shows up to blow up, it's ugly. Actually in that experience, our adrenal glands release cortisol. These stress hormones attack your hippocampus injuring and or killing brain cells. As chronic showdowns, anger expressed in rage can contribute to brain diseases such as Alzheimer's and dementia. When anger becomes a chronic pattern or style of relating, it's bad. Without safe connection between your significant partner and your co-workers, you risk a fractured trust–the cornerstone on which all relationships are built. When you stay curious about anger and what is to be discovered by it, your relationships deepen, your attachments become more secure, and your experience in life is more and more to embrace learning moments. There are no mistakes when you think of anger in a frame of vulnerability. Develop an ease to ask questions of yourself and others, and you are guaranteed more longevity in life and love.

Thoughts on anger:

1. When anger is bad, your brain releases cortisol, adrenaline, and the results are you can't concentrate. You will feel more and more irritable and unhappy over time.
2. When anger is ugly and chronic, serious consequences can result with long-term impacts to the hippocampus (learning centers of the brain). You will start feeling more and more isolated and less and less satisfied in all aspects of your life. You can unwittingly fracture the most precious relationships that give your life meaning. When anger is really ugly, you may end up at a police station.

3. When anger is good, your brain is stimulated to produce norepinephrine, which improves your concentration, mood and stimulates learning. When you use a step-by-step process as suggested above, you will gain insight from the discomfort of anger.

4. Your brain is always trying to find homeostasis (a return to calm). So when anger is not expressed with emotional safety, you will naturally fight or withdraw. If you continually block yourself from expressing anger, or tolerating hearing other people's anger, you will likely end up re-reading the previous chapter on anxiety!

If anger has become your habit, you've been feeling irritable or easily triggered; it would be prudent to assess your level of stress. Here, you'll find clues that you are headed towards burn out. Take the opportunity to take a look at your lifestyle routines. Have you got time set aside for yourself every day? Are the activities you focus on currently providing you with the outcomes you want? Are you running in reaction to your life rather than proactively planning it? Are you getting enough sleep? A recent study of 9,000 four year olds found that children who had less than average sleep times were more inclined to anger, aggression and impulsivity (8). Health habits start in childhood. As you commit to better sleep hygiene habits, you set your partner, your children, and quite possibly their children up in these same ways.

Because we need a perception of some personal control in our lives, when we go through breakups or come to significant life stages such as: adolescence, early adulthood, early parenting and mid-life, anger can start to bite us in the butt. Be preventative during these stages of your life by scheduling regular check-ins with people who matter to you at home or work. How are they experiencing you? How do you experience them? Dr. Rollin McCraty, a researcher of heart-brain coherence developed a science-based tool to measure the energy we transmit to each other through the heart-brain connection (Neurocardiology). His work suggests that we measurably affect each other in an immediate way through the contagion of emotional processing, but also in a global way. His research through the Institute of Noetic Sciences has looked at emotional impacts through natural disasters such as hurricanes and tsunamis, but also non-natural impacts of the 911 terrorist attacks on the World Trade Centers. His work is also reported in Tom Shadyac's documentary "I Am", a compelling film which proposed two questions: "What's wrong with our World" and "what can we do?" We can start to seek deeper understanding of each other! We can make a big difference if we seek to understand the underpinnings of our own anger, talk and then heal the confusion that exists. If the stories you are telling yourself about your former partner or yourself, is blaming, shaming, or without forgiveness, you aren't helping yourself, your family, your friends, your community and (according to Dr. McCraty's research), our planet!

Chronic unexpressed anger can also lead you down a path towards addiction. Because you are holding your feelings in, you may be coping by using addictive escapes like habitual drinking, shopping, over working, gambling, sexting, or over exercising. You can take flight using any of these ways out of your emotions temporarily, but if you do, you will be on a road that leads you to anxiety, depression and another relationship ending.

Take some time out to ask yourself: "what does this (situation) mean to me?" In order to answer this question, you may need to take a few stacked breaths until your clear thinking returns. The bottom line is anger can be an active initiator of change. So don't run away from it. Check in with yourself if anger has been overwhelming you lately.

****

Breakthrough Tips for Anger:

1. Notice you feel angry in your body: tight chest, burning feeling in your head? This is the start of the fight or flight feeling. Break the pattern here.
2. Give yourself a chance to breathe and release, so your parasympathetic system has a chance to kick in.
3. Ask yourself "what does this (the thing that happened) mean to me?"

4. Speak from personal insight "I felt ____". When you begin with an "I" statement, you can't go wrong. The other person won't feel attacked and generally a deeper connection and understanding results.

5. Make sure you are not polarizing your experience with words such as "always or never". Use words such as "some of the time".

6. Take some personal time to be curious about yourself and the communications of each day. Are there any repeating stories, personal themes showing up? What could you do differently to shift paradigms?

7. Have closure to all disagreements. Try to say to yourself, "can I get better at… (Whatever your partner has described as upsetting)?"

8. Don't build a case using every piece of historical evidence against the other. Winning or being right, you will end up on your own… again.

9. Writing in a journal is a great way to release and figure out what is important about your upset.

****

Overall, stay connected with your anger and be curious about other people's anger too. Remember, anger is just information and you can't close the door to the past without some insight of your own fears and vulnerabilities. Remember that the traits of your former partner that drive you crazy are usually a mirror of your own lost self.

You are normal if you've been feeling more angry than usual. Anger is a stage of grief. Become an expert on all your feelings. As door number one (the former relationship) closes, door number two (A life swamped in anger) may not be the right door to your best life. Door number Three (Forgiveness and Reintegration) is! The next chapter is about morphing a family after a marriage breakup. If you are breaking up without the complexities of children, it's still a helpful chapter because it may give you insight on what your friends, family members, or maybe even a future partner, may be going through.

CHAPTER 8

DIVORCE & THE BLENDED FAMILY

The truth is, getting over a breakup when children are involved, is really hard. No matter which side of the fence you sit on (being left, doing the leaving, or deciding together that your marriage is over) it will take some time to heal the ending of your marriage because it's not just about you. When you have children, no matter which way you look at it, you and your family are entering a newly imperfect world. For many, the imperfect world is a whole lot better than the prior devastatingly horrible world you were in. You may feel totally relieved to be out of your marriage misery especially if there were dynamics of abuse or neglect. In this case you are congratulating yourself for a brave commitment of family safety and health. And you still will be worried about your children's future as they try to navigate two parents in divide. Divorce rates are happily on the decline (in Canada and the U.S.) shifting from a 50% divorce rate to a 43% divorce statistic according to 2006 census reports.

It's interesting to know that the mean age for men who divorce is 44, and for women 41. So it seems midlife is when we all take a second look at "I do" or "I do NOT". A more recent report tells us in Canada 4 out of 10 1st marriages end in divorce, and 18.6 per cent of children live with only one parent and 14.6 per cent of children live with common-law parents as a result. By the way, the Canadian 2006 census was the first to report on same-sex marriages and 16.5 per cent of same-sex couples now marry (reported by CBC News October 4, 2010). We are in an era of healthy change. Of divorcing couples in the U.S., the average longevity for first time marriages to is about 8 years, and the average time between first marriage and second marriage is 3 ½ years according to the U.S. Census Bureau (2012). As a general rule it seems people still want to get married because of traditionally held values, to have children with the same family name, because they feel it makes economic sense, and because they value the ritual of marriage itself. We continue to be a pair bonding species and there are some times when it takes a few retakes on marriages to find the right bond. Wouldn't it be great if every couple was required to do some pre-marital counseling before marriage to discover each other's personality traits, emotional health, values, attitudes and beliefs? Imagine still if there was a test, like a drivers exam, before having children? You might ask yourself questions such as:

1. What is his or her relationship like with his or her parent(s)?
2. Is he or she an introvert or an extrovert?
3. Is he or she an eldest, middle, or youngest in family of origin learning?
4. Will we like the life we make together?
5. Do we have common interests?
6. Do I feel fully accepted by him or her? Or does it feel like I need to change?
7. How do we talk through difficult conversations?
8. Is there a lot of emotional cut off in his or her history with family or friends?

These types of questions would be helpful to answer in pre-marital counseling. In the absence of such things, great advice is to own a dog with your loved one for three years. Share the grunt work and the pleasures to see how you and your partner's traits, emotional processes, values, attitudes and beliefs show up before you conceive.

If you are moving through divorce right now and you have children, this chapter is to help you manage through the stresses of your separation and divorce, and gain some relief and freedom from all the anger, resentment and angst that is typical of a divorcing family, especially when children are involved. As the road ahead can feel full of ups and downs, keep your center.

In all of the responsibilities you are wading through as a parent, as you safeguard your children's adjustments, take time to process your own stages of grief. Focusing on your values reduces stress. If you were the one who was left, focus on the "values" you can hold in striving for the healthiest possible family morphing. If you were the one who left your marriage, keep reminding yourself of the core "values" that motivated the dissolution. Your values might be "children come first", "take the high road", or "live truthfully". In so doing, you will be more engaged with your right-brain and have an easier time negotiating grief as you integrate coming to terms with your 'new normal' life. In case you are wondering, the left-brain is the part of your brain that organizes your time and all the 'details' of your life. The right brain is the part of your functioning that considers 'the big picture'; what you stand for as a human being and as a parent. If you take a second right now and hold your hand in front of your face and focus on your hand, you will notice the details of your skin, your knuckles, etc., and the rest of the background will look out of focus. That is your left-brain engaged right now. Then refocus on the surrounding details of the background and notice that your finger becomes blurred. This is your right brain functioning. Your right brain processes the values that engaged your separation: commitment to live more honestly, value in feeling more empowered, less stressed, healthier, less conflicted, more playful, less or more materialistic or providing a happier model of living for your children, to name a few. Write whatever values have motivated the change or can inform your ability to walk through this unknown time. You will discover a 'values exercise' you can do in the chapter on boundaries. Focusing on your 'big picture' values will be calming and help you over-ride the anxiety and immediacy of 'next steps' towards divorce. You know you will get through this time. Many others just like you have done it. You will too.

If you were left, you may have values in providing a brave role model, to be a great example of healthy divorce, of living a more heart-centered life in the future, or to live a life of compassion and forgiveness. When you identify which values you can live by through this time of transition, you will feel less stressed, less reactive, and more resilient as you adjust with your children. As you define your values for living through this, you will be more able to honestly release the emotional binds of your former partner— your 'Wasbund' or 'Waswife'.

Your left brain is the functional, the part of you that needs control, feels discombobulated with the stresses of the new life in process – getting your children organized to go to the other parent's home, getting the bills paid, sorting new lifestyle habits, and over all coping. Your right brain is the 'bigger picture' process. It helps you see the context of your 'whole' life, keeping you future oriented to opening a new door to your best life. And statistically we know that, unless you choose not to, you will very likely be in a new relationship commitment three years from now. Playing a musical instrument, singing, listening to music, dancing, painting, drawing, playing games are all ways you can engage your right brain. Practicing meditation, yoga or other mindful exercises in breathing or walking actually strengthens the connective tissue (corpus callosum) between the right and left hemisphere. These types of brain gym habits will make a huge difference in your breakup breakthrough as you re-story loss into a new beginning.

I've seen clients who, (sadly because they haven't moved through their relationship grief), ten years after their breakup from their former partner, are still agonizing in the guilt and shame that goes with what they have locked into as being their 'greatest failure'. They report feeling frozen in the responsibility and failing to their children. Why is this? Well, when you think about the information from the previous chapter on anger, schemas and scripts, they may have started with 'feelings of failure' and then developed a whole story 'I am a Failure'. What you don't talk about and heal, you can end up wearing for life! We are a win-oriented culture and divorce (especially when you have children) is still seen by many as a smudge of character, a lack of substance, a loss of self-trust/ other trust, a breech of family commitment...You may feel you can even add to this list of judgments right now. The angrier you feel, the more these stories will continue to lock you into your past and prevent you from closing the 'Big Pain Door'.

I love Marianne Williamson's suggestion that if someone has hurt you, pray for him or her. She suggests that you will either manifest change for the one who has hurt you or the pain they have caused you won't matter to you anymore. Your intention through praying, leads to a full perspective shift and reframe out of sadness into "I'm so grateful my former partner ended the marriage/ I left the marriage". This sounds like an impossible idea but when you give this inspiration some thought, you will realize that in praying for your former partner, you also train yourself into a fresh positive, 'other focused' perspective. You will start to lighten the fixation that 'you feel betrayed' and you will begin to understand how your former partner's behaviors were 'human' after all, considering their unique life experience. You will begin to develop empathy and empathy then sets you free from resentment. It starts you on a path of forgiveness. If you forgive him or her, you can start to forgive yourself. It's the combination of conscious intent through journaling, shared feelings and talk therapy, along with the passage of time and development of personal insight; you free yourself and your family emotionally.

Have you noticed that your most frightening critic of you is you…especially at 2:00 in the morning? If you have been hard on yourself, isn't it time to breakthrough that self-sabotage? In the way a bully might corrupt your community or workplace with satellites of people to side against you, you can unwittingly set up satellites against yourself by walking in the constriction of shame and blame. You give yourself a kind of soul sickness you may really struggle to crawl out of because instead of praying for forgiveness, you are practicing everything negative. You'll find yourself looking for every flawed moment and dwelling on all the ways you have lost control in your life. In the day, you may be afraid to talk to anyone about your pain and grief and in the night you worry about everything unresolved. This then manifests in negativity and reactivity towards and around your children! Your children forget to make their bed, and you swear in a language foreign even to you! Your children forget to clear their dishes off the kitchen table, and you blow your top. You may start over functioning and obsessing to ensure your children's' homework is done, that they are doing their best at school or in their sports. You're over functioning then leads to a multitude of anxious calls to their teachers at school. Then their teachers, invited into your personal Hell, start feeling anxious about your children too! At the slightest sign of distraction, your child is singled out as 'troubled'. This is how the spiral of anxiety spreads. Did you know that an anxious person, just in sitting beside you, can actually make your blood pressure go up?! Try to remind yourself that your children are healthy and whole. Your lives are changing but their school, teachers and friends have not. They are still very able and may find the school setting is a place where they can feel 'normal' and feel relief in spending time with friends and teachers.

Try to manage your anxieties. Don't hover over your children's social and academic life. The more you fear for them, the more hopeless they will feel about themselves in their own world. There is so much research that says the way you see your children as able or disable, has significant and enduring impacts. As you expect, so it will be. Your children will come to you if they need you. Their teachers will call you if their academic performance is dropping. Its good to let the school know that there are two family homes now so that newsletters can be directed to two email addresses. Make it as easy as possible for both parents to continue to be involved and aware of your children's school activities. Outside of those types of logistics, trust your children have the same resiliency as you do. They also have the same social supports through their friends as you do. If you see your children becoming withdrawn, angry, reactive or see their academic marks drop, you may want to seek family therapy.

The more you feel you have been 'a failure' the more your children will adopt similar scripts in living too. They will start wearing your emotional shame. It's subtle how this can happen. You may be less involved in the parent participation at their school. Or you may get into an anxious pattern of asking your children "are you ok?.. Was school hard today?" Instead of seeing them as the able children they are and have been. Your questions for resiliency might be "What was the best and the worst thing that happened today?" This inquiry assumes that it's normal to experience both and there is no expectation of worse first. Don't get caught in the typical post divorce fused shrink-wrap of worry for children's well being? Children are just as resilient as you are. Look at what is going right for you and your children, not just at the fears of what 'might' go wrong. I think that may be how one creates 'Hell' on earth.

Whenever fear goes up, anger and conflict rises too. It's why I put the chapter on Anger before this chapter on marriage endings. This chapter is to help you move through your marriage ending when children are involved. You CAN move through your inevitable divorce in a hopeful perspective of learning and growth, and not get stuck in chronic blame, shame, guilt or anger. What you are going through is completely normal and as you now know, a very common phenomena! There is as much support as you will ever need and a lot of it is just a 'Google' away. You only need to Google Divorce to find an assortment of research on the topic. You can Google Douglas Darnell & 'Parental Alienation', or Judith Wallerstein & 'outcomes for children of Divorce'; to motivate you to not put your former partner down. Just do your best as you walk through this big change in your life. Your children are resilient and will move through this transition with you. Children model in your shadow, so your anger; grief, resentment, fear or ambivalence will be their experience too. Children learn from what you do, not necessarily by what you say. If you move through this time with a plan (when your left brain is so important), your (right brain) feelings will integrate a balanced perspective of 'new normal' clarity and understanding. If you are still feeling locked into fear and anger:

1. Talk to a friend or hire a psychotherapist to help you with these feelings.
2. Join a support group for separation and divorce. Having others to talk to can be so healing. You are not alone in this process of change. 4 out of 10 people you know have gone through this or will go through this just like you!

It's so true that forgiveness sets you free. There are unique and obvious reasons that you and your former partner have gone your separate ways. One of the most challenging aspects of moving through separation and divorce is managing the impacts to children. The fear that you and your former partner have negatively impacted your children's lives is one of the core blocks to forgiveness. No question, life would be simpler for your children and yourself, if you weren't breaking up at all. Your children's magical minds are probably wishing that these changes were just a bad dream that they will wake up from. Research suggests that even in situations where children are acutely aware of their parents' conflict, at all ages, they may have hopes that their parents will reconcile. Stay steadfast in hearing your children's fears and pain. Try to be patient and empathic not judging anything they share with you. As much as possible, try to simply keep forward focusing with assuring comments such as "I know you wish 'Mommy'/ 'Daddy' were not divorcing. You wish we things could go back to the way we were". Try to reassure them that you and your former partner will be more caring for each other living in two homes; that you are still a family; that you and the other parent will be more able to be better parents to them in this new 'two home family'.

In being empathic to your children's fears, and redirecting your children's thoughts to some of the positive advantages – that they get to have 'two bedrooms' now, that (if possible) they will keep their same schools, same friends, and a lot of the same routines. You can remind them that you and your former partner love them and they themselves are living proof of the love between you and the other parent. (Even if that's not a totally honestly felt truth for you right now, you may gain a more positive perspective with time. Forgiveness shines through with the passage of time. The idea to 'fake it till you make it', works). The truth is you love your children and it will feel calming for your children to gain an impression that you actually don't resent the other parent (even if right now, you honestly do). This is a time to stretch yourself emotionally.

∗∗∗∗∗∗∗∗∗∗∗

Here's a **10-Day Forgiveness Challenge** to get you into a 'stretch' perspective.

First, write out ten things you most resent about your former partner right now.

Put the piece of paper with the ten resentments beside your bed before you go to sleep.

In the morning, take another look at the page. Cross one thing out on your sheet.

Write the opposite perspective of the resentment on a small piece of paper and put it in your shoe today and literally wear it for the day!

So here's an example: You might resent your former (husband) for being so negative. You write, "I resent (him) for his negativity". The positive opposite would be "I appreciate how critical (he) was because (he) made me grow".

You then walk through your day with this piece of paper that says, "I am open to judgment and criticism". Notice how you feel during the day as you think about being that person who embraces criticism and judgment (even the things your former partner was negative about) because it welcomes a curious mind and personal growth. Notice; are you more open to others? Are you walking a little more intentionally? Is there a new calm in you? Do you notice a new patience in the way you are showing up? What does this new perspective bring to your life?

At the end of the day, write out a statement of forgiveness and gratitude. "I forgive (him) for being so negative. (His) negativity has made me grow in….(write out 3 things you noticed about yourself in walking with this growth through the day). In some of the negativity, was there room for personal growth as you have reflected through your day?

The next morning cross one new thing on your list. It could be that (he) was self-absorbed. You write on a piece of paper in the morning "I am giving". Do the same steps as above. In the night, you might write, "I learned to be more giving because my former (husband) was so self-absorbed. I forgive (him) and I am grateful to be such a capable person because of (him). Repeat this until all ten things have been crossed off your list.

This exercise actively moves you into forgiveness and gratitude. Clients love the freedom in letting go of resentment and its dark energy, which clogs your good spirit from shining light.

Life takes surprising turns and if you have a map to move alone your winding road in this transition out of your marriage and you will feel a lot better through the all the inevitable changes if you can forgive his or her failings. And of course, the next step is to forgive you!

Do the 10-Day Forgiveness Challenge about you now. What do you wish you had been better at through your marriage? Write out 10 things and follow all the steps from the previous exercise.

****

Now its time to get your parenting routines ironed out. As soon as possible, go on line and 'Google' parenting plan. It should include what to do when your child is sick? It should outline holidays and birthdays. Of course it will outline a schedule for your children to maintain easy and constant access to both parents when and if possible. The best-case scenario, unless there is a history of abuse or neglect, is that your children have equal access and time with both you and the other parent. Try to have consistent parenting structures in both homes so that your children can regain a calm in their new living arrangements.

Be encouraging of your former partner's attempts to adjust right now. Try to be compassionate and understanding if he or she makes mistakes or forgets important things. Do your best and try to see your former partner as doing their best as well. Your children need to feel good about both parts of who they are—that's who you are and who your former partner is. In my practice, working with families who are moving through separation and divorce, I often ask the children when they are here, to hop down the long hallway leading to my office, on one foot. While their two parents watch, I often ask the children, 'how did that feel'? What I usually hear is, "that was hard", "my leg hurts", "I almost fell", and "I felt stupid". This simple exercise is such an effective way to really take in this message – we all need two legs to stand, hop, and dance in our lives. Your children do too. To have a healthy self-concept, your children need you and their other parent to continue to be positive supports in their lives.

There are some circumstances such as family abuse, death and addiction, when this is not always possible. Hillary Clinton was right that it takes "a village to bring up a child" and I'd say it helps to count extended family and community members as your family supports right now too. You want your children to dance through their lives with purpose, and love. Practice patience. This process of morphing your family will test you to your bones. Just do your best. If you did the 10-Day exercise and you still feel hopelessly angry and resentful of your former partner, maintain strong boundaries (refer to the boundary chapter), and have as little contact as possible. Don't say the things that are top of mind. Any "You" statement will not land in a helpful way. This is a good time to rely on email or text messages to coordinate childcare and maintain your parenting plan.

Work on setting up a predictable schedule as soon as possible. If this is not coming together, you may need to seek legal support. You need to have a predictable schedule of how to handle school, sports activities, special occasions, and illness. In the shared access, take time out to heal. Use your time away from your children to do things that feel nourishing to you. You might go for long walks in natural spaces, go for a swim, play a sport, or learn to play a musical instrument (which engages the right brain). Dancing and music are two great activities that help your brain heal from grief because they engage both hemispheres of the brain. Its hard to be apart from your children when you are going through these changing times, but you will find they benefit from having parents who are cherishing their time with them and who are also refueled from their time alone. If you try to be 'on' 24/7, you are bound to burn out. This can be a highly emotional time for you.

****

Practice asking for support! Here's an exercise to identify your supports.

Sit down with a big white sheet in front of you.

Draw a circle in the middle and put a photo of you in it.

Then draw a bigger circle around that and paste photos of you and your children on that line.

Draw a bigger circle and paste photos of your extended family (try to include your former partners' family too).

Then draw a bigger circle around that and paste photos of your closest friends.

Put this poster board up in your family room. You might ask your children if they can think of others who they include as being supportive loving members of their life. They will probably say 'Mommy' or 'Daddy'. Yes, it's normal to 'forget' to put the other parent in there too. Your children may feel relieved to be able to put him or her in the chart too. You can't move through this in a healthy way without everyone in on the change. So, unless he or she has been abusive or neglectful, go on and paste your former partner on the graph too. You might ask your children, 'where do you think we should put 'Mommy' or 'Daddy'? This is just another way; you get to talk about the adjustments everyone is going through. You can decide together as a family where you want to keep this poster board up. You can add telephone numbers. Your children then have a community of healthy supportive contacts they can easily call. You will too!

****

You also will need time to set up your future life with new hobbies, activities and health habits that feed your body, mind and spirit. Stress signs can be: irritability, trouble sleeping, loss of interest in things you normally love, trouble concentrating, losing your keys or other important paraphernalia, weight loss or weight gain (appetite changes in either direction). Don't wait until you get burned out. Talk about the changes you are noticing about yourself. You might ask your children what they are noticing about themselves. You aren't burdening them in these conversations. You are actually helping them have access to their feelings and a sense of when they might need more support.

Typical changes for school aged children can be: less interest in social activities, change in appetite, lack of academic focus, aggression at school, trouble concentrating, lack of participation in home chores, magical mind conversations about 'when' the other parent might be coming home. In all these ways, conversations at dinnertime can be so helpful to alleviate fears or insecurities that may be showing up. It can be helpful to have some shared family dinners with your children's friends and their parents. These social gatherings help your children feel more secure in the new normal of life in two homes. Set yourself up for success by accessing the supports available to you in friends, your children's schools, and with extended family. The more you invite extended family to dinners and special outings, the more well adjusted and supported your children will be. The more you sense your children are adjusting, the more your own anxieties will disappear.

Talk to your physician if you or your children are not sleeping properly. Everyone needs their sleep and sleep interruptions are easily overcome with new well-defined bedtime routines. The more you and your children talk at dinner, the more you will fine they and you get back to sleeping well again.

It's common to discover yourself and your children doing a lot of dreaming.

You may want to start a **dream journal**, as these can be great avenues for conversation. Dreams are a way that your psyche lets go of unspoken anxieties. The more you talk, the better your sleep patterns. If you are seeing a counselor, it can be helpful to bring your journal with you to your sessions. This gives your professional a window into what your fears may be. For example, if you had been dreaming about a truck running you over, this stress dream might signify perhaps a loss of control in your life. Your counselor would then help you work through ways you can regain personal control. You might look at how this learning of 'powerlessness' started, through your marriage with your former partner, and possibly in your family of origin. He or she can guide you to ways your thinking and communicating can give you more solid footing to feel a sense you have some power in your life today. Repeated dreams are wonderful tools to heal your psyche. Everything you dream about is all part of your own unconscious self. For example, in the truck dream: you are the truck, you are the person being backed up over, and you are the road. When you think of your dreams in this way, you start your own healing process. You may fear moving forward (being the truck/a move of residence), being run over (fear of your former partners' actions), that you are the road (this time shall pass and lead to new places).

At a basic level, the dream is your psyche saying your stress has come to overload and its time to take better care of yourself. Keeping a dream journal is a great way to process this time of transition. Even the act of writing your dream down, you will release and understand the fears scorching your sleep.

Many clients try to rebuild their ego strength by displacing their feelings of failure in their marriage, by projecting them on their former partner. Try to catch yourself from falling into this kind of blame game. This is natural and human, but can have lifelong negative impacts on all concerned. The truth is, while you are moving through your divorce you are treading imperfect, turbulent waters no matter what you do, say or feel. You can't control how your 'Wasband' or 'Waswife' will navigate the emotional storms. Just do your best to maintain parallel or complementary objectives. Do your best to provide optimism and encouragement, rather than entrenched negative case building and faultfinding. Take the high road. It will lead you to your best life. What is he or she doing right? Look for the ways he or she is trying to collaborate. Don't get hung up on hanging on to the nick knack material things. Swap your possessions out in a fair and equal distribution. Try to think of this process like you are exchanging baseball cards. He picks, you pick, he picks, and you pick. In looking for a win-win result, your children will see you both working to do your best to be kind, caring and resilient. What do you want your children to grow up knowing about you through this process?

Otherwise your complicated feelings will load up your children's emotional states, making it difficult for them to constructively evolve and engage in their own lives, academically, athletically and socially. Its always best for them to gain a sense of equal playing fields for both you and your former partner if possible. In this way they see you both as empowered and good parents who they themselves can count on. They also need to feel as equally comfortable in both living situations. The more insecurity they develop about one parent or the other, the more insecurity they will feel within themselves for a lifetime. The best thing you can do is to ensure that you manage your grief process constructively. Whenever necessary, seek a counselor to help you process your resentments and regrets. Try overall, to assume the best intentions for all concerned. In this imperfect world, everyone is attempting to find new footing. Your grace will bring out the best in others.

Judith Wallerstein, a psychologist who passed away in 2012 at the venerable age of ninety, conducted a number of landmark longitudinal research projects looking at outcomes for children of divorced parents. Her findings support a trend that children of separation and divorce have a more difficult time when it comes to forging their own long term relationships (9). Her research confirms that you should do your best to keep your children out of the crossfire in the divorce process. Resolve the separation agreement as well as the division of assets and come to a fair resolution as soon as possible. Look for a fair deal that you can both provide balance from.

When my marriage ended, I started at my own ground zero. My former husband and I had sold our home and we were debt free. Our children were starting university and we all launched out of the nest. When I was on my own, I felt remarkably free. I recall starting my therapy practice at that time with one cell phone I used for work and home. I shared an office with a family physician friend. At home I lived minimally without television, cable, or Internet. It's incredible how easy it can be to simplify. The less you need, the less pressure you will feel. My daughter and I made some key changes that helped a lot. Ashley switched from a being a foreign student at Queens University (which cost approximately 20K per year including school and living expenses), to living with me and going to University of British Columbia (for about 9K). Ashley's father paid for her university tuition and I covered her room and board and gave her a monthly allowance to cover her books, clothes and sundries. She also worked at a local restaurant part time. In many ways, this became our "Gilmour Girls" time and was actually a really fun stage of life.

Our son Justin was on a full ride tennis scholarship in the U.S., so overall financially life was relatively simple. Michael and I were aligned in our support for our children, and our children were doing well. We got together for birthdays and on milestone holidays like Christmas for a few years. This helped to take the drama out of our break up and gave our children the confident sense that we were still a family and that they still had our solid collaborative support, no matter what. Michael and I even gave each other hugs when we saw each other. I think it was pretty clear to our children that we would actually care better for each other in our new separateness.

Holidays are times when break-up blues often leak in whether you were married with no children, married with children, or partnered and not married. It's in the high holiday rituals such as Christmas, Hanukah, Yom Kippur, Rosh Hashanah, Passover, Ramadan, Chinese New Year, Bikrami Samvat (Hindu New Year), (to name a few) when you may feel a little more stuck than ever. You will know what is healthiest for you going forward, by how you intuitively feel at this stage of your break-up. Depending on how long you were together and how immersed in your family system your former was, you might decide to have your first post break-up gathering together. This may take the sting out for you and the rest of your family, who may also be feeling the loss since your break-up.

On the other hand, if you feel overwhelmed by that idea, it may be best to keep it simple. Return to your boundaries and celebrate these festivities without the worry of potential conflict or stress. What you should always ask yourself is, 'does this help me to move on'? The better you are able to adapt right now, the better the rest of your tribe will be as well. Remember that the less contact you have with your former partner, the sooner you will adapt to being single again, and the sooner you will be able to integrate that change into your whole family, your circle of friendships, and your other relevant community systems.

For some couples, time spent together after a break up helps ease the drama of change. For others, clear boundaries to cut the cords of attachment, prevents tearing the scabs off all over again.

The best way to get to the other side of a painful process is to focus on a win – win attitude and, as best you can, on improving yourself. At the end of the day, try to be a model of grace. You can't control whether your former partner will rise up with your win – win attitude, but you can control your own feelings of good Karma coming out of a difficult time. Model grace and acceptance by re-cycling anger and resentment into a journal or talk therapy of some kind. So here's the tricky part of this commitment to grace. What do you do about letting go of your anger if you are committed to not put the other parent down? It's an emotional bind like no other. And, what if your former partner is not as committed as you are about not gossiping?

One of the greatest hurdles for many couples who divorce, is coping with the gossip. We were very involved in our community because of our children's sports and academics and our professional contributions in our work. I found it so challenging to have the sense that I, or my family, was the center of any speculative conversation. Whether it's positive or negative, everyone seems to have their own thesis about you and your family troubles; especially when you don't say much about why your marriage ended. My former husband and I had agreed to maintain the benign explanation that "we simply outgrew each other". I feel good that I maintained my promise in this regard. Many people did their best to find out more about the rest of our story, but I was steadfast in adhering to the simple explanation we had put out there. It was a protective measure for both our children, and each other. The patience and grace I feel I held to with this, has paid off in a good Karma kind of way. I believe there are times we just have to hold on to faith in a higher place and trust that things will heal with time.

It's been a big insight for me to realize the benefit of not worrying about things I can't control; the freedom of practicing acceptance. This attitude creates loving space in my life. My mother who was a big time worrier when I was growing up, now at 91 years old has Alzheimer's. While she was a little difficult to grow up with because she was a big time worrier, she is so much happier living life in the opportunities of being present in the 'now'. For my Mother today – every moment is a new moment. We fondly call her the 'love machine'. She has given us all a life lesson about the benefits of living in the absolute present. Live your life knowing that every moment is a new moment. Every time you see your former partner, make it a fresh start. Let go of how it went yesterday and be open to the fresh possibility that comes to you today.

It's sadly a strange human phenomenon that you can be so attracted to gossip (either perpetuating it or retaliating from it). It's a given, as humans, your behaviors will often be flawed. You are learning. We are all learning. All you can do is learn from your actions in the past, be curious about your impacts, integrate new learning into new daily practices and commit to striving to become a better human being. The more shame you carry from your past mistakes, the more angry and unhealthy your life.

****

Signs of un-health can be:

1. The experience of anxiety or full-blown panic attacks.
2. Having repeated nightmares and disrupted sleep.
3. Trouble concentrating.
4. Forgetfulness.
5. Losing your keys.
6. Forgetting appointments.
7. Feeling irritable for no reason.

****

What would you most dread someone knew about you? Is it really that terrible or is there something to be learned and to grow from? (Boundaries, a fear of rejection, a family history of addiction, a fear of failure...) We all have some soft spots to grow into. What are yours? There is a little excellence to be felt in the perfection of imperfection. Shame blocks you from personal discovery.

What you don't talk about, you can't get better at. There is grace in sharing your truth and being present without judgment from others. Peace comes from acceptance. Stop the gossip! Start journaling. Seek the help of a counselor or psychologist who can give you healthier perspectives about your marriage ending and what can open up for your children as a result. After you close the door to the past and move through your grief in a healthy way, there is a world of possibility for you and your children.

The single piece of wisdom that kept me sane was to know that what others say about you or your former partner is actually just information about them and their own fears and inadequacies. We experience life and all that is in it because we have scripts (how we see things or organize our thinking) and schemas (how we expect things to happen according to our past, so we select out information that is not congruent with our own learning and select in what is) from the past to draw from as we experience the present (10). We are actually mirrors to each other. I am confident that this theory holds true for both positive and negative discourse. I call this the mirror technique; not to be confused with mirror neurons discussed later.

Don't take my word for it. Try this yourself! When someone says something to you, reflect the comment back to him/her as a question. For example even with something simple like "I like your hair", you might ask him or her if they have been thinking of a hairstyle change. They will likely say, "Yes, how did you know?"

If someone asks you if you are tired, they are likely struggling with some sort of sleep difficulty. We have scripts and schemas that make us attend to and retain certain information and delete others. It's our own mind that shapes our questions and thinking in the present.

So when you see darkness in others, consider that it is probably coming from darkness inside you. Get your projector-meter out! Figure out why you are looking for the negative. Don't whip out your words from your dark. They injure and re-injure others and then they continue your trail of darkness. Deal with your darkness. When you see lightness in others, it comes from lightness in you. When you see light, speak up. The world needs you! When you see dark, check in with yourself. The world needs you to.

Keep your rose colored glasses on despite the challenges of friends and acquaintances that may disappoint you. Time heals all as your story loses its headlines and someone else's story replaces yours. Do your best. Rise above the gossip and if you intuit or hear that someone is making up stories, just let it slide. If you think about it, whatever it is, it's probably something they have experienced or it's congruent to their own character. Let your behaviors and actions speak for themselves. Do your best. That's all you can do.

It's also a good idea to look after your physical health. Keep a steady dose of endorphins going with regular exercise because a healthy brain state gives you a more positive outlook. Get your sleep and eat well. We cannot change anyone else, but we can change ourselves. As Mahatma Ghandi once said, "You must be the change that you want to see in others" (11). Your dedication to a healthy process will flow and with flow, grow!

Whenever anyone goes through change, fear goes up. This is an important time to set up family meetings with your children. If you are on good terms with your former husband or wife, include him or her on the weekly meeting too. You may want to meet in a neutral place like at a park or at a coffee shop. If your separation is mutual and there is a healthy dose of regard between you and your former partner, you might meet at each other's residence. Start with meeting once per week. Let everyone at the table have a turn to say what is going right, and what is going wrong. There are some families that use a type of 'talking stick' or an object you can pass around. As you hold an object such as that, it reminds everyone else to just listen. Additionally for men, and boys, the brain is more relaxed having something tangible to connect with. Try to set a planned time to have your meetings. You are setting up structures that will allow your children to feel they have 'two homes', 'two loving parents who can love each other better from two different homes', and a world that is going to feel less stressed over time.

In the months following, you can develop a bi-weekly, monthly, and then bi-monthly schedule. Take your time in the first year. Let your children's feelings just be what they are, no matter what. So if he or she says, "I hate you", just empathize "It's hard to hear you hate me right now, and I love you just the same". If your child says, "Why can't you and Mommy (or Daddy) live together?" just assure him or her reframing "You would really like us to live together again. And you have two homes now. We love you more than ever in both homes". These types of empathic and reframing statements remind your children, they are loved. They can count on you both. Their feelings are so important to you no matter what they are.

Take time out to have fun with each one of your children on their own as much as possible. The time you spend in play together will help them know you in an unstressed way, and will help them get used to having two family homes with two parents. I recommend couples find an activity like running, tennis, golf, skiing, hiking, or some active aerobic type of sport you can share. What they tell me is that it's easier to talk through things after they have played together. An up side of going through this process is that in having a parenting plan, you will get to have time with your children and time out to heal. You need both. Time with your children is healing to your brain and gives you a sense of identity – you are always Mother or Father to your children no matter what. Research shows that just being in contact with your offspring, calms your nervous system.

You may also notice that your children have some difficulty concentrating at school in the first year post separation. If its possible to go for a run together before school, or walk them to school, it can really help set them up with a better brain state that is less stressed and therefore ready to learn. Exercise isn't the only panacea for feeling better. You can share the idea of journal writing too. It can be helpful to have a routine in both homes where you all take fifteen minutes after your evening abolitions and write in your private journals as a family. Playing board games or cards is a great way to connect and also to let emotions out. Try to keep the same routines if possible in both homes. Again this generates this idea of still being a family. It's a less dramatic change for your children and it helps develop healthy lifestyle habits.

If you are in a parenting plan of one week on, and one week off and your child wants to talk to the other parent, try to facilitate the connection. If your child wants to see the other parent, try to reassure and be empathic "You really want to see Mommy right now, and this is my special time with you. You will see Mommy on Friday (whatever day that is)". By acknowledging the feelings and reassuring with the committed schedule, your child will adapt with the comfort of a reliable structure.

Be patient with yourself. You can't heal faster than you already are attempting. It's hard to morph a family and often your own healing is delayed because you are concentrating on your children so much. You won't want your children to see you fall apart because they need your strength to buoy them up. You will need to take your time to grieve with someone who can help you gain a healthy perspective on why, how, and what has gone sideways between you and your former partner. When I was going through my own divorce, I wrote in a number of journals. I talked to a counselor. And I had many mornings where my eyes were so puffy from crying all night that it took about three hours and a walk with dark sunglasses on for me to be able to get into my day. Morphing a family, you will discover strength in you that you may never have ever realized before. Morphing a family, you will discover a weakness in you that you may never have ever realized. Morphing a family, you will discover all of 'you'. Truthful, integral, patient, caring, loving, challenged, angry, sad, bitter, frustrated, kind, and developing YOU!

****

Breakthrough tips for Morphing Families:

1. Focus your first year on your children, they need you. Who you are as a father or a mother is one of the most solid identities you will have in your life. No matter what happens, you will always be your children's first love. Research shows huge benefits to your brain in just being in the company of your offspring during times of grief. Your children need you when the family breaks up, and the benefit to you of dedicating the transition year to them is huge and lasting. They will need a

safe witness to process their grief. This transition year, providing your time, is hugely preventative to their wellbeing long term. You either put the time in now, or you will be putting the time in latter when they start acting out repressed feelings in self destructive actions, and an inability to attach in their own future relationships.

2. Find mutually fun ways to get exercise with your children. These shared physical activities help put the brain in a state that fosters communication and lets feelings go. The shared positive experience helps in the process of setting up a 'new normal' for everyone.

3. Work on your mirror technique. This tool is a lifesaver when you are moving through your dark tunnel fears, inadequacies, and grief.

4. Journal your feelings so that you don't bottle up. Sharing thoughts and fears with your friends or a psychotherapist can make a huge difference in rebuilding.

5. Write a list of things you are grateful for. This is also a fun exercise to do at dinner when your children are with you. They can also write out their own. This helps shift your cognitions towards the positive, progressive, future possibilities.

****

CHAPTER 9

FEELING GUILTY

This is such an important chapter. One of the reasons you may be stuck from taking full action to close the door to the past is that you are feeling guilty for blowing it in your past relationship. Feelings of guilt are actually quite helpful to our well being to the extent that they motivate us to live in alignment with our integrity and values. What do you value most? How were your values upheld in the way you were in your former relationship? Our feelings help steer us away from making dumb decisions and from otherwise undermining our lives. Feelings of guilt can be powerful agents of behavior change. When we feel guilty, we often adjust our behaviors so that they are more congruent with our integrity. However, feelings of guilt can also lead to obsessive ruminations in a downward self-defeating spiral. YUK. You won't be doing anything helpful or productive while in that mental space. Your negative distressing thoughts are formed in your left-brain and you rescript and heal them through the emotional processing done in your right brain (crying). This is why a journal, a good friend or a therapist can be a big help. Avoiding your feelings by keeping busy, proving yourself at work, or jumping into a rebound relationship right away doesn't change your pattern of thinking and deep distress. These are only temporary fixes. You will need to unpack your own emotional cycle.

When you go through a relationship break-up, there is no doubt that you experience a type of trauma. For this reason, it is imperative that you seek professional counseling so that you process and learn from what you are going through. Otherwise, similar to symptoms resulting from any experience of post-traumatic stress, (PTS), your grief from the breakup can stay trapped in a chronic flashbacks and rehearsing of all the "if only's", "what if's", and "why ME's". After retreading along all these negative pathways, you will start to feel like you have become the problem. The experience of guilt results from recognizing you have taken an action that has caused a negative outcome, either to yourself or to another. By the way, when I am referring to 'guilt' in this context of a relationship breakup, I am not talking about the kind of doctrinal, belief-based guilt that is prominent in many religions. I am referring only to the experience of guilt that flows from a sense of failure to perform well enough or acting outside your value system in the just-ended relationship that might be a barrier to being successful in future relationships.

When you go through a break up, you can fall into a crisis of identity—a demoralizing experience wherein you may think that you are not good enough. One of the key factors contributing to this self-imposed dark pit of guilt (where you experience angst drawn from a perceived multitude of perceived deficit behaviors) and shame (where you see yourself as inadequate), may result from the fact too often you understand yourself only in comparison to others. Is my writing style good or bad? Am I a good writer or a bad writer compared to other commentators? Our educational system is set up in a way that we measure our success against others.

Dr. Brene Brown, a noted researcher and author in the area of shame and vulnerability, discusses her research findings on the subject of guilt and shame in her lecture series The Power of Vulnerability (12). Dr. Brown studied men and women (with a mean age of forty), gathering data through interviews conducted over the past eleven years. She found that eighty-five percent of all men and women recalled a shaming experience around their creativity in childhood. Dr. Brown analyzes what is known as the "creativity slump", that happens to students in grades four or five as a result of children whose creative openness can be harmed by teachers who subjectively grade children one against the other. This same destructive process can also happen within families when parents compare siblings to each other or to others in their peer group. One child may be identified by a parent as the 'star academic' and another the 'star athlete'. These comparisons can result in a significant loss of childhood self-image to the child who is being compared unfavorably to others. This comparing process represents a significant deficit in our educational system and family systems because it sets an early trap for children who start to internalize a self image that can create a slippery slope to lifelong tendencies of feeling guilt and shame. Children surrender their freedom to be innovative to their growing fears they may not be good enough after all.

I would suggest that the fear of being compared to others and not coming out as good enough can load up our psyche with negative drag that gets in the way of successfully navigating through relationship endings. Aside from the pain of the loss itself (which can feel like a death) and the stages of grief, this childhood training in comparison of our value to others is one of the reasons why it is so difficult to move forward from a relationship ending. Growing up with a construct of brilliance or embarrassment based on comparisons with others in our peer group, we are at great risk when a relationship ends. Deep in our human spirit resides the successful or unsuccessful child who has either made the grade or has failed. Coming from a lifetime of misconceptions about the self as a manifestation of who we are rather than who we are in relation to others, it follows that when our relationship fails at any age, we drop into our own lifetime design of win or lose. As an aside this may be especially true for competitive athletes whose identity is defined by how the game ends. The pressure to win can be a barrier to intimacy and wholehearted living. When the experience of a failed relationship sinks deeply into our psyche, the greater danger is that we might start to identify ourselves as being a loser, whether we have been left or even when we do the leaving. In this way, a relationship ending can lead to an even greater trauma of loss of solid identity.

In order to heal from any trauma, you should not dwell on the trauma site. You will move through the pain of your losses in all the stages of grief, and it helps to manage what you pay attention to most. In the context of a relationship breakup (as in any traumatic experience), you are much better off to direct your thinking to the positive actions that occurred in your life as a result, and to what changes you can make that will be preventative for you in your future. Otherwise, you can be re-traumatizing and deepening the thinking that your life will be out of control forever. Although it may feel that way now, every day and every month you will start to notice the ways everything that has happened starts to have meaning. For example, in the summer of 2013, one of the worst man-made disasters in Canadian history occurred. An unmanned runaway train carrying oil derailed in the center of the town of Lac-Megantic, Quebec. There were thirty-eight people who were killed in the catastrophe, and with many people who are still missing. This was devastating news around the world and an unthinkable loss for those whose family members are tragically gone forever. We can focus on the horror of the tragedy, which might terrorize us to the extent we may decide to never go near a train track again. Or we can focus on the need for more safety precautions in moving dangerous cargo. We can also focus on the heroic efforts of rescuers and outpouring of caring by people across the country to the victims of this tragedy.

In the wake of any trauma, large or small, it is always helpful to talk about the event as much and as soon as possible. Debriefing the event helps release rather than lock on to negative runaway thoughts about it. In talking things through with someone we trust, we find out we are not alone. One dilemma in the wake of a relationship break-up is that if you are trying to preserve the confidence and privacy of the other person, (for whatever reason), you won't want to share your breakup experience with your close friends because they know you former partner too! But this silence creates a psychological barrier. It locks in an inner dialogue that, in turn, can give those gremlins of self-doubt, open season to harm your psyche. Chronic rehearsing of guilt can lead to imbedding negative core beliefs within you that will be very difficult to escape from later in your life. So my strong advice is that you make sure you seek weekly counseling immediately following your breakup, for a period of at least three months, so you can move forward.

Feelings of guilt often rise when the pressure that we feel to be perfect gets out of control. We all live within a tension between the person we are, (our authentic self), and the person we wish to be (our ideal self). Our ideal self never makes mistakes, never makes a poor judgment, and never utters a statement that we later wish we could take back. But the simple truth is that we are imperfect, flawed, and it's our humanness that actually makes us most loveable! It's hard to love a rock! The truth is we are not inanimate rocks. We are complex beings that engage in some good and some not so good practices. We all are learning as we go. We could all be more caring. I find myself humming the Beatles song "Imagine".

We all live within this gap between our authentic and ideal selves. The significance of this dichotomy is if the gap becomes too great, our anxiety level and even our feelings of self-loathing will go up. When this starts happening we also start experiencing a host of difficulties such as getting a good night's sleep, concentrating, functioning, eating, relating, working, and even breathing! It's healthy to have enough of a gap between our authentic and ideal selves that we are motivated to grow and get better in life. But it becomes unhealthy if you develop so much of a gap that your biggest secret is that you don't like yourself! So we need to manage our expectations around perfection or else risk falling into the abyss of depression and anxiety. If you feel possessed with guilt, for example that you 'blew it' in your relationship, then you are well-advised to go back to the 3 R's exercise and expand all three areas. It is high time then, to process your thoughts with someone you know and trust as being both compassionate and wise.

Guilt is a self-imposed emotion that can cause profound damage to your capacity to navigate through difficult periods in your life. Guilt can distract you from appreciating where you went wrong and how you can avoid this mistaken pathway in the future. The experience of guilt can dominate your life and end up owning you!

The experience of shame, which happens when you actually start to identify yourself as being the problem, rather than understanding what you have gone through as choosing a behavior that you know is contrary to your core values. Shame can be a debilitating force that can lead you into downward, negative spiral of behavior with disastrous consequences for you and others. Shame is the foundation of all addiction. Shame is the most powerful driver steering you into avoidant coping behaviors such as drinking, smoking, shopping, or sexing.

So whatever your failings have been, don't wallow in guilt or shame. Own your choices and understand ways you can get better in your life practices. Commit to the tools and skills you need to put to practice to get better. Don't hang out in the failings of your past. Don't put yourself down because of them. It's actually kind of arrogant to think you won't make mistakes in life. Of course you will. We all will. We create our own reputations and if you find yourself constantly apologizing because you feel guilty, eventually others will start to lose sight of your goodness and focus on your deficits too. Attention grows where attention goes. If you think of personal relationships as vessels of growth as this book is describing, there is never any one person at fault, absolutely wrong, or in full blame. Two people create the dynamics of change. Partnerships are, by design fifty-fifty! At every stage, from conception through commitment, the fifty–fifty equation for responsible change holds true.

Human cognitions often tend to bias towards the negative. One manifestation of this tendency is that it is easier for us to recall what we have done wrong than what we have done right. For that reason we feel more guilt about things than would be objectively warranted.

If you are still beating yourself up after your Three R's (above), here's another challenge to 'force quit' your negative bias. Write down the reasons you blame and shame yourself on one side of a page in your journal. Keep track for a whole day. At the end of the day, write down both the positive and negative version of the past day's experience.

I can think of an example from my own personal history. I did not cook gourmet meals when I was married to my former husband. I saw my lack in cooking skills as a negative personal attribution. I was an unimaginative cook who might have taken a cooking class to become more diverse and skilled at cooking (negative bias – me, the lazy gourmet), but I did not take any such class.

On the opposite side of the page I would write: "I cooked most of the meals during my parenting years as part of a positive caring for my family. They were meals without sauces. These days such meal planning and preparation would be referred to as 'clean nutrition'. Considering today's trend of 'clean food', I was way ahead of my time giving high nutrition/low fat nurturance". None of that kind of reframing could have happened for me if I had not taken the opportunity to talk to others about my guilt and deficit feelings around my need to cook better meals. Because I did get this help, I am able to recall my cooking career with a positive rather than negative perspective.

I anchored my learning with curiosity in my family of origin. My father grew up on a farm in Alberta. I can't remember seeing him cook anything but pancakes on Sunday. My mother cooked delicious but very simple farm-style meals. She was a little controlling in the kitchen, so it wasn't a place in our home that invited learning; with the exception of making bread. I had the fun of watching the dough rise and then the opportunity of pounding the dough back down into a ball again. When I think of the smell of fresh bread, I smile and I think of her fondly.

If you have been a harsh self-critic who is constantly reminding yourself of all the ways you failed to do your part in your last relationship, write out a list of these personal revelations. And you should also include the ways you saw your virtues, strengths, passions and caring behaviors operating in the relationship.

****

You might include in this **relationship balance sheet** items like the following:

How were you a positive influence in your significant other's life?

What are you grateful for from that relationship?

How did the relationship help to develop a better you?

What strengths showed up in you through the experience of the relationship?

****

This exercise will help you to regain emotional homeostasis and a more positive self-concept. This, in turn, will help you to become more creative, helpful, nurturing and connecting with others in the future. Why beat yourself up when it's to no one's benefit to do so? At the same time, you should not hold on to your regrets in your private bubble of shame. Share your personal learning. Obviously it takes two for a relationship to end. Own your part in the need for growth. There are always things you could have done better in your past relationship. Don't kid yourself by projecting your learning points on your former partner. We can all get better. When you identify your learning, talk about your learning with a professional counselor or trusted friend. It takes healthy ego strength to identify ways that you have fallen short.

Own your deficits and practice new thinking and behaviors to get better. Hiding out in your shame or your fear, you will be frozen in the past. Imagine a big ice carving of sad and emotionally stuck you propped at your front doorstep. As you slowly melt, the drips of you flood your whole home. Mold sets in! How's that for a metaphor? You can't avoid personal accountability no matter what happened in your past relationship. Shame is one of the core feelings associated with anger and the cycle of addiction. We are all learning and growing…even you!

To use another example from my personal life, I could say: "I am a failure because my twenty year marriage ended". Or I can give that statement a more positive reframing: "My marriage was a twenty year success" and focus on our positive attributions and strengths as parents and partners. I could say "Michael and I fell out of love" or I could say "we loved each other enough to let go". The truth is I fell out of love with who I was in the relationship with Michael once our children had completed school, and were not my primary focus any more. I could have been more confident in taking a stand for what I believed, felt and what I needed. I could have been more differentiated when it came to difficult conversations instead of placating Michael to keep the peace. I wanted a more spiritual and less pressured relationship with Michael and possibly I could have held my spiritual ground with him. I could have devised a lifestyle more conducive to "time in" instead of rushing… so much. I could have managed my anxiety better, and slowed down a lot more. My boundaries could have been so much stronger if I had 'just said no', even some of the time. I could have been more proactive in lots of ways, but I wasn't.

Different aspects of our personality come out with different people. Michael and I were pretty competitive in our relationship together. I recall in one of our children's elementary school year, when our children's school principal joined us for dinner. We had a Ping-Pong table at the time. The three of us started playing Ping-Pong with our then ten-year-old son Justin. Michael partnered with Justin and I partnered with the principal. It still makes me laugh as I remember how Michael and I started with a 'whack' of sturdy competition. I thought everyone played Ping Pong to win. The principal and our son simply kept the ball in play. It was hilarious to see the contrast of play to play, versus play to win. It was such a revelation to think of just keeping the ball in play rather than always trying to win.

Relationships are more in sync when we align ourselves in this kind of win-win attitude. Young Justin and his school principal drove this point home for me in that moment. I've never forgotten it. Since that time, Justin has become a force on the tennis court. His undergraduate degree was supported by a full-ride tennis scholarship in an NCAA Division I school in the United States. For him, 'play to play', evolved into 'play to win' as his elite status in tennis grew. Yet today in the balance between Justin the lawyer and Justin the tennis player, he has rediscovered his ten-year-old style of playing happy tennis and he is playing better than ever. He doesn't have the pressure of winning a match for his University; he is just playing to play. He's still that competitive guy that I can see as both his Father and myself, but without the external pressures of his coach and team, he wins more tennis games now than ever. He plays wholeheartedly in all aspects of his life as a lawyer and as a tennis player.

Honing our skills and maintaining our spirit in the joy of play for play's sake may be the secret to loving life, our jobs, our partners and our selves. With a 'play for play' attitude you won't be frozen in guilt, and you won't get stuck in the ruminations of your past. No more sleepless nights, no more turning over and over wrestling with those gremlin dialogues of personal guilt and deep regret. Figure out what you might have done differently in your past relationship. Possibly share your learning with your former partner. Think about how you can get better in the future. Do your best. Emotional freedom will get you back to contributing to others again.

"Keep your face always toward the sunshine – and shadows will fall behind you" – Walt Whitman

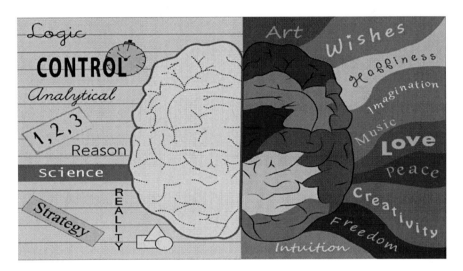

Guilt and the Human Brain

There is lots of research about the differences between the male and female brain. (I am not referring to earlier brain research that was done primarily on male cadavers and under the assumption that the male and female brains were the same). More recently there has been a surge of research supporting the fact that the brains of men and women actually work quite differently. Men and women may experience guilt and grief differently as well. Earlier brain research did not include the study of female brain because it was discovered that the fluctuation of hormones presented a problem in confounding results. In the past few years, research has shown that men tend to be single focused because of the way the male brain is hardwired. In contrast, women are hardwired to be lateral, multi-focused thinkers.

What we now know is that even in doing simple acts like picking up a cup, the male brain is activated in the hemisphere opposite to the physical action. So if you were to interrupt the male brain in a single task of picking up a cup, a man would not be able to pick up the cup. Likewise, it may follow if a man is stuck in guilt or shame, he may have a very difficult time functioning. His singular focus would turn his deep freeze up. By way of contrast, research shows that in women both hemispheres of the brain light up on the same action of picking up a cup. Women have the same left-brain to right side of the body action process. But if you interrupt a woman's brain, she can still manage the task because the other hemisphere will kick into operation. This amazing discovery has lead me to thinking more seriously about how important it is for men to practice out of negative thinking. So men, you should keep a journal of any negative thinking you experience and practice re-scripting yourself into more positive thoughts.

With respect to women's unique wiring, how does this factor into how a woman moves through the stages of grief and guilt? Do women do this differently than men when a relationship ends? If women can access their brain bi-laterally, they may have an easier time coping through grief stages when guilt and shame cycles often are manifest. Women who are processing guilt and shame may have greater ability than men to multi-focus, despite where they are in their grief.

Men may have a harder time at this stage of guilt and shame because they may not be able to manage all the changes that occur when a deep relationship ends, because men are wired to just think of one thing at a time. Accordingly, the likelihood is that women handle the big picture and the multiple adjustments that occur with a break up with greater ease. But women also may get stuck in negative case building theories. Women may become entrenched in case building based on everything that has 'ever' happened through time. This case-built wall of perceived and tallied deficits may then block many women from moving forward. These are questions that cry out for future research. When it comes to feeling guilt and grief, the male brain may have a harder time adapting to change, especially if that male is not the initiator of change.

In terms of gender differences in emotional processing, a man tends to struggle after a breakup with the intendant sense that he 'is a failure', and that he is 'not acceptable'. Coping with relationship loss, he is most likely to avoid his feelings and withdraw into activities such as work. A woman struggles more with the overall emotional loss and social impacts of her breakup. She is more likely to struggle with anxiety especially if she isolates herself in the loss.

Brain specificity may have implications for how we move through stages of breakup recovery. I call these stages: infatuation (the longing for the past), power struggle (whose fault is it, certainly not me), reflection (on second thought we weren't a very good fit after all), re-evaluation (I can learn and grow from this loss), transformation (I am better because of this breakup), commitment (I am going to live my best life), acceptance (I am so grateful I was with my former partner for a time), and reconciliation (I hope my former partner has the best life too).

Women have larger frontal lobes (which is where problem solving occurs). Men have larger amygdala (the part of the brain which regulates sexual behavior) than female brains. Women have ten percent more white matter (which helps connect the right and left hemisphere). Men have 6.5 percent more grey matter (which is used for information processing) (13). It makes sense that these distinct differences between men and women may play out as factors that would impact breakup recovery.

We are living in an exciting time as we are increasingly discovering new insights about brain function through more sophisticated scientific investigation. Louann Brizendine, M.D., reminds us that the male capacity to produce oxytocin (the attachment hormone) increases with age while the production of testosterone decreases (14). For a man, breakups may be more difficult to handle the older he is because with more oxytocin and less testosterone, he may feel more attached to the way things were and less proactive in change. For a woman with the fluctuations of estrogen, progesterone, and testosterone in perimenopause and menopause, she may feel things more than she has in the past. This then may cause more pronounced expectations as "the vision-obscuring veil created by the hormones of reproduction begins to lift, a woman's youthful fire and spirit are often rekindled, together with long-sublimated desires and creative drives. Midlife fuels those drives with a volcanic energy that demands an outlet" (15). Gender and age effects may impact which party initiates break ups with which frequency at different stages of life (men in young adult years, women in later years) with these hormone shifts. Certainly, we are living in a very interesting time as we discover more about the human brain and how it impacts everything in our lives. The brain is social. We need to experience each other to create change. The more safely connected you feel within yourself, the less reactive you will feel with others. The more you communicate, ask for help, practice new ways of thinking, the more your brain will expand positive new pathways that reinforce the knowing that you are not alone, that you are loveable, and that you are generally safe in the world. As you create your own safety by embracing all your feelings and living honestly with what you experience, the more relationship ready you will become. Meditation, exercise, eating well, getting enough sleep, and healthy social connections are the ingredient practices for better brain health. The more you connect your emotional world with your world of logic and reason (right and left hemisphere), the bigger your brain will grow. Listen to music, dance (right brain examples) and journal, set goals for yourself (left brain examples). Engage both sides of your brain in your process of moving forward.

****

Whether you have a male or female brain, here are some breakup-breakthrough suggestions that I believe will help you get unstuck from spiraling feelings of grief and guilt:

1. Make sure you have closure with your former partner and that you are clear about your part in the demise of the relationship. If you feel guilty because you think that you should have been more caring, patient, loving, and/or communicative with him/her; or if you feel resentful because he/she should have been more caring, patient, loving, and/or

communicative with you, you should revisit the Three "R's". Repeat the exercise on your own by writing letters (not actually sent) or by journaling.

2. You may want to hire a psychotherapist or a life coach who can help you step over the psychic blocks of feeling guilty.

3. Take all the time you may need to move through your grief. But you should also give yourself a time framework, or a series of achievable milestones, within which you can complete this process. One reasonable time frame would be to set aside one month for every year you were together.

4. Process your grief and talk about your feelings of guilt with your long-standing dear friends. But also balance your time talking about this with some new friends in order to have a fresh break and get a new perspective on life.

5. Try to achieve balance about what you think about. Don't allow yourself to dwell on one thing too long. When you think of your body right now, do you have any localized pain at this moment in time? Give the pain a scale of intensity 0 – 10. Now close your eyes and consider all the feelings in your whole body. Start at the top and work your way down to your toes. How do you feel... everywhere? Now think of that localized pain. What number would you give it after you do this whole body-scan? You probably will notice that your pain has abated. This is what happens when you manage your thinking and what you are attending to. Having integrity means being 'whole'. You are the 'whole' of your behaviors—some good and some not as good... but all are loveable and part of learning. Whole thinking dissipates guilt because you will learn to embrace your imperfection and create new emotional space to learn. Your natural emotional state is to feel peaceful, not guilty.

6. Ask your friends what they tend to feel guilty about? This exercise will help you to realize that you too are normal and it will also give you a perspective of what it looks like to be such a harsh personal self-critic. Talk through your guilt feelings as much as you need to. As you say your thoughts out loud, you will notice you are being 'over the top'. Your friends can guide you away from obsessive negative fearful loops that can block you from being more present with them.

7. If you are a parent, and you are feeling guilty that your children's lives are forever changed since you and the other parent have split up, you should spend more time with your children in a fun physical activity. Let them talk about their fears, resentments, sorrow, and anger. Listen without an agenda. Just be empathic and hold the space. With the positive chemistry that physical exercise produces, the brain is naturally able to shift stuck thinking, taking on more positive resiliency.

8. If you are single with no children, set a personal goal to refocus your attention on something that actively redirects your thinking. Challenge yourself physically, artistically, and mentally. You might learn photography, try sailing lessons, and learn how to play a guitar, or take up a new yoga practice. You might even train for a half or full marathon or enter a Grand Fondo cycle event.

9. If you are still blaming yourself or still stuck in guilt, reframe your negative thoughts to their positive opposite by saying them out loud. Become your own personal promoter. For example, if you are with a friend and she says she is getting married in a few months, your thoughts may go to, "I just want to hide because life is passing me by and I am such a loser". But you say out loud, "I am so happy for you. How can I help you with the wedding preparations?" Saying positive thoughts out loud and taking a positive action is how you can change your brain so that you can to get away from guilt and get into a positive state of happier resonance.

10. Write out a list with two columns: on the first column identify your irrational negative beliefs (It's ALL my fault); on the second column list positive opposite beliefs (I've learned things about myself that I can get better at next time). Whatever forces are keeping you trapped in negative ruminations, (such as unprocessed emotional grief, financial fears, or residential haunts), you should identify, and put them on a list of negative self talk. This exercise will take some practice, but it definitely works!

11. Then get whatever help you need to move on, see them in a better perspective, or completely put the negativity in the past. The sooner you do so, the sooner you are going to start your healing process. Remember, significant others around you, may be impacted by your breakup breakdown too. Your family and your friends are waiting for you. Life is short and there are whole new stories of life and love ahead

of you. Friends will help you if you ask them. Ask for their support to help you see through your blind spots. If they sense you are getting stuck, you should give them carte blanche permission to give you feedback and a giant nudge forward (or even a good kick in the butt) if they think you need it.

****

Time to get on with knowing who you really are! Who are you becoming? Who do you want to become? Just like an eagle, it's time to spread your wings.

CHAPTER 10

RELATIONSHIP PATTERNS

N ow that you are better able to process anxiety, anger, guilt, and anger, you will be keen to get back in the cat seat of love. This chapter helps you look at your patterns of engagement when it comes to relationships. This will help you gain insight about your patterns of falling in and out of love too fast or too soon. Do you tend to rush into relationships over and over again? I remember watching a cartoon called The Road Runner when I was a child. In this television program, Wile E. Coyote chased the ever-elusive Road Runner wherever it went. With the speed of light, their relationship inevitably landed Wile E. at the bottom of some cliff under an ACME Anvil. This chapter will help you understand why it's so important to look for love inside of you first, instead of chasing coyote.

I recall a thirty something client of mine 'Wile E.', who was heart-broken after the ending of a series of relationships that would start in a starburst of infatuation and love chemistry, proceed with a pattern of rapid acceleration, and then hit the wall with a splat!

We may think that a 'Wile E Coyote' experience is funny to watch when we are six years old. But feeling our adult heart go splat is very painful. In 'Wile E.'s case, he had some insight but no control over repetitious past relationship patterns. He'd fall in love, have frequent sleepovers, and within a few months invite his new girlfriend to move in with him. But after this starburst beginning, things would start to go sour. In the adjustments of living together, conflict would ensue and the relationship would then come to an end. He could see this sequence over and over again and yet it just kept happening. "I guess love is blind," he'd say as he held his head and heart, his confidence level about being in love in tatters. 'Wile E' didn't have structures in place to slow himself down when it came to the launch of prospective new loves. He also saw a certain lack of ability to manage his relationships at work, within his family of origin and even in the way that he organized his daily activities. If this sounds like you too, then, you may want to consider learning how to pace yourself in your own relationships. One useful guiding rule might be to equate length of time in relationship to how many times per week you have sleepovers. So for example, if you have known each other one month, you might restrict yourself to only have one sleep over per month or week. Two months might equate to two sleepovers per month or per week. Whatever you decide, make your schedule with conscious intention.

To set a sustainable pace in a relationship you should first consider how you divide up your leisure time. If you are maintaining other structures in your life that are nurturing to you (such as friendships with other people, time with your family, time in sports and leisure activities), chances are your relationship will be better equipped to proceed at a pace that will facilitate a secure attachment that has a better chance of a longer life span rather than an anxious attachment that will likely flame out with another heart-wrenching ending.

How this might play out in the real world for example, is that if your partner is distracted from your relationship because of things happening in his/her life such as work, health, financial or family stresses, you wouldn't be upset because he/she is less emotionally or physically available to you. Consequently you (unlike Wile E) will be less likely to head over your own emotional cliff and you will avoid wild drop offs in your own level of love interest as trust builds between you and your partner.

Typically when your stress level goes up, the capacity of your brain to process loving feelings goes down. The more stressed your potential partner is, the more aggressively you will tend to pursue connection (like Wile E. Coyote). This is because you may take his/her withdrawal personally and perceive this act of withdrawal as critical information about the relative health of the relationship. But these kinds of roller coaster feelings can then lead you over an emotional cliff. The more you lean on one person as THE resource for fulfillment in your life, the more likely you will be let down, and the more likely you will drive them away. However, if you have alternative ways to find personal fulfillment, such as other friend-ships, hobbies and interests external to the relationship, the more secure you will be in yourself and the better you will be able to manage yourself in relation to the ups and downs of your partners' life. The more security that you have within yourself, the more stable and enduring your love will be for your partner. (As the cartoon character Wile E Coyote shows, it's hard to survive repeated falls off cliffs without receiving emotional scars that over time can fracture trust.)

I believe that it is important that in the early stages you get to know each other well spiritually and emotionally before developing your sexual con-nection. The better your verbal communication skills, the more pleasurable and fulfilling your physical connection will be. The less self-conscious you are the more playful and curious you will be. As you develop intimacy through your growing friendship, you will gain more trust and security. With more trust, you will have a better sexual connection. Couples, who delay sexual intimacy early on, allow communication to become the foun-dation of their attraction. This helps ensure longevity of your bond(15).

When your relationship moves into the 'sleep over stages', you may want to design a graduated pace that works for you. It's a big change to wake up together, share bathroom spit, and even get a restful sleep in a shared and sometimes different bed. This is where the one sleep over for every month you've been together policy pays off. You need your sleep. So does he or she. The point is not to be prudish but rather prudent about how to set a sustainable pace for your relationship.

Another critical step in the evolution of the relationship is the decision about when to introduce your new love to your family and friends. Anxi-eties can go up when either of you fear being judged. The more you know your partner; the less this will be a factor. I recall introducing my husband at a family dinner at my sister Carol's, and she said to Joe "You better not hurt Jo-Anne or I'll break your knees with a baseball bat!" Rest assured Carol has never hurt anyone but does have a big personality with a corre-spondingly big sense of humor. I felt totally relaxed knowing that this zany sister moment could not distract from my relationship with Joe. We were so comfortable with each other by then that he could also trust that he could laugh about it rather than worry about my sister and baseball bats! But this story serves to highlight the sense that if you are secure in the rela-tionship, these off-the-wall experiences that we all tell at weddings, won't deter love from evolving. If we hurry the process of integrating our extended friends and family, there is a chance for stresses to rise and anxious attachment to result. So, go slow. The more authentic and real you feel with your partner, the more you are ready to introduce new stressors. This is not to say that our friends are stressful, but chances are they may feel somewhat protective of you and assess the potential harm or benefit to you that may accompany your new partner.

If you are Wile E. Coyote and have had a few crashes of the heart, get your feet on the ground and choose the speed of your step. Pace yourself. You're in charge… aren't you?

There are amazing ways your body speaks up to make sure you go slowly and do not accelerate and maybe fall victim to your anxieties. Compare how you feel on a Ferris wheel versus a roller coaster. If you pay attention to what your body is telling you as you pace yourself in a growing relationship, you will access your 'built in' body regulator that guides you towards a balance of body, mind and spirit. For example, when you take on too many changes too fast; you will notice anxiety symptoms such as racing heart rate, sweaty palms, and even dizziness. Clients often try to mask these presenting symptoms through taking medication. The far better way is to embrace your best friend – your body and its inherent wisdom in order to slow down the pace of change in your emotional life.

Even your breath works with you to slow you down! It turns out when you are stressed out, your breath will become unpleasant. Britain's Loughborough University and Imperial College London took breath samples from twenty-two young adults, in both relaxed and stressed states. Two compounds in the breath – 2-methyl pentadecane and indole – increased following the stress exercise (16). This research reports from a small sample, but it occurs to me that our bad breath (which repels) may be doing us a favor to slow down the number of people we are in contact with during the day when we need to have some time in. In any case, stay connected with the wisdom of your best friend – your body. If you don't want to slow down, chew gum! Here's a little nickel knowledge: according to current research, chewing gum improves your brain function and mood by increasing your circulation and blood flow to your brain (17).

****

Breakthrough Tips:

1. Don't lose you and your favorite lifestyle habits when you start dating. If you have a practice of running in the morning and your new date wants to meet for coffee, just say no. Covet the time you habitually set aside to keep you physically and emotionally healthy. If you have been accustomed to meet with friends, don't stop meeting them altogether just to free up time for a date. You may want to modify your habits and routines, but stay connected with your body, mind, and spirit resources.

2. If you start having sleepovers, try using a formula of one night for every month or two months you have been together. This ensures your autonomy and a decent night's sleep! Remember, learning to sleep well with a significant other takes time.

3. Meet equally in both homes – yours' and his/hers. Most people feel more autonomous and calm in their own space. Be thoughtful and fair to yourself and your new partner.

4. If finances have been part of a learning curve for you in the past, you may want to share the cost of dates. This can help maintain autonomy and emotional equilibrium. To save any awkwardness in splitting the bill, you might like to download an app such as "check please" which figures out your tip and splits the bill for you easily.

5. Keep one night a week all to yourself. Make space in your Day-Timer to date YOU.

****

CHAPTER 11

ESCAPE FROM AN AFFAIR

Another fallout pattern for people who jump before they walk, leap before they look, and who need to learn to slow down before they crash, can be affairs. Its been estimated that roughly 30 – 60% of all married individuals will have an affair at some point in their marriage (18). 2 – 3% of all children are the product of infidelity (19). This chapter is to help you avoid one of life's greatest traps of integrity, guilt, and shame. There is a big difference between traits and behaviors. Our personality traits affect our behaviors in positive and negative ways. We have a kaleidoscope of personality traits that come out in different contexts. When you are frustrated or feeling unloved, your survival style (of behavior) comes forward. Some may call this your "dark side". Your personality is fairly unchanging through time and, if you don't have your personal crackerjack executive team running your show, you may become immersed in unhealthy actions that don't reflect your core values. Affairs often happen like a perfect storm. Batten down the hatches of your lifeboat. This chapter will help you sail past this freak of human nature and learn better ways to navigate a life you can reflect upon with joy, not shame.

Affairs are most common in times of significant life stage change: early twenties, early thirties, early forties, mid-life, and to a lesser extent in latter life. When there has been a sudden death, a sudden illness, a new job, a lost employment, you can feel like you have lost your personal compass. When major change happens in life, the anchors you have counted on as you're true north or true south, all may seem to spin. You may be fearful of your own mortality, or the mortality of your loved ones. So if you look at affairs through the lens of addiction, it starts with the emotional trigger (life stage), then progresses to the craving (to feel good), then the ritual (the affair itself), then the guilt that follows (telling lies to maintain the affair), then the shame (loss of core belief in self). This sad pattern results in a cycle that can be devastating. We all know the movie 'Fatal Attraction'.

Then there is the type of affair that starts from compassion. I once worked with a client who was helping a neighbor whose wife was suffering terminal cancer. The husband was dedicated to his wife's care, and felt validated and supported by my client who showed up initially with prepared meals and general support. The affair started in the blurred boundaries and shared grief of the inevitable passing of this man's wife, who was also my neighbor's good friend. Certainly on its face, one might say what's the matter with that? This sounds like a beautiful love story. And it was for the first year. However, the new relationship never developed a life of its own even after this man's wife passed. Their love was born and held in the context of loss. Even after death, the relationship would always have the energy of a triangle.

In some ways, affairs can be seen as a type of communication triangle. When you don't feel loved by your partner, you might seek someone else to feel loved by. The difficulty here again is that it's you that needs to know you are whole, creative, and loveable. Having another impermanent resource that is external to you, will only serve you as a Band-Aid soon to leave your wounds exposed and you again unloved.

If someone you have been in relationship with has an affair, the same triangle principal holds. You can project all the deficits of your marriage on the object of the affair (the other person), but in truth your energy should be placed on your marriage and your relationship. An affair is always a symptom of lacking self-esteem, self-concept, and vulnerability. When you know that you are worth loving, you can totally ask for what you want with the person you need it from – your true love – you. We need to be responsible for our needs and feelings.

Affairs, as all addictions are, can be driven by primary feelings of shame. At the core, if you feel your needs are 'not that important', you are 'embarrassed to ask' or that you 'can't control the behavior even though you know it will risk everything', you have the ingredients of addiction. I recall a female client I worked with 'Brenda' whose husband 'Bob' had multiple affairs during their thirty years of marriage. When 'Brenda' first came to see me, it was over her decision to have one herself. 'Brenda' confessed, "Why not have an affair? 'Bob's been doing it for years!" 'Brenda's anger driven behavior was also, at her core, shame. 'Brenda' held the belief that her husband's pattern of affairs was her fault. She thought she had not loved 'Bob' well enough, that she herself wasn't attractive anymore. Otherwise he wouldn't continue to wound and offend her this way. She actually did end her marriage and we worked through her feelings of herself as a woman, as a mother, and as someone who had loved her husband so much that she would do anything it took to keep him. Fortunately, she came to see me before she had actually had the much-planned out affair herself.

For 'Brenda' and 'Bob' a 360 change in their lives was what it took to start to live honestly. I still recall 'Brenda' coming into my therapy room six months later. "I can't believe how good I feel. I really don't know what I was thinking staying with 'Bob' all that time". In fact 'Brenda' had never exercised her inner rebel. Taking the steps to end her marriage, she returned to an unmet stage in her own adolescence. 'Brenda' had always been the good eldest daughter. Her parents had been married for fifty years. She had four siblings, all of whom were happily married. 'Brenda' self esteem and core strength was always under the surface. The only reason 'Brenda' hadn't left her marriage earlier was because of her values of staying in a marriage no matter what. Here we see where the values of integrity and commitment need to be broken. There are times in our life when even the most honored and cherished values for living need reassessing. Certainly being the co-dependent in an addicted relationship is not a life to be loved.

If you have been involved in an affair, my advice to you is that you engage in a '3C' exercise with yourself: (i) Show some **Compassion** for yourself, because the affair has happened for a reason that may illustrate a weakness in you that you need to come to grips with; (ii) get better at brutally honest

Communication, because you need to talk about it and the needs and feelings that led to the affair, in order for you to find a way out; and (iii) **Commitment,** you need to make a promise to yourself that you will take whatever steps are needed to get out of the grips of the affair, including immediately going through a cold turkey exit from the scene.

Participants in affairs illustrate the symptoms of an **insecure attachment style**. Often people, who have repeated affairs, have childhood attachment wounds where there has been a loss of care due to parental or childhood illness, loss, or family addiction. People with insecure attachment styles are highly reactive, tend to have a locked on needy way of connecting with others. The greater yourself-esteem, the less possibility you will ever have an affair. The greater confidence you have to express your feelings, the greater chance you will have of experiencing a life-long relationship.

If you have got stuck in an affair trap, my advice to you is that you first assume responsibility for your part in it and then get yourself out of it as soon as possible. The future of an affair is not bright. Even if the affair relationship works out in your favor, you will always be reminded of your own breach of integrity by engaging in the affair in the first place. That is not likely going to be a life you will love, no matter which that potential 'one' is. Moreover, if he or she has had an affair with you, he or she will likely betray you in the future too. So until he or she is truly single, you should move on!

If you have a habit of getting into affairs, you should stop dating for a while and seek the help of a psychotherapist. The underlying drivers for getting into habitual affairs can be your low self-esteem, e.g., your need to win someone who is unavailable in a 'choose me' kind of way. This may be the manifestation of a lack of inner confidence that you deserve more or that you are going through some kind of life stage crisis. Sometimes it is that you simply are in the wrong place at the wrong time! This perfect storm then brings about a convergence of your life stage factors with those of other party in the affair. The results are the tangled, usually painful, and by definition deceitful dynamics of an affair. How much fun is that??

If either of your parents had an affair, you may even have unresolved feelings of betrayal you are working out. When a parent engages in an affair, children go through the betrayal too. There can be a loss of confidence that you can trust men (if your Father had an affair) or women (if your Mother had an affair). Rather than blindly cycle in and out of affairs, my advice to you is to spend some time to figure out why the pattern is happening, rather than see yourself-esteem dwindle with each misplaced experience.

I recall working with a thirty-something client in my practice'Curious George'. Curious George was in love with a married woman with whom he had been having an affair with for two years. She had promised him she would leave her husband and for two years he had maintained their secret relationship. Little wonder his self-esteem and confidence sank as weeks, months and years went by without the promised change. As long as he was on her sidelines, he was constantly reminded that he was second string. The longer he maintained his benched status, the more damage to his integrity, and emotional health.

If you played a team sport as a child, how long would you have continued to show up for practice or games if you knew you were always going to sit on the bench? Why then, as adults, would you make these self-destructive choices in your relationship? It takes courage to wait for the right game, for the right partner to come along, and then to fully step into a new life partnership. Getting involved with someone who is married is often the quintessential pathway to unhappiness. Even if such a potential love mate actually leaves their marriage, you will always be reminded of their (and your) lack of integrity of carrying on an affair with you while they were married to someone else. Going forward you will likely live with the nagging worry they are just as likely to step out or leave you when the doldrums hit or greener pastures present.

In the case of 'Curious George', he was on his way to go skiing after our session and I asked him:

"When you ski, do you 'sort of ski'?"

"I'm not sure.," he said. "What do you mean?"

"I mean what would sort of skiing look like?"

He still looked puzzled.

"Well, would you be motivated if you didn't have a complete set of skis, boots, poles? Would you stand at the top and just look at others skiing?… despite the cold."

"No. Definitely I always have everything I need and head down the mountain. I love the feeling. It's thrilling."

I then asked him "why do you 'sort of' do this relationship, choosing a woman who is not available? Aren't you left in the cold most nights?"

To really get what he was doing to himself in his habit, I had to connect him to an action he wasn't as invested in. If you have a friend who is stuck in an affair, try to make the analogy by comparing what he or she is doing with half doing the activity that he or she loves. It can be such a frustrating experience to witness someone you care about, participate in this type of out of control habit.

The Bottom Line about Affairs with Married People

We all make choices about our way of thinking and acting. And these choices produce feelings that lead to cold, unsatisfied dead end ways of being, or to new wonderful, even thrilling experiences. If you are stuck in the dynamics of an unrealizable affair with an unavailable lover, you should take a big breath and ask yourself "how long do I want to feel badly"? You can feel badly for one month, one year, or even decades, as long as you choose. We actively choose the lives we want to lead. If you truly want to be happy, then choose a partner who is fully available.

If you find yourself in a pattern of being attracted to people who are not available, you should consider whether the allure is coming from the competitor within yourself. Are you living your life in pursuit of—the need to win, or are you looking to love and be loved? Sadly, the former life game plan can be because you are caught in a trap of low self-esteem. Your hunger to 'win' in a 'choose me' way can be driven from a childhood experience of not being chosen. The truly sad part of this kind of 'love life' is the damage that you will do to all the people who you leave in your trail of destruction.

To get out of this dead end life plan, it will be helpful to write out a timeline of your historical infatuations. On one side of the line put the object of your hot pursuit (his or her name) and on the other side of the line put a list of what else was going on in your life at the time. I bet that you will see stressors showing up that correspond with the patterns of attraction. Often if you are a competitive personality type and you have the sense of loss in some aspect of your life at work or home, you may be re-directing your feelings into these types of conquests instead of simply grieving or processing the feelings at large. If this exercise of writing out this timeline is giving you insight, you should take your insights to a psychotherapist, counselor or psychologist. With some help, you can break your pattern of chaotic living and develop a more integral life.

****

Breakthrough Tips if you are Stuck in an Affair:

1. Make a list of the compromises you have had to make during the affair and negative impacts to you as a result.
2. Make a list of the compromises she/he has had to make during the affair and negative impact to her/him as a result.
3. Write out a timeline of your relationship – what was happening in your life when the attraction began? Were you in a transition of any kind: a death or loss? Was he/she? Significant loss can feed a driving need for attachment.

4. When you think of the duration of the affair, ask yourself how long you want to continue to feel terrible? Actually draw a timeline to consider this.
5. Go Cold Turkey! Stop all contact. Think of the affair as an addiction.
6. Find a hobby that involves something that makes you feel good about yourself so that you can start to build confidence (e.g., running or yoga).
7. Tell yourself you should be someone's Number One!
8. Ask for support from a trusted friend or family.

****

CHAPTER 12

SETTING BOUNDARIES

Developing healthy boundaries is the best way to live your best life. This chapter helps you get them and live them! Boundaries are the guidelines you choose to define your limits for communication, behavior, and lifestyle. Boundaries are referred to as being: diffuse (not very clear), rigid (impenetrable and isolating) or flexible (clear but defined as needed). This chapter follows what you have learned about addictive behaviors and affairs because one of the primary causal factors for addictive behaviors and affairs to set up, is having a lack of defined boundaries. Without setting and understanding your boundaries, you may feel progressively overwhelmed and out of control through life, your career, and your relationships. Which are all the preconditions for addiction and burnout to set up in your psyche.

As you work towards closing your door to the past, you will want to understand how you can set up and define your boundaries, which will allow you to move on. Whether you initiated the breakup or whether your former partner initiated the ending, you need to develop clear boundaries so you don't get stuck living in the past. If you are having a difficult time moving forward, you will feel so much better when you put this chapter to practice.

It's so hard to move on from a love relationship. To close the door, you are closing the door to the possibility that it's not really over. It's especially difficult to close the door when there are children, family, and friends involved. You may feel currently that every time you hear your former partner's name, your heart skips a beat or a cold sweat breaks out on your face. When you see your former partner at a social event, you may find yourself returning to all the mixed emotions of your breakup. It can feel like you are back at Chapter One all over again. Don't worry. Eventually you will be able to see him or her in those situations and you will probably feel like you are seeing an old friend or family member. So if you've been struggling to be firm about closing the door to your past, start setting stronger boundaries. This is especially true if your split up was a contentious one with lots of anger.

Think about the concept of boundaries as a metaphor. If your neighbor had a vicious dog, you might build yourself a fence for protection. If the dog jumped over the fence and bit you, causing you pain or scaring you, you might say something to your neighbor. If there were no resolution, you'd move. Boundaries are like fences. The more pain someone causes you, the greater your need to strengthen boundaries between him or her and you. If the break up is recent, and the feelings are raw, the taller your fence needs to be. The stronger your boundaries are, the better. If the break up is old and vaguely painful, the lower the fence, the more diffuse the boundaries.

If you aren't sure how raw or healed you feel at this stage, err on the taller/ stronger choice of boundaries. Take down the photos of him/her. Reassign your status as single on Facebook! Get your things back from his/her place and/or if he/she has his/her things at your place, give them back today! These actions help you be clear, to yourself and to your former, in setting strong boundaries. They are healthy processes in closure, and they give you an emotional freedom to move forward in your life, solo.

Give yourself a maximum of one-two hour(s) a day to think about the grief. Journal. Play music you feel comforted by during this time. Go for long walks. Breathe in your world around you and breathe out your loss. You will start to notice resiliency in things around you – the way an ant carries a load of bread crumbs five times its size, a child will fall and you see it run to his Mother for comfort, a man at the side of the road changes a flat tire. You are just as strong as the ant, as loved as the child, as capable as the man with the new tire. In those quiet times alone, you naturally will be guided to notice others who master the challenge of change, loss and resiliency.

If you need to contact your former partner to process some learning or shared pain, do it in that time. Email is probably an easier modality for communication though because you can detach from the micro expressions that we all tend to ruminate about. (I wonder what that look was… why did he/she say that??) These types of thoughts won't improve your sleep or enhance the process of letting go.

I think many of my clients get caught in a trap of re-traumatizing themselves by pouring over old photo albums. Although it can give you some comfort to look over your photos, you can get stuck there too. Look through your albums knowing that all the best memories will be yours forever and the memories are true for all time, even though the relationship is over. Many clients however, look at their photo albums and get triggered by a certain photo with certain people in it, to follow up with friends and family members to ask why they think this or that happened? This is torture for you and for your friend! Another trap is to start your own detective work researching what your former partner is doing now? You can get caught wondering if there is someone else the person has started dating, or worrying about how they are feeling. Every time you think these thoughts, they take your psyche back to what you don't want — more pain and no gain. It's going to take time for your pain to heal. I've always been a fan for letting wounds air-dry—no Band-Aids. What I mean to say is give your pain air, be strong like the ant, be loved like the child, and resilient like the man changing his tire. The less you are emotionally tied to the old relationship by obsessing about your former partner, the more you will discover someone new… the new and improved YOU! Remember this is probably the only time you will have to be on your own, so enjoy your freedom.

Gradually with this perspective of strong boundaries, you will notice that a few days have gone by and you haven't thought about the other person at all. In a few weeks and/or months depending on how long you were together in the relationship, you will notice more and more freedom and distance from the loss. In a few years you will probably notice that you will be able to be in a social setting with your former partner. You will feel as if he or she is an old family member you care for, but you no longer grieve their absence or the intimacy they brought into your life. You can't cut yourself off from your losses, but you can develop your knowledge of the love you knew in that relationship. You can channel your learning so that you are better able to love others more fully because of them. Once you have loved someone, they become forever a part of the weave of your heart learning; of who you have been, who you are, and who you are becoming. At that stage, the stories and memories of your relationships will feel like the landscapes seen from your life sailboat. You see the past with a fondness, but you aren't living in it any longer.

The most amazing thing is that the qualities you have loved in your partner are all within you. You may have given yourself permission to enjoy the freedom of being like-minded with your former partner, but it's really been you all the time. Do you know the English translation to the lyrics of O Sole Mio?

What a beautiful thing is a sunny day!

The air is serene after a storm,

The air is so fresh that it already feels like a celebration.

What a beautiful thing is a sunny day!

But another sun that's brighter still,

It's my own sun that's upon your face!

The sun, my own sun, it's upon your face!

It's upon your face!

When night comes and the sun has gone down,

I almost start feeling melancholy;

I'd stay below your window

When night comes and the sun has gone down.

But another sun that's brighter still,

It's my own sun that's upon your face!

The sun, my own sun, it's upon your face!

It's upon your face!

Emotional boundaries are strengthened in a practice of 'the mirror technique'. Recall the folklore of vampire literature, when you hold up a mirror to a vampire, they disappear. In the same way you can re-direct emotional missiles from others. When you are the target of negativity, re-direct what the person is saying back to the sender. In those moments you can be empathic, but well boundaried if it is feeling like a war zone. This is a soul saving tool if you are in a contentious split. With the emotional safety and space of time, you take the various 'missile war heads' and undetonated them to determine if there is learning to grow from or more damage to your soul. From your sailboat you can also simply, empathically leave the dead missile(s) on the beach. Not exercising boundaries means that you are not worth respecting and want to be target practice. I don't think so!

Physical boundaries may be set in blocking a phone number, email address, or when you change the locks on your residence. These actions may be simple healthy processes that make it clear to you and your other that the relationship has transitioned. Physical boundaries can be set when you decide how much physical space you will share socially. For a period of time you may want to share some social events (flexible boundaries) or go cold turkey (rigid boundaries) with no contact. This may have impacts on your shared friendship circles. You are the best resource to determine how strong or diffuse your boundaries need to be at this stage. Trust your feelings.

Spiritual boundaries may be seen as: take off a ring or other jewelry, which you identify with the relationship, take down photos, change your name, residence, all of which happen uniquely, in a pace that feels right for you. Check in with your body. Your feelings will guide you in pacing the nature and extent of your boundaries. If you have anxiety, your body may be telling you to either slow down or speed up! Follow your intuition and have care in how your process may affect others in your life, your former partner, your children, your friends and your community. For many years, even until recently, I double barreled my last name as it was unsetting for my daughter if she and I didn't have the same name. These things never bothered my son, but each had their own experience. There are no absolutes in how you transition. Differentiate your way.

Intellectual boundaries may be set when you sit back for a while to determine who, what and where you want to put your energies. In this time, you are discovering how to live honestly. Ask yourself how you feel after you spend time with whomever you spend your time with. Ask yourself if the activities you have been doing are still nourishing to you or if you want to try something new. What is stimulating to you at this stage of your life? Do you want to read, explore, dance, meditate, grow things in a garden, go back to school, volunteer in a Third World country, or write a book?

Anything you put your attention to will grow if you set some defined time around your intention.

∗∗∗∗∗∗∗∗∗∗∗∗

Breakthrough Tips on Setting Boundaries:

1. Take some time to consider what your values are in life. Your values are a great way to gain clarity and commitment.
2. Think about it…What is important to you? Family, Relationship, Connection, Being of Service, Love, Passion, Challenge, Novelty, Imagination, Play, Health, Personal Development, Giving Back, Team, Honesty, Organization, Integrity, Fitness, Independence, Beauty, Spirit,

Humor, Respect, Positivity? When you have a list of 5 that are most important to you, put them in priority sequence.

3. Ask yourself how much your values actually show up in the day-to-day? Give each value a scale of 0 – 10. 10 I live there completely/ 0 this value is missing right now.

4. What do you notice? Often clients are surprised to find that the values they most cherish have the lowest scores in day-to-day practice. If that is true for you, how can you set new boundaries to bump up your score on that value to 10!

5. Which value is most important to you right now? Does your intention strengthen your ability to set boundaries? What do you need to say "NO" to so that you open up space for the things you value?

****

When you say yes sometimes, and no other times, you will notice a whole new level of freedom in your life. You will notice that it gets easier to enjoy your job, your relationships, your health commitments, and just about everything! You will find yourself feeling in the zone again. It's the way you can up the anti on "Be'ing" in your life rather than "Do'ing" all the chaotic endless tasks that lead to burn out. In fact if you've been feeling chaotic, its probably because you have been operating from everyone else's agenda and not taking time out to figure in what is important to you right now.

If you are a pleaser here's a great one-line lifesaver: "As much as I'd love to, I really have to say no." Saying no, without explanation, may be your greatest challenge, but it's your greatest resource. Setting verbal boundaries is easy when you have some stand by power lines. Someone says something hurtful, and you say "Why would you say that?" "What's your point?" Someone keeps calling you when you don't return the first call, and you say "Why do you think you call me so many times when I don't answer right away?" "Why do you think you do that?"

In the process of starting a new relationship, it can be truly difficult to maintain your integrity to say no some of the time because you may not want to let anyone down. In the same way, it's important to be skilled at observing the other's need for boundaries as you set up new relationship rhythms and ways to regulate yourself and attune to your other (20). The more conscious and skilled you become in setting and adhering to these new boundaries, the more your energy will rise. See for yourself! You will also notice less conflict as you develop greater intra and inter-personal security and trust. Time heals all. We live in the most abundant, stimulating world. You will get to choose what's in yours.

Note to self with respect to boundaries as you move into the next two parts of this book and you are ready to start dating again... Remember all the ways you have grown, as you fully understand and integrate ways you can strengthen your boundaries. From your break up, you have discovered the value in saying no sometimes. You now know how to differentiate and define your needs from your other by using the mirror technique or the tools in the anger chapter. You have the ability to express your feelings as unique and valid using the tools in the anxiety chapter. You can consider what he or she says, what you will take on and grow from, and what you may empathically hear but not take on from the communication dialogues, from your new journal practice and because you have five friends on your home team. As you finally close the door to the past, and get ready to love you in part two, you are a boundary master! Boundary setting will always be a Key to your future relationship happiness. Be a master at Boundaries and you will unlock Happiness. The more clarity you have in understanding the principals of boundaries, the quicker you will be able to spot the personality traits of potential mates that are good or not a good fits for you.

For example as one client reported: "He seemed a little 'over the top' upset with that waitress when she brought us the wrong drinks last night". She may like a 'take charge guy', many women do. But she sat back to consider he may be easily triggered to anger with you as well over time. We are who we are in every day moments.

Another client said of his girlfriend, "She seems to have no idea about what she wants in her life. It's a little frustrating". He sat back to consider that she may not clear when it comes to the longevity of loving him over time either, which may suggest she is not 'date ready' yet.

Examples such as these would be warning signs that the potential partner you are considering is a little under developed and you may be in for an emotional roller coaster ride going forward. Being an observer of people's behavior is another way of managing boundaries. You can talk these situations through, but the chances are these types of patterns will continue to show up and be stressful to deal with if they are worrisome to you now. Being in **emotional symbiosis** you are in a type of co-dependence to fix your partner's deficits. In the first example, the relationship symbiosis would be seen in the girlfriend managing her boyfriend's aggression in restaurants. In the second example the symbiosis is seen in the boyfriend needing to help his girlfriend be more confident and clearer about what she wants. When we start out in life we are naturally completely symbiotic with our caregiver(s). A child who is breastfeeding is symbiotic with his mother because he can't survive without her nursing him. In adult symbiotic relationships, the boundaries are blurred and the relationship can be headed for high drama because there is so much at risk all the time. This is why relationships work best when two people have the same level of differentiation. The more whole you feel, the more of a whole partner you will attract. The more whole your partner, the more at ease you will feel because he or she is not putting pressure on you to give more time, energy, emotion than you naturally feel comfortable with. Why not choose someone who is naturally more simpatico with you?

Knowing your boundaries and learning to define them is one of the biggest secretes to living a life you will love. As you continue to say no to what you don't want, all the things you do want, show up. You then attract your best upgrade in partnership because you have set your own bar higher, or simply one that is naturally more in line with you. You deserve...everything you can imagine! Why not?! Just watch as your energy starts to flow into everything in your life. With a deeper understanding of boundaries, you will discover: renewed creativity at work, renewed energy to play, and a life where everything starts to sparkle for you again. The more comfortable and alive you feel in your relationship, the more energy and imagination you will experience in all parts of your life.

This is exciting because when your new 'Right One' shows up, he or she will be a reinforcing experience in your life, rather than a drain. You will be released from the bog of power struggles and misfit personalities. You will be released from a pattern of 'fixing' your partner, (and or) from your partner wanting to 'fix' you. Say good-bye to negativity and frustration. Love is now energizing, reinforcing and… easy. Its not that you won't have confusion some of the time, but you will have an easier way to consider your experience and that of your partner. You have Boundaries! Just say no to what's not congruent with your values list and say yes to what you really want more of right now. And if you still aren't sure if you want to say yes in any moment someone over steps, try "Give me some time to think about it" or "That's a great idea. Let me get back to you on it".

CHAPTER 13

STILL AFRAID TO CLOSE THE DOOR?

If you still feel stuck in the past, this is your final kick in your but to close that door! When you get physically constipated, your physician will suggest you drink more water to get your bowels moving. This is also a great way to flush the stress hormones (the results of emotional constipation) out of your system. Cortisol otherwise can accumulate in your kidneys. Bottom line: (pardon my expression) time to get your shit moving! If you are still feeling stuck, you are like many, who love deeply and just take longer to move through grief.

Carolyn Myss has a compelling metaphor for emotional pain as a physical wound. When you cut yourself and you see a scab growing, you don't pull the scab back to watch the wound bleed (21). Why then would you dwell on the painful experience of conduct that you wish you hadn't done, about the decisions you regret, and about the insulting behaviors you resent? After you've done your 3 "R's" exercise, you should put aside these reminiscences, good and bad. Get unstuck, and let yourself heal and move past the wounds of the breakup. Put your thoughts about your old relationship in an imagined book that you can put away, until such a time as you are well on your way to experience a new life on your own.

In this respect go back to some of the concrete steps that you did before: did you put your old relationship photos away? Did you stop checking your former partner's Facebook status updates? Have you can changed your social routines? If you haven't, try a new fitness gym and take yourself out to a restaurant you have never been to. Have you modified and updated your friendship circles so that you are not constantly reminded of your old relationship? It's important in all these changes of context and routine that you maintain your contact with, and build even deeper rapport with old friends (they nourish and support you). But you should also balance this with making some time for new friends (who won't remind you of your grief). A final note on the benefits of changing your environment based on what I have learned from my practice is that when couples split up, the one who stays in the once-shared residence grieves longer because of all the daily (and nightly) emotional triggers that can chain them to what was.

When you go through a breakup, grief is often accompanied by a sense that you are no longer able to control your life. If this perceived loss of control prevents you from engaging in a progressive forward process, try a few simple defined tasks like cleaning out your sock drawer, your closet, or your desk. Wash your car. Do a good deed for someone (in a pay-it-forward style) without acknowledgement (22). These tasks can give you a sense of relief with each completed thing. Doing a task, which has a clear start and a finish to it, is a great boost for your psyche when you are trying to let go in your heart. It can also help if you engage in a 'gratitude exercise' every morning or night. If you think of one thing you are grateful for, notice the feelings you get in your body when you think of it, and you will train your brain to be happy again.

Think back to a time you recall when you had felt life in relative ease. Maybe it was when you were starting that new job. Possibly it was when you graduated from school, college or university? It could be how you felt at the end of a run last week. Think of something you know you are good at. What is it? When were you last doing it? Close your eyes and think of it now. What do you feel in your body as you recall it? Happy? Powerful? Joyful? Playful? Where do you feel those feelings exactly? Are the feelings in your heart? Are they in your stomach? Do you feel it in your arms? How does it feel—tingly, sparkly, warm, comforting, cool, exhilarating? You know how you feel. Let yourself be in that feeling right now. Practice bringing those feelings to mind and body first thing in the morning tomorrow. Do this mini-meditation again at lunch. Do it one more time before bed.

If your heart is still aching because you were left, know that it is hardest for the one who is left and its also hard for the one who left. Often, however the one who did the leaving doesn't process the feelings of grief until much later. Typically just when you are feeling over it all, your former partner will be in the thick of his or her own process. If you haven't got boundaries established from the previous chapter, you can get caught in the back and forth pining of the past. You start out calling her in that two-hour window you set aside. Three months or three years later, you are feeling free and breezy again. Then you get a call from your former partner and they are in their two-hour window of the day missing you. Boundaries will set you both free. Make sure you aren't in this crazy frustrating back and forth about the past.

This is chapter thirteen, your final chapter to process your past. You don't need to spend another second thinking about him or her now. So go on, stop talking about him or her. Focus instead on you – a YOU with Courage, a YOU with Clarity, and a YOU with the Confidence you just felt when you did the previous meditation. Courage is your conviction to move forward. You know why you outgrew each other. And if you aren't sure you really do, go back to repeat the 3 "R's" exercise. Sometimes when you do these exercises the first time, you may not be as honest as you are when you do them for the second time. I think the reason for that is that as you get stronger, you gain ego strength to really list out your regrets, resentments and find a new lighter solace in the remembrances – like looking at the scenery from your sailboat as you chart new adventures ahead. It does take time. I did these exercises several times myself. I think I was a slow learner and a little resistant to really let go. In the first year post separation, I did my 3 R's about once per week. As I recall my journal days and my lists, the knots in my stomach and heart let go of the grip they had on me. I know I wouldn't have been fully able to love Joe if I hadn't gone through this heart wrenching process in the years before we met. Clarity of mind ensures that you will not be lured back into an idealized picture of the relationship you are now breaking out of. Confidence comes with time.

It takes time for you to develop a routine wherein you wean yourself out of the big and little things you used to do as a couple. These habits are outdated because they were built on the shared dream that is now deceased. And the repetition of those habits can only serve to reinforce the message of pain and loss you are trying to overwrite. You need to process your pain and loss rather than get stuck in it and miss your life in the process. You are the only one who can choose to move you out of grief. Recall the poignant movie "Message in a Bottle" in which Kevin Costner plays the part of a widowed shipbuilder whose wife passed away in an untimely death (23). I loved that film. It touched the hearts of many because we have all experienced this to some extent. No wonder it was a blockbuster box office hit.

Movies, by the way, can provide great therapeutic benefits. Message in a Bottle is a moving example of what being stuck in loss and grief looks like. Watching a movie like this can be so helpful; seeing 'yourself' so well portrayed on screen gives you fresh perspective and a greater resolve to break out of grief. No one has confidence in the transition of letting go. If they tell you it is easy, you should know they are covering up the fact that actually it is rather hard. Many spend lifetimes writing letters to their past. Our memories of our lives and love experiences are encoded in our hippocampus (in our brain). Each time we see something, it connects us to a stream of thought that brings us back to our original experiences. We have a broad network of neural connections that can be morphed or intentionally rewired with better behavior choices and the cultivation of new contexts and better outcomes!

There are some simple things you might do to rewire yourself: change your environment, move your bed, paint your walls, drive to work by a new route, ride your bike instead of driving. Change up as much of your daily routine as possible. Put your energies into areas where you can guarantee good results – to your health, to your work, to your family, to your home, or to your community. See a new part of the world. Take a road trip. Start setting up new memories. Start a new photo album.

I loved my time as "Gilmour Girls" living with my daughter in her second year of business school at university. When she was going through the intense study regime of becoming a chartered accountant, I suggested we train for a marathon. Running the New York City Marathon in 2009 with Ashley was a bucket list event for me, and helped to ease her through the stresses of a very intense academic stage of professional development. I feel I was a positive support for her and I cherish that time with her as an up side of separation and divorce. You may find that your relationships with your children or friends soar in this difficult time of transition. It's a side benefit that you'll be grateful for. It's all in the process of reintegration. If you have children, they will need your time. Your first date should be with them. Its tough to begin to feel better yourself until you know your children are bouncing back too. If you don't have children, you might spend time with your extended family. Your parents, and your siblings will probably experience the grief of your relationship ending. Your former partner was in their life too and they may miss seeing you together as a couple. The ease your family discovers to release their own grief adjustments seeing you as a single person, (whether you were left or you did the leaving), the less you be triggered and be able to steadily keep moving forward.

Confidence grows from being aware of the 'you' in your past relationship(s), and in the re-grouping of your whole self so that you can develop new relationship habits in present and future. It's a time of personal stock-taking and reflection about your light and dark sides. If you don't show up differently in your next relationship, you will have a good chance of repeating the kind of dependent/independent, internalized/externalized behaviors. If pleasing patterns were your downfall, and emotional withdrawal did you in, make sure you set yourself a plan to outgrow those habits. In Part two you will learn about how your birth order affects how you relate with others. You will also start to consider the influence your caregivers have had. You'll see how your shoulder saboteur undermines your creativity. Be curious about who you really are, your true self is not the chameleon who fits into any space. When you really know your 'whole' self, you will feel confident warts and all! You are the combination of past, present and future— branches of all the members of your family; of your culture; of your education and all your friendships. Who are you becoming? Well that's entirely up to you!

By the way, when it comes to romantic landmark times such as Valentine's Day, my advice is to just get out of Dodge! Give yourself a fresh perspective in a new environment. Or, celebrate with your close friends who love you.

****

Here are some helpful breakthrough exercises:

1. Write a letter to yourself
    Dear Me,
    a. Identify your strengths and ways you have grown since your break up
    b. Isn't it amazing how much support you have had from a), b), and c)
    c. What is one way you will challenge yourself this year? (Body, mind, spirit goals)
    d. What will it feel like when you master that challenge?
2. Seal and stamp the letter and give it to a trusted friend who can mail it to you three months from today. In this way, you double the benefits to your brain as you adapt and integrate change in two stages:
    a. By writing it.
    b. By receiving it three months later, you have the opportunity of accountability. In so doing, you reinforce the wisdom/support of your own insights and personal assessment of your strengths.
    The power in the letter is the fact that it is written by you— THE most positive and impactful coach ever. This also enlists your trusted friend in collaborating with you to move forward from pain to gain. Partnering up with a friend on any commitment is shown in research time and time again, as a key to success.
3. Do something nice for someone else. This 'pay it forward' idea has been shown over and over again to increase feelings of happiness. The best way to move forward from pain can be putting your attention to helping others. Just thinking of ideas of things you can do for others is probably already lifting your spirits.
4. If you have other single friends who are motivated to do some self-improvement with you or work through any personal goals, you might

start a Breakup Breakthrough Group. Join my blog at joanne-weiler.com.

****

CHAPTER 14

LEARNING OUTCOMES FROM PART ONE

You are starting to see how dynamic you are in your life and the relationship(s) in it. You now have some powerful tools to help you when you feel overwhelmed. You also know how important it is going to be for you to have supportive relationships in your life with people who you can be honest with and share your needs and feelings. When you do, you will be breaking through old negative internal stories that may be telling you that you are: powerless, flawed or unloved. You are powerful. We all are! And the more you learn about your internal patterns and how they shape your external behaviors, the more access you will have to greater intimacy and deeper more meaningful connection with yourself and others. You may be realizing that your feelings are your guide to the inner knowing you deserve more. You always have.

You may be starting to understand why you've been angry, anxious, sad, and resentful or impulsively racing to prove your worth in the references of others. The more you run away from your feelings, the more you continue to reinforce the negative internal stories that have constricted your life experiences with others. Are you noticing moments in time when you know that negative self-talk is wrong? Everyone deserves to be loved unconditionally. No matter what has happened in your past relationship(s), they are keys to understanding how you can set yourself up with reparative unconditional positive self regard. You know how to self-sooth your feelings now, and how you can ask for help.

You are now ready to deepen your learning to find out where your negative internal and inter-personal patterns have anchored. The anchors came well before you met the partner you just broke up with. Deep down, you probably already knew that! The next part of this book will help you understand the foundations of undeserving so that you can shift your internal and inter-personal patterns forever. It's time for something new. You may be starting to be more curious about the internal schemas you've been rehearsing about yourself and others. I'm sure you are starting to feel less stuck the breakup, and more spacious curiosity about what you are learning. From a new internal curiosity and open perspective, your options will start to expand. You may start to realize that love is inside of you, not outside of you. That's personal power!

You'll notice that your new practices of journal writing and meditation bring you new internal spiritual strength and calm. All the fears, judgments and disappointments that came with your relationship loss, have started to melt. Your confidence is on the rise. You probably understand how much you have interacted in your own cycle of behaviors; the ones that maintained loneliness, abandonment, anger, anxiety and grief. As you let go of old stories that you failed or weren't good enough, you will also start to wonder why you ever got so stuck rehearsing hopelessness? As you look back you may see now that in trying to force your old relationship to work, you had been robbing yourself of the love and joy that is your birthright. Here are some powerful questions to ask yourself at this time:

What has opened up for you as a result of your relationship ending?

What has changed in your life as you stand in your new perspective as a single person?

What do your friends tell you about what they see in you today?

You have probably met some new friends through this process. You may be realizing that almost everyone around you has had some experience similar to your relationship pain. You fully know are not alone in this journey. I think that's really a comforting thought. Somehow knowing that we all go through breakups provides a kind of soft collective landing while you are regaining your true footing. I bet, the most surprising friendships are starting to show up for you. Have you got anyone working with you as you journey through the chapters yet (friends or a professional counselor/guide)? Is there a friend you know who may benefit from working through the next part with you? You are almost through Part One, closing the door to grief, inviting inside change. In Part Two coming up, you will be putting your toes into a design of new possibilities of thinking and feeling.

From Part one you are probably starting to realize that without the experience of the pain you've been through, you would have less motivation to grow and evolve. I think it was Jane Fonda who came up with the original statement when she produced her exercise videos: "no pain, no gain" and "feel the burn". Her 1982 workout wisdom applies to resiliency and your heart today.

Right about now, you are probably thinking enough pain and growth already! I'm lonely and I want to feel joy again. Relationship endings are difficult enough when you are the one feeling your way through the dark in it all. You are going through an experience that everyone goes through at some time in his or her life. It is a little like labour, with all the same contractions that as you breathe and contract, you think are going to kill you. You are giving birth to a new a new and improved version of you, and you now realize its not killing you, it's birthing you. You are a miracle.

When you think of things you feel are your contributions in your life, you will recall they have come from an experience of personal pain. Thich Nhat Hanh tells us that even the lotus grows from mud. I am with you in this. I know pain. Whether this pain comes from giving birth to babies (painful and exhilarating), getting a Master's Degree in of Psychology (challenging and fascinating), running two full and two half marathons (exhausting and exhilarating), I wouldn't trade my pain away for anything. What have been your greatest endeavors, challenges, and life contributions? One of the most painful experiences in my life was by far the transformative moving on from my twenty-year marriage. And the attendant sense that I had not fulfilled a life promise made on my wedding day (painful, humbling but liberating).

The term revolution comes from the Latin word 'conversio', meaning "a turn-around". And there is no doubt that the end of your relationship is a critical turning point in your life. But this pivotal experience will also lead to huge gains in your future life. You can successfully navigate this transitional experience. I hope that this book brings you a boatload of positive impacts on the revolutionary experience in your mind body and spirit as you heal from your breakup and you choose what positive gains you will achieve from this admittedly difficult time.

I was in a yoga retreat in Sayulita, Mexico last February with my sister Carol. My yoga instructor Jim Gallas started our first group session with a large yoga YUM (which in yoga Sanskrit terms means LOVE). It sounds like yum as in yummy food. In any case we all joined in a massive YUM chant that still resonates with me as I recall the sound of fifteen of us collectively turning inwards and sharing outwards our collective expression of caring. My wish is that this book will generate a similar vibration that reminds you that love is inside of you and when you learn to access it, you can start to begin a truly delicious life.

We all go through losses in love. The only way we learn how to get better at loving is by experiencing and growing from the euphoria of falling in love, (the chemical intoxication of dopamine, serotonin and phenylethylamine) and surviving the piercing pain of love endings (and the chemical release of the stress hormone cortisol). If love has let you down, practice new perspectives to help you start looking inward in order to be able to look forward to something different and better in love. Have you ever been gifted a painting that you don't really like? Rather than put it in storage, you might try putting it in a new frame in order to experience a new perspective and hopefully a new appreciation of the painting. The same is true with your experience of a love relationship that has failed. How do you move on from what feels like such a deep cut to your heart into the frame of what might be next?

With new supports and a fresh perspective, you may be surprised at the shift within you as you begin to understand what was wrong with the old love and what you are well advised to look for in both yourself and a new love partner so you can be successful the next time around. But in order to do this, you must be brutally honest with yourself. Here are some questions to take to the mattress tonight:

What will you do differently in all relationships in your future?

What is one new insight about you, which you can now become a master of?

Since your breakup, what new experiences have opened up for you?

What are your greatest strengths and weaknesses?

For me regarding the last one, it's asking for help. I am still working on getting better at that.

At the yoga retreat in Sayulita, I was attempting a yoga pose called "Pigeon" (which I will do on request but I truthfully have always hated it). Seeing my discomfort, the yoga instructor kindly passed me a yoga block… so my limbs wouldn't fall off and I could lift myself out of the pain position that I was in. (I'm a little tight in my hips from thirty years of running!) Who knew a yoga block would open up all this new possibility in my body? With the aid of the yoga block, my hips lifted in a way I hadn't experienced before.

If you are open to ask for help, it will become easier for you and others will enjoy the opportunity of providing you support. The literature of psychology names '**the open limbic system**' which refers to being in a healthy brain state, where our stress centers and our adrenal glands aren't working overdrive to pump cortisol (the stress hormone) through our bodies. This adrenalized state of being is the 'human doing' system, which drives us to do, do, do more, but results in isolation. There is actually electricity that our brain emits when we are living in this stress state and we affect others around us in a type of emotional contagion that is either positive or negative. So much happens implicitly in the brain. When we create the emotional safety to bring our fears, insecurities, or pain into real time conversations, we develop stronger attachments and more positive brain pathways. Dan Goleman suggests we can practice ourselves out of unhealthy brain states, and which results in a **limbic revision** (actual physiological changes to our brain pathways) (24). These positive changes are contagious to those around us. Just imagine what the world would feel like if we practiced walking, talking and Being more caring every day.

At the Yoga retreat, I wondered if my calm yoga energy gave me the opportunity for Jim to notice I needed help. None of us wants to be "fixed" because the premise of that idea would be that we are broken. Am I broken? No. Neither are you. I am, we are, learning on this adventure called life and love.

Whether we need "fixing" or not, our lives will be better if we help each other out a little more. Practice asking for assistance this week, instead of being so shyly, self-contained... insular. I think I made Jim's day when he saw his yoga block give me such a positive return. Yoga is a great way to get more inner balance and be much more in synch generally. In my clinical practice, my male clients often think meditation is 'fringe' and 'for sissies' or for 'counterculture types', so they just won't try it. They miss out on what is now becoming increasingly a well-accepted health habit. Yoga and meditation are excellent ways to gain more access to your 'whole' self. Care in and care out. Breathe in and breathe out. Sun rise, sun set. All things in health and love are balanced in their reciprocity. Quite possibly, in a few more decades, those who don't practice some type of 'inside' exercise will be the ones living on the fringe.

If you keep focusing on the things you can't control: (the him or her that got away or hurt you/ how he or she hurt you), you will get stuck in an endless trap of grief and therefore heighten dissonance. With a reframe, I'm not saying you shouldn't experience your feelings. You need to feel your loss, but for how long? Some say the grief of a relationship ending takes approximately one month for every year you have been in the relationship. Sometimes though, you can get stuck being a victim of pain for life. It can require a push in a positive direction to lift yourself out of the black hole of mounting insecurities. Like trauma, it's good to talk about it in the initial stages to reduce symptoms that are similar to PTSD, but dwelling on the rehearsal of blood and broken glass detail, is just re-traumatizing. When I process trauma with clients, I take them to the details of their survival, to who showed up to help at the scene and to the strengths within them at the time. Post car accident, it's risky business to be guided through the horror again and again. It's healing to focus towards those who helped at the scene (you are not alone), how you survived (you have strength) and how the rules for the road have changed (there is something to be gained) since the incident.

I work with clients who are rebuilding after a breakup in this same way. To do otherwise, you can become fixated on the notion that you weren't smart enough, beautiful enough, charismatic enough, interesting enough, patient enough, generous enough, active enough (versus you are enough and enough is enough) … it's easy to head down this slippery slope of imagined inadequacies. Use this book to help you recognize and harness your inner strengths and become a more real, powerful, and loving you.

When you think about your former relationship ending, could it be that you both were absolutely perfect, but imperfectly matched in an impossible relationship? The flawed synergy of your personalities may have produced an unremitting grind of unhappiness, brightened only periodically by the willow-the-wisp of wishful thinking. Either way, the sooner you accept that the past is past, the sooner you can start your own personal boot camp back to your best spiritual, physical, and emotional self.

Lets go back to Jane's workout – no pain, no gain. Think of how much pain you have after a big physical workout. When you lift weights, you actually tear muscle fiber. It's as your muscle fiber rebuilds, that you gain muscle definition. You know how painful it is to walk or lift anything after you have loaded up your workout the day before. But you feel stronger and with a rest day, you end up being able to lift heavier and heavier weights. This same principal is true when it comes to relationships. Breakups are so deeply painful whether you are left or you do the leaving. It's a little like shredding your heart for sure. Train your attention to what you have learned, and how you will be better in the future, expect more from others, develop better life and relationship strategies, and you are guaranteed to look back one day with great fondness for the gifts of the painful break up. Train your thinking and behaviors, and you will have a life better than you could have ever imagined it to be. Eventually you will have a true lifetime partnership in an ultimate journey to agape, other focused, evolved, and universal, love. You write the software and upgrades of your own life.

★★★★★★★★★★★★

Learning Outcomes from Part One: Closing the Door

1. You can learn from your patterns in previous significant relationships? Just write out a timeline of two, five or ten year segments depending on your age. On one side of the time line, put the name of every person you have had a significant relationship with.

2. On the other side of the line write out what you learned about yourself because of that person. (Include your parents and siblings on the time-line. They are your first relationships). Looking at the things you learned about yourself, how have you changed your behaviors because of that learning? What have been your blind spots? How have these relationships given you personal growth? Is there any repeated behavior pattern you notice now? (Some examples might be: a lack of boundaries, a pattern of pleasing, a pattern of withdrawing, a lack of confidence, a lack of life balance, a lack of financial planning, a lack of patience, a lack of play, a lack of exercise or self-care)

3. You can be more strategic in relationships, based on what you see from your relationship timeline exercise.

4. A change in your behaviors will change you.

5. You can dramatically shift all your relationship outcomes in your future.

6. Feeling sad, anxious, angry, guilty, and longing are all normal parts of this process in moving forward.

7. When you ask for help, you can do things you never thought possible.

8. Boundaries are protective of your emotions, your time, and your physical health. Boundaries guard your freedom!

9. Anxiety is your best friend, shaking you, giving you information to speak up.

10. Anger is intimate. It reveals the vulnerable self, and with healthy tools and emotional safety, it will lead you to closer connection with others.

11. Guilt can be protective as a guide towards decisions congruent with your values. Shame is the unhealthy identification with the negative itself (Shame is a core emotional driver when it comes to all addiction).
12. You need to close one door before you can open another.

****

PART 2

INTEGRATION, LEARNING TO LOVE YOU AGAIN

CHAPTER 15

BODY, MIND, SPIRIT REBOOT

You are probably starting to realize that it is all about you. It always has been. And at this point you may also still be feeling so numbed out by this major change in your life that it's impossible to think about ever feeling good again. This chapter is designed to give you a few quick fixes, which help boost your chemistry, reboot your mojo, and bring your anxieties down so that you will become more curious about what you now have to gain versus, remain stuck in what you have lost. The more you realize the changes you can put to practice and the insights you can develop from, the more empowered you will feel.

1. Engage in some sort of exercise routine. You need to give your brain a boost! Endorphin and norepinephrine are hormones released in exercise, which make you, feel good. These hormones are identified in study after study as major contributors to lifting symptoms of depression (25). Your choice of exercise should be something that gives you heart-pumping cardio, where you are building a sweat for at least twenty minutes. If you are not typically someone who would naturally enjoy exercise, add your favorite music to motivate you.

   Everything you do should be working towards your goal to feel better. Choose music that is energizing and inspiring. This may not be the time to be listening to achy breaky country music for example. Still finding it hard to commit? Join a cardio group, fitness, or spin class, which will put you in contact with a proactive, and possibly supportive, peer group. (Always check with your physician before engaging a new exercise routine.) You may resist this idea because it's not anything you have ever done before. Remember that this is about doing things differently so just fake it till you make it!

2. Get social. Think about spending time with your most positive friends, and your most nourishing family members. Set a goal to get together with someone this weekend. Avoid the allure to continue to hide out. No caves! Even though you don't feel like it, once you are out and about, you just may find your smile again.

3. It's also a good idea to find yourself a wingman— someone who has your best interests in mind, who can be your compass and confidante. In this time of being on your own, it's easy to feel lost in the post relationship non-structure. This type of partnership can be soul saving. While you get your feet on the ground, you may really appreciate having a friend as a trusted sounding board for your ideas and reflections. For many, the fear of being on your own for the first time causes a type of brain freeze. It can feel as if you don't know anything anymore. The stress of change can actually rev up your adrenals and limbic system, which makes it difficult to process information. During this time, your judgment may be slightly off. Check in with your wingman "what do you think about this idea…?" I totally remember feeling this way in the early months of being on my own. I think I experienced a similar 'brain freeze' in the early months of having our first baby. I was so afraid of making a mistake, to complete even the most simple task (like bathing our newborn), that I had the nurses in the hospital show me all the basic infant care 'how to's' three times! I'm sure they were happy to see us leave the hospital! If you are a worrier or tend to fear making mistakes, you can probably identify with your own need to have a wingman!

4. Start sleeping! If you have developed chronic sleep troubles since the break-up (difficulty falling asleep due to obsessive thoughts that keep you up), it may be a good idea to start writing in a journal before you go to sleep. If you find yourself some nights lying in bed ruminating, stop torturing yourself winding through those negative thoughts. Write the intrusive thoughts down so you can let them go and get back to sleep. This simple act of discharging your worries to the page, allows your brain to stop interfering with your sleep. Things always feel worse at night. In the morning, you may wake up with a fresh perspective on

what has been torturing you through the night. Have you ever found solutions or insight in the dark?

The second thing to consider is your pre-sleep routines. You shared many bedtime routines with your partner, so you may find these same routines act as triggers that remind you of the relationship just before bed. These old relationship pre-sleep routines become sequences can trigger you to be sad and then launch the worry cycles that drive you crazy. Switch things up. You might call a friend to talk through your day, or plan an evening walk around the block with a neighbor. You may find that simple things like which side of the bed you slept on can trigger sad memories. You may want to move your bed to another part of the room. You might want to get some new bed linens or paint your bedroom. You could start sleeping in the middle of the bed. If you've always had showers before bed, you might start having a bath before bed instead. There is lots of research, which suggests aromatherapy provides benefits in relaxation and wellness (26). You might invest in some lavender essential oils (which have a calming effect on the brain). If you have never meditated before, try a breathing meditation routine before bed. Here's an example:

a. Close your eyes. Breathe in, breathe out. Let go. Breathe in, breathe out. Let go. Say these two statements a few times and then focus your attention on your feet. Feel the connection between you and the ground. Imagine in your mind's eye that you can set roots into the ground…spread them solidly. Set your roots as an individual – all the facets of you as a person developing spiritually, physically, and intellectually. Imagine that you have roots so that you won't blow over at the first wind or stormy day. How do you want to define yourself as a man/woman, professionally, artistically, as a father/mother, sister/brother, friend, etc.?

A wide root base holds you when the winds rock. You are a tree; firmly planted in your developing, newly single identity. The roots support the metaphor of all the branches of yourself-discovery in this time of being one. Who are you? I am a .., a …, a …., I am. Breathe in, breathe out.

Take home thought from the meditation: Is there one part of your root base on which you want to focus more attention? Who are you in family, who are you in career, who are you in spirit, and who are you in intellect? Are you emotionally intelligent? Who are you in your physical self? What would nourish you most at this stage of your life if you focused more attention on it?

The more you practice this meditation, the more your attention and energy is drawn to the multi-faceted parts of your identity as a loving human being. In the day, you will find yourself feeling stronger and more solid, and in the night, you just might find yourself sleeping well again.

b. If you are a more hands on active person, you may find that a tapping trick will get you to sleep. Lie on your back, close your eyes, place your hands on your collarbone and begin firmly tapping alternately. Breathe in breathe out. Continue the tapping without interruption for five minutes then hold your hands in place and you will feel a calming release of oxytocin (the attachment hormone which is associated with feelings of calm and connection). (27).

Sweet dreams.

If none of these ideas are helping you get back to healthy sleep patterns, see your family physician for a sleeping pill. I hesitate to recommend medication, but not sleeping can cause a full-blown psychosis! Get your sleep no matter what it takes. Your brain consolidates new information when you are sleeping. We need everything working FOR you now.

Getting a good sleep is part of your core work in rebuilding amazing you and your new cognitions to get there. There are natural remedies for sleep as well that a naturopath may advise you on. For example taking magnesium before bed can help with sleep. Sublingual vitamin B12 taken first thing in the morning can help with improved mood. Both are available at most vitamin or grocery stores.

5. Consider your chemistry. To do a rudimentary self-assessment, track your morning mood over a couple of weeks. Check in with yourself first thing in the morning to give a mood score 0 – 10. The higher the score, the higher your mood. This subjective rating guide provides a snapshot of your chemistry because on waking, nothing has happened yet. It's a quick way of knowing your baseline chemistry and mood trends. If you are assessing yourself in the low range more mornings than not, and are finding it impossible to commit to a morning cardio exercise routine, and you are finding yourself unable to lift yourself

into your day, you may want to consider asking your family physician about prescribing an anti-depressant. He/she will give you a more thorough assessment using The Beck's Depression Inventory (28) or some similar tool. If you have been having suicidal thoughts, go to your nearest hospital Emergency where you will be fast tracked to see a psychiatrist. The feelings that overwhelm you at times will pass. In the meantime you need to be safe. If your experience is more described as feeling blue, tearful, and sad, get started on a new commitment to cardio exercise to boost your naturally occurring endorphin. Get more exercise to lift your chemistry and lighten your thinking towards new possibilities. Exercise will also help you sleep at night. To some extent, if the body isn't exercised, it may not want to let you sleep because it hasn't been physically challenged in the day.

6. Get outside in the natural light first thing in the morning. The blast of bright light trips your occipital lobe (sight center of your brain), which regulates your sleep clock. Being outside first thing in the morning also helps to give you a 'big picture' perspective of life moving forward. The grass is growing. The sun is shining or it's raining. The world smells green, musty, alive, and clean. It sounds noisy, quiet, buzzing, beeping, chirping, and crunching. Be alive and in the moment. Let your senses develop more emotional resilience.

CHAPTER 16

PROJECTIONS VERSUS REALITY

This chapter is to help you make sure you are staring in your own best movie. Projections are the powerful ways we see people in our lives. Sigmund Freud identified projections as being a defense mechanism human beings use when you see the unacceptable attributions of yourself in other people. Instead of being curious about yourself and growing, 'everyone' else seems to be full of deficits. You may for example, fear your partner will have an affair, while unconsciously you may want to have one yourself. You might be critical of a friend's embarrassing social comment when its actually you that fears judgment. Another example might be that you feel guilty your relationship failed and you project your own failing on your former partner. We can project guilt, shame, anger, fear, vulnerability, inadequacy, and hopelessness…basically anything that you don't like about yourself, you may potentially project as a distasteful quality on someone else.

Often people who bully others feel huge insecurities within themselves. Someone who describes his or her partner as controlling is often hiding their own desire to be more controlling themselves. This comes back to my point earlier, that what ever others say to you is actually information about them selves. This chapter will help you be more self reflective rather than 'other' projective!

'Lucy In the Sky with Diamonds', a client I once worked with described her feelings of loneliness in her fifteen-year marriage. Her husband 'Doug' was a successful businessman. 'Doug' was so busy in his career, and with his sports, that 'Lucy' felt abandoned and alone most of the day. She worried 'Doug' might be having an affair. Why else was he not interested in physical affection? When 'Lucy' came to see me, she was in the process of deciding whether she should leave her marriage. 'Lucy' and 'Doug' had three children together, all of whom were now in their teens and generally well-adjusted young academics. 'Lucy' felt that, despite her efforts to get her husband's attention, she would always come last on his list. 'Lucy' couldn't remember the last time she and her husband had been intimate. When her father recently passed away, 'Lucy' was reminded that life is short. I asked her if she had been close to her father and this question unlocked a floodgate.

'Lucy's father travelled a lot when she was growing up. When he came home, there was so much tension between her father and mother because of financial and emotional deficits, that 'Lucy' "never really felt loved by him". As a daughter, she longed for his attention and learned to cope by pouring into academics, not expressing her needs, not expecting anything, and in that way she felt she would never be disappointed. This avoidant attachment style was driven by the belief that she wasn't truly loved by her father so she shouldn't expect to be loved by any man. Her feelings of isolation in her marriage were actually a 'projection' of her own withdraw emotionally. 'Lucy' had never learned how to give or receive love and in her marriage, though she and 'Doug' were a highly functional couple as parents, 'Doug' had learned to make the best of 'Lucy's withdrawing behaviors by keeping busy with his sports and work. This is how projections impact healthy relationships in unhealthy ways over time. 'Lucy' and 'Doug' started out as an affectionate couple. However as 'Lucy' started looking for evidence that 'Doug' didn't love her, she came to feel more and more resentful over time. In the fifteen years of her marriage, 'Lucy' was expert at pleasing 'Doug' while expecting nothing in return. Over time, it's little wonder that her confusion of childhood became a self-fulfilling prophecy. Our work together required that she explore why her father may have been so emotionally absent when she was growing up. She came to understand that when he worked out of the home, he wasn't intending to abandon her. Her grief work was processed through letter writing and some family research with her siblings. These inquiries opened up new thinking for 'Lucy', which helped resolve and re-story the thought of herself as unlovable, into herself as loveable.

She began to look for new information that her husband loved her. The more she looked for positive moments, the better she felt and the more loving she was able to be with her husband. She confessed near the end of treatment, that it was she that had secretly fantasized about having an affair, though she had confronted 'Doug' many times that he must be having an affair if he's not pursuing her for affection. Her fears were a projection of her own fantasy that she could find love in being attractive to someone outside of her marriage. The more she accused 'Doug' of having an affair, the more anxious and withdrawn he became. Fortunately through her curiosity about her family learning and the grief and loss of her own Father, she discovered 'Doug' was the love of her life. As she looked back on their history together, she saw a multitude of ways he had been saying, "I love you". The affirmation and feedback that she started to give him about the positive things she noticed going forward, motivated him to step up his loving behaviors and stay home more. This led to a whole new positive connection in their marriage.

It's so important to feel current and resolved with the parents you grew up with. Otherwise your historical hurts with them may show up as projections into your present and your future relationships. It isn't always possible to have those difficult healing conversations when loved ones have passed away, but in the process of expressing your feelings as an adults (in letter writing or empty chair exercises) you can free yourself up to be less complicated as a life partner.

The only way 'Lucy' had known her father had loved her was when he brought home gifts from his travels. Because her father had lived through the Depression, money was scarce, and therefore gift giving was also scarce. 'Lucy' had come to believe, as a result, that love itself was scarce. In the present she had avoided expressing needs because she didn't want to upset the little time she had with her father. As a result she spent a lot of her childhood time sad and lonely in her bedroom. As an adult, she continued a learned sequence – "when I'm upset, I go inside. It just doesn't occur to me that I can talk to him." This pattern gave her husband little chance to find a way into her heart. When she understood this, there was an immediate shift towards valuing her needs and honoring her feelings not only with her husband, but also with all men.

'Lucy's father missed out on the opportunity to be more present in her life when he was alive. She was very motivated as an adult to make sure she did the work in her marriage so that her children could benefit from more giving and receiving of abundant and unconditional love. It's so important that your children see you as a fully expressive, and connected partner. Children learn how to be in their own lives in their futures based on witnessing how you and your partner relate. If 'Lucy' had not become more aware of her projection (that she was not worth loving), versus the truth that she needed to learn how to love, their children would also grow up with detached styles of relating to others.

Today 'Lucy' makes love a priority. She is intentional about expressing her needs and her feelings and her husband feels his love is received in a less complicated way. She has learned to be more 'other' focused and asks 'Doug' what he needs and how she can be a more compassionate, intuitive partner. Fortunately 'Doug' has welcomed her invitations. Their relationship has gone through a metamorphosis. Never under estimate the power you have to create the relationship you dream about.

If you identify with 'Lucy' because you tend to withdraw 'to your room' with your needs and feelings, what feelings are you denying airtime, or rejecting entirely? What are you feeling right now? What is your body saying? You might pay attention to how you are feeling when you walk through each doorway. How do your shoulders feel? Are you hunched? Are your shoulders expressing overwhelm or burden? Do you feet hurt? Are you feeling irritable rushing so much? (Have you become a human do'ing again)"? My yoga instructor reminds, our feet (52 bones and 100 muscles in each) connect to and impact the way our whole body lines up. Interesting to think that sore feet may be your lesson to live in better alignment and better balance.

The body teaches you, and your feelings guide you. The more balance you develop, the more creativity you will attract. The more creativity you have, the more loving be'ings you will become. These are 'love in, love out' lessons your feelings and body can bring to your life when you become more "self" conscious.

✱✱✱✱✱✱✱✱✱✱✱

'LOVE IN, LOVE OUT' LESSONS

1. When you wake up, notice how you feel in your body. It's fun to think of your body as your dear friend. Does she/he need anything?
2. If you are like 'Lucy', start a journal. Write out what you are discovering about your feelings and thinking. This first step will help you get clear about what you will need from your future partner.
3. It's also helpful to return to old pages in your journal. If you leave one side of the journal blank, you can write on the blank side of the page, the ways your feelings have changed or not changed since your first entry. This creates a learning process for you, which increases insight and develops more positive cognitions with practice.
4. Remember to practice gratitude. I love to think about one thing I'm grateful for from the day before, or something that I have to look forward to today. This practice puts my rose colored glasses on. It makes me attend to more positive things through my day.
5. Check in again with your body (your dear friend …) during the day. She/he needs you to communicate with her/him. This attention of care is a big step towards wholeness. If you notice anxiety in your stomach or heart, you might take three minutes to do a breath release or a quick tap (mentioned earlier). If you notice your back is tight, you might do a quick stretch and reconsider the number of responsibilities you have loaded up on your day planner. Is this a reminder to delegate or ask for help, like 'Lucy'?
6. Is your jaw clenched or are you carrying your hands in fists? These can be trigger points that close us up and heighten stress responses in the brain. By practicing open hands and letting the tongue touch the roof of your mouth, you can calm the nervous system down. I like using

doorways as cues to do a body check. Do you have places in your body where you tend to close up in response to stress: shoulders, hands, jaw, stomach, feet?

****

Get Inside Yourself to Get Outside Yourself

What this means, in other words, is that you can't provide love to another person until you have healed the gap in your own heart from past relationship wounds and fully understood your own behavior patterns in relationships. Body mind and spirit, what have you learned?

Your body messages

If you become more conscious of what your body is expressing, you can be more aware that you are withdrawing (like 'Lucy') when you actually want to practicing staying more engaged. If you are like 'Lucy' and you have a habit of withdrawing, you might start to notice how your body looks constricted when you walk. Do you walk with your shoulders back, your eyes forward, and your hips moving naturally? Notice who you are in your body. The capacity to love comes from understanding who you are, whom you have been, and in the practice of who you will be in love the next time. If you don't change, there is a good chance you will repeat the same painful patterns and wind up with the same sad endings.

I have come to a deeper understanding of my body as my guide and my closest friend in maintaining a state of kindness, compassion, delight and equanimity. Shoulders down, I'm in alignment with my day and the people in it. Hands open, I'm relaxed and connecting. My body is my teacher. I am a student in learning how to care for and pay attention to her needs for balance, posture, play, strength, nurturance and companionship. I have also come to an understanding that loving relationships are what motivate every part of my life, to the best of my ability each day.

Mind messages

It's such a tempting practice to continue to cut down your former partner but it's to your huge disadvantage! Your conversation will become absolutely boring to your friends, while you rehearse a trench load of loss that you may be forgotten in. The more you continue, add nausea, resentments, the more you will attract all the bleakest evidence of life. It's as if the past unlucky turn of events in your life have un-keyed life-long misery because you are training your thinking to fifty shades of black... (Not grey)!

Develop an awareness of your projections. Whenever conflict brings you to tears or fury, there is probably a projection of unresolved family relationship(s) feeding the intensity of your emotions. When it happens, you experience both primary emotional pain in the present relationship and secondary, physical pain in your body. This can be experienced as back, neck, and shoulder or stomach constriction. The idea of projecting the unresolved difficulties of our formative parent/child relationships on our adult partner is well researched and described in much of the self-help literature (29). It is a part of our human conditioning to unconsciously choose a partner who has some of the qualities of our parent(s).

Your feelings of love and the thinking that takes you through Cupid's door to fall in love again will be shaped, to a great degree, by your attraction to the positive, to fresh experiences, to new intellectual and emotional learning about yourself. So if you want to talk about someone, talk about yourself and what you have learned. This will train your mind into positivity and accountability where you feel powerful and confidant again. Ideally your parents preconditioned you for love. As we experience our parent's positivity with regards to themselves and each other, we are set up for success. We naturally then choose friends and potential mates that have congruent styles of thinking. Living in a caring state towards all, may be the most important action we can take towards body, mind and spiritual health individually, within partnerships, communities (and at the risk of sounding too sucky or idealistic), globally.

Spirit messages

When you are taking care of yourself, your spirit will radiate love through your body. Whether yourself-care is found through your friendships, your yoga, your jogging, cycling, or hiking habits, take care of yourself. I recall reading a book 'Celestine Prophecy' many years ago and its premise about the exchange of energy systems between human beings and plant life. Whether we consider our energy systems or the actual engineering of oxygen and carbon dioxide from plants to human life, simply being outside is a great way to be in spiritual balance. How much time do you spend in the natural light of our planet?

On my yoga retreat, my guru Jim Gallas reminded us of Buddhist teaching and a quote by the Dalai Lama "My religion is kindness". In Chip Hartranft's translation of the Yoga Sutras, we learn about the heavenly abodes or Brahma, which are kindness, compassion, delight, and equanimity (30). May we all have plenty of each! Have you noticed that when you are living in life balance, people around you seem happier and more inviting?

Sharing your body, mind and spiritual self

It's human nature to re-live the unresolved issues through unwitting choices of love and life mates. If you can resolve previous confusion through your 'him or her' in the present, you will heal your past. In doing so you actually heal your brain pathways. This is where emotionally focused couples therapy can be so powerful. With emotionally focused therapy and in the safe holding of your current partner, you can re-experience your fear of separation, punishment, judgment, or rejection, which may have originated in early childhood. In this type of healing experience, your brain pathways actually heal and your cognitions around conflict shift. In a reparative experience, you will begin to think of anger as intimate and safe.

Ideally, as a child you you experienced relationship stress in a safe learning context. Your parents asked you what your motivations were in doing the 'wrong' behavior and explained what should have been a more ideal choice of action. Ideally you knew you were loved unconditionally, but your behavior wasn't. Anxiety shows up when you are fearful of losing love if you make a mistake. The fear of your separateness because of 'mistakes' causes the release from the protection of your caregivers. Not making mistakes then becomes a condition of survival. In a perfect world you are cared for unconditionally until you are ready to push your caregivers away. When this stage of individuation doesn't happen in a ready-safe sequence, you may project the unresolved feelings on an unsuspecting partner or friend as adults, later in life. The trouble is your partner or friends aren't necessarily going to consider this fair play! This is when couples therapy or individual counseling can be ideal. Otherwise, caught in the turmoil of unresolved historical hurts, you can undermine the process of healthy safe attachment (31). The more insecurity undermines you, the less loving feelings develop. You will move, instead, into relationship patterns of survival or fight and flight.

It's helpful to consider how your growing up has shaped you. Birth order effects are addressed in more depth later. Simply put, as an eldest, everyone knows they can count on you. Eldest tend to over function. They take on a lot of extra responsibility, which can lead to burn out. Some may experience an eldest as controlling. The middle child is the sweet center of the Girl Guide cookie. They tend to be easy to get along with but sometimes can suffer the invisible child syndrome, disappearing into the leadership of the eldest or lost in the caring of the youngest. The youngest tends to be adaptable as they observe the family dynamics the most. As a youngest you may be a little easier going, knowing you have an eldest and a middle child to pave the way for you. If you are a youngest you may fall into dependent patterns with others. There is some research to suggest that birth order effects are less significant when the gap in age is five years or more. Growing up may be learning to move between all three-birth orders; developing access to the acumen of all your other siblings' birth order styles of relationships. In partnerships it's helpful to choose a partner who is in the same birth order as you. In this way, you will be more inclined to develop rather than sit back in the controlling, invisible or dependent patterns of your siblings.

****

The best way to broaden your capacity from your birth order learning is to try out your sibling(s) styles and communicate through the process of integrating your whole self as an eldest, middle, youngest and only child. You might do a little research or invite your sibling's opinion of ways you can share in this growing up process! Ask questions about how they might handle certain situations. If you have a particularly challenging brother or sister who you feel triggered by (because they are 'so controlling' or 'so victimized' or 'so under-functioning'), take the risk to have that difficult conversation about how you experience him or her and how he or she experiences you.

1. Try to avoid using global statements such as "you always...", "you never..." Instead say "some of the time...", or "quite often..."
2. Start with saying something affirming of the other person. He or she needs to know you love and respect them, so that they can be open and not defensive when they hear the problem.
3. Stick to one issue. Don't build the tsunami of all the ways you feel they've let you down in the past. You aren't building a case.

****

The objective in these sibling conversations is to grow up, to develop the capacity for more loving, honest, connections in your relationships. Your sibling relationship(s) is/are your longest relationship(s) you will ever have. They are your Source, your wellspring of childhood memories and your most enduring guides through the dark tunnels life can present. Resource yourself in knowing and integrating all the wisdom they can offer you. Remember too, like you, they are also changing, growing, and shifting their thinking through their adult experiences, just like you. You may never have gotten along in childhood, but stay open to the possibility that this relationship could change for the better in adulthood.

Remember that one of the most powerful styles of communicating with siblings so that you don't carry historical baggage is in the practice of 'not knowing' them today and discovering them as adults, unobstructed by who either of you was in the past. When you don't pre-know your siblings, parents, partners, and childhood friends, on the basis of outdated relational patterns and prejudices, the present becomes a miracle of possibilities. Your openness and curiosity, managing projections, keeps you alive and growing.

CHAPTER 17

YOUR FIRST LOVE CREATES A LASTING IMPRESSION

The first insight towards knowing yourself is to know how influential and powerful your first love experience is. Typically, you may recall your first infatuation or love lost from childhood. Did you know that this single experience could be so imprinting that it formed a script, which makes you repeat the same relationship pattern through your lifetime? That's why you see people marrying the same type of person over and over again. Elizabeth Taylor, who married eight times, married Richard Burton twice. It's not easy to build deep, enduring, attachments in a Hollywood life style, but why did Elizabeth Taylor marry so many times and even the same man twice? Certainly eight marriage losses and transitions would have taken a physical and emotional toll. Too often, when confronted with a loss or the prospect of loss, we don't step back to question ourselves, or our relationship patterns. You can't change something you aren't aware of. You need to know your own emotional patterns; how you impact your own experience in relationship with others. You need to be smart to be lucky in love.

You developed a script from your first love experience in childhood. Then your childhood emotional instincts (or wisdoms) led your heart and thinking in life up until now. In Elizabeth Taylor's example, could it have been that her first marriage to Nicky Hilton (which reportedly may have been physically and emotionally abusive) set her on a path of not trusting men? It may have been that she continued to be off balanced by men because she never stepped back to be self-reflective. She might have learned to express her boundaries with men. She might have been more curious about the emotion of anger itself. Instead she spent her life in a fight or flight habit with men. When it came to following her passions in love, she really was a "Cat on a Hot Tin Roof" (1958). Her lack of emotional differentiation may have landed her on the roller coaster of her life, in and out of love. On the other hand, she was also an inspiration to live passionately, fully engaged, from one marriage to the next.

Another example of emotional impacts building scripts (to contrast) can be described; if your first boyfriend or girlfriend cheated on you, that loss of trust may set you up to develop anxious attachments with others. These insecurities then lead you to the same ending, over and over again. The more you worry you will be hurt, the less you are spiritually present to be loved. Your preconditioned anxiety makes your future partner anxious and the relationship inevitably becomes more work than it's worth. Stress notches up and loving feelings tank. Your fears and anxieties, from emotional wounding in old relationships, can actually abrupt you ability to experience secure attachments moving forward. The loss of trust can prevent your future relationships from developing into deep secure connections.

This is a good time to start to recognize, heal and move forward from the hurts of your childhood. Consider that you can trust that if the partnership is right, it will naturally evolve, as it should. No flow, no go. You will need to take a risk and a leap of faith to trust at some point. If you don't trust, you will project your own insecurities on others and end up being so difficult to love that you end up being left over and over again.
Another consideration is the type of partner you have been choosing. If you proactively choose a different personality style from the man (or woman) you were wounded by in the past, there may be a lot more hope that you will experience a better love outcome and therefore regain the capacity to trust. This is why knowing and loving yourself, healing the wounds of your past, and developing new healthy scripts for your relationships, is so important.

Researchers such as John Bowlby and Eleanor Ames published landmark studies looking at attachment styles seen in neonate bonding and children who have been adopted from orphanages. These and other studies, show us that our first relationships with our caregivers during our critical stages of development are so fundamental to our lifelong capacity to make attachments in secure, insecure, or avoidant styles. If you have had the constancy of nurturing care in your childhood, you were set up to make secure attachments with your future mates. This means you can easily express your feelings and needs. You can cope when those needs are not met. You can self-sooth and self-regulate. Even if you have had great childhood experiences with your parents, however, the wounding of your heart in your teens or adult life can start with someone who comes into your life carrying the emotional baggage of unresolved insecure attachment styles from their own childhood care deficit.

****

Love can become so complicated by these experiences that you then develop avoidant attachment styles, not wanting to risk being hurt. Don't let yourself become one of the walking wounded! If you have a pattern of self-sabotaging by pulling back when you sense you are getting too close for comfort, talk about it with your partner. You might let your potential partner in on your patterns of withdraw and invite him/her to let you know when he/she senses that is happening. Invitations for change are so powerful because they say:

1. I accept perfectly imperfect me
2. I accept all of you unconditionally
3. I don't know what I don't know
4. I trust you (because you feel safe)
5. Let's see where our dance takes us

****

Relationships are invitations for change when you think about it. Entering a relationship we are at risk of pain, growth, loss and love. We choose our partners based on familiar family features, and unconscious recognition that we will be in safe holding. As human beings we assess for future safety to know our offspring will have good genes, as well as physical, financial, and emotional safety. We unconsciously make sure that our partners will be able to provide constancy of care, and that our life goals are mutual. Once we make the decision to love, we flip our 'love switch' to 'on' and thereafter try to embrace all the forthcoming elements.

The Past versus Present

Love has the aliveness of a thunderstorm at times. No? Did you know that crops grow better in a field that has been struck by lightning after a thunderstorm? The electricity promotes better soil and therefore growth accelerates. *Love is electric.*

If you think about the seeds of a tree, it's only with a fire that seeds are able to grow into trees. *Love is like fire.*

Waves, which are caused by wind, clean up the debris that collects at our shorelines. *Love islike the force of wind.*

I can think of many metaphors in nature that teach us that to love is to take a big risk. But to love is also to be alive. If we are alive and growing we are saying we are willing to share the most precious gift we have to give – our time. Life as we know it is finite, so the time we spend together should be thought of as a gift more precious than any material thing. It's through spending time and risking love that we change old scripts of the past. If you fear trusting, you can only outgrow that fear by risking trusting again. How choose a better partner to trust this time? This is where your intuition and body knowledge come into play.

If you pay attention to how you feel in your body when you are with certain people, you will start to recognize the energy differences. When you think back on your day tonight, consider whom you've come into contact with. Take out a piece of paper and write down everyone you recall. Then give them a number ranking 0 – 10 for how enriched 7 - 10 or drained 2 – 5 you felt in their presence. With a little practice you will begin to develop effective radar for who is simpatico and healthy for you to be around. It's not that you need to avoid those you know drain you, but you can manage your time and/or interaction better and start to be more body aware of who feels enriching or light, and who feels draining and dark energetically. This idea speaks to current research in brain electricity and toxicity. Living with this awareness is like taking vitamin D to feed health and longevity.

We know from research that we can actually heal our disrupted brain pathways physiologically by re-engaging and re-scripting from the confusion of a relationship gone wrong. An interesting research project was done on rats (as human beings, we are actually quite similar to rats in our DNA). In this research rats were put on a pad that had been electrified in one section of the pad. The rats soon learned not to go to the electrified section of the pad. Then the experiment turned off the electrified section and tried to encourage the rats to go to the section that had been electrified. They encouraged the rats with food and even cocaine to venture on the part of the pad that had just once been electrified. They did this over many trials and with no results! Finally they put another rat (which had not had this electric conditioning) on the pad and it went straight for the food. When the other rats saw the unconditioned rat venture to the food, they all moved forward to the food. This research speaks to the power of relationships in neural integration.

The single most powerful way to change our brain is through healthy relationships. If you've been burned on a past relationship, the only way you will heal and undo the pain is through a healing relationship. Stay engaged with your heart. Dan Siegel in his book Mindsight refers to the value of taking 'time in' (32). We need to cultivate a practice of meditation or quiet reflection so that we can regulate the way we perceive information as well. Our brain shapes the information flow. So it's not just about choosing a healthy partner, it's also about being healthy in our selves so that we don't project old baggage and damage each other. This is why it's good in a relationship to make time to be on your own in order to be able to differentiate emotional experiences and honor each other's differences.

The bottom line? Feel your feelings in your body, through quiet reflection, understand what the feelings are telling you, and finally, talk about what you are feeling. Express your needs until they find safe landing with someone as loving and loveable as you. You can actually create changes in your neural pathways in the way they fire up your brain and your body.

Think of love in the context of four elements of earth:

1. Be grounded, practice self-care so you contribute to health,
2. Be like wind; communicate so you can come to emotional rescue when needed,
3. Be like fire; passionate, alive, engaged and growing,
4. Be like water; clear out and wash away old patterns of heart confusion.

Authenticity

Even considering the idea of being authentic, we may be inauthentic. Authenticity is an oxymoron, because it contradicts itself! When you are not self-conscious or guarding your behaviors, you are probably being authentic. Many couples tend to forge an inauthentic self at the early stages of meeting because they adopt a pleasing intuition about what might be attractive. Do you tend to ask your best friend what you should wear, say, do on that first date? At that point, believe it or not, you are already headed for heartbreak! In a Cyrano de Bergerac style, you are hiding yourself, trying to win your potential partner's heart, in the style of your friend! Be yourself. If you're not yourself, you will either get tired of keeping up a pleasing façade, or your partner will see through the contrived you, and the relationship will eventually end. You also run the risk of losing yourself, being so focused on pleasing the other that the false life will not only become tiresome, even exhausting, but you will lose sight of who you really are, who you want to become. It's no fun being someone you're not, especially when you can be who you really are with someone who is thrilled with the authentic you.

This is where body learning can be so valuable. If you consider whom you are when you are on holidays, you may sense more of your authentic self.

On holiday, as a rule, you are likely to be sleeping, eating and exercising well. When you think about the types of holidays that you enjoy most, are they relaxing on a beach, attending a learning event, exploring in a foreign culture, challenging your body in a physical environment, diving into the deep, exploring an archeological dig, or famous museum ... are you most alive when relaxing, learning, dancing, or adventuring? As you think about these times, you will probably discover your authentic self. The self you love most. The self that feels most at home. One of my clients said to me once about falling in love, that they felt they had come home. I think that's such a beautiful way to express love. Being at home in the self may be what discovering your authentic self is like.

I like me when I am creative, relaxed, in touch with my playful self and learning something new. I will admit I am a junky for learning. I know I feel good around the ocean because I love to swim. I enjoy being with people. I love music and dancing. When these factors are present I feel most alive and at home with me. It's then I feel open, connected, loving and expansive. When I feel stuck in my body, mind and spirit it's usually because I am rushing too much, over functioning at work or in my relationships with others, and not taking time to be outside. In those times, I tend to withdraw and become more closed. My creativity goes down and I am less loving.

****

I think we need to be as aware of our personality strengths as we are our blood type! Do you know what blood type you are? Knowing your strengths is the best way out of the dark tunnel of fear.

1. What are your best personality strengths?
2. How do your strengths show up at work, home, in relationship with others?
3. What is one thing you could do differently that would support you more?

If you think about your siblings and your parents, what are their strengths?

1. How are these strengths showing up in your life?
2. What is one thing you could do differently that would support you more?

If you think about your family of origin, when were you happiest?

1. As a sibling, what is a favorite memory?
2. As a daughter or son, what is a favorite memory?
3. As a family, what is a favorite memory?
4. What is one thing you could do differently to engage some of these activities?

****

So often when I see clients who report they have lost their libido, it's because they have lost a sense of who they are. They have become so busy in the day-to-day practice of work, eat, sleep, work, eat, sleep, that they actually feel numb to the bone. I can see it in their eyes. The aliveness of our spirit shows up in our contact. The eyes, by the way, can be a great way to spot health. You'll notice that you engage eye contact more when you feel good. The same is true for others. Not in an eye glaring kind of way, but in an openhearted kindness you see in the micro expressions of a smile that is seen in the outer creases of the eyes. When you are stressed your limbic system fires up and as your adrenals are activated your body closes up. You therefore develop the micro expressions that say 'back off' – less eye contact, closed hands, rounded shoulders; hips slung forward or back, shoulders hiked up. These are all body signals that tell others to distance from you. They also send a message to your brain to release more cortisol (stress hormone) and so on and so on. When that defensive process occurs there is less blood flow to the skin, skin ailments show up, your immune system shuts down, and sexual dysfunction shows up. You will become unmotivated, indecisive, and very reactive to others. A morning meditation or practice of cardio exercise may lengthen your life and quite possibly change your world. Any kind of body movement you can practice through the day to make you more conscious will help you get back in balance. Did you know that by simply looking up you could raise your energy? Or if you are feeling a little scattered, try looking down to feel more grounded. If you need to calm yourself, put your attention to the smells in the room. There are so many great ways you can practice to **self-regulate** and allow your authentic self to show up more of the time.

Keep Your Feet on the Ground

Are you typically 'swept away' by love? In this situation you crave the bliss of the love cocktail— a 'high' induced by the chemistry of dopamine, endorphin, serotonin, and oxytocin. In this experience, you let yourself be literally intoxicated by the addictive chemicals of love. If your parents had a short courtship or other family members tended to fall in love fast, you may be inclined to expect the same. The trouble with this pattern is that if you fall into love quickly, you may also fall out of love quickly. These intense patterns of high and low love living can take a toll on your capacity to trust and value yourself moving forward. After a few months or years of intense beginnings and endings, you may wake up realizing that love itself is a mistake. That is just not true. You just need to slow down!

The object of your passion may be striking, charismatic, and alluring, but you may come to recognize that he/she is also annoying, irritating, unreliable, and self-centered as you spend more and more time together. Or perhaps that shy, reserved, steady quality you once found so endearing is now resoundingly boring! You may start to wonder why you are doing less and less together and the erstwhile object of your desire begins to feel more and more uncomfortable in your friendship circles.

The rational brain helps you love smart if you can consider a few things while your relationship is unfolding. You can love many people over your lifetime, but will you love the life you will live together with this ONE? The truth is if financial or family stressors are a factor, the brain's capacity to function in its upper cortical loving centers goes down. The more stress in your life, the less loving feelings you will experience. The more stresses that flood into your relationship, the more the relationship will lose its luster over time. So slow down and get back to you!

Slow your body down

Feel your feet on the ground. Notice all ten toes... your heels. Feel your body center in your pelvis. Notice your stomach, your chest, your shoulders, and your neck...your head. Notice your breath. Notice when your head is thrusting forward and you are rushing. Notice when your shoulders are rounding and you're collapsing. Notice the connection between you and the earth, you and the Divine. I love the focus of imagining in your mind's eye, loving hands on your shoulders. Feel the connection of a caring spirit between you and others and good intention between all.

Slow your mind down

Remember that the excitement and energy you are feeling is within you, not outside of you. So as you start dating someone new, make sure you continue to date you. Think about the strengths within you that you listed a few pages ago. The fun loving joyful person who is showing his or her face right now, is you. Keep up your practice of journaling that you started earlier. Write down all the positive attributions you love about the other person and identify those qualities in you.

Slow your spirit down

Continue your practice of meditation. This is a great way to connect with yourself spiritually. Practice gratitude for the privilege of being you. When you meditate, be an observer of you as you recall your previous day or week. Let yourself recognize and appreciate love within you.

Having a daily ritual can help maintain your spiritual health. This may be a fifteen-minute morning meditation or a one-hour jog. It could be a mindfull walk at the end of your day. For some, it's a simple practice of breathing deeply while you sit at your desk. It can be the practice of prayer and sending well wishes to someone you care about. If you think about previous generations, you may recall seeing your parents or grandparents have 'martini' hour before dinner. While, alcohol can be a negative force in some families because of addiction, a glass of wine at the end of the day can be a healthy ritual, which gains some more spiritual access.

The Power of Family

You are a combination of your whole family. Work towards having the best possible relationship with your whole complex family group. Everyone has some type of 'complexities' in their family. Bumps in life cause complex survival patterns of behavior. Most families can track generations back to sudden deaths, losses, bankruptcies, divorce, or chronic illness. When these life events happen, the family system is impacted and survival strategies prevail. Some of these survival strategies may include, withdraw/pursue, abusive anger, depression, anxiety, blame and shame or other less than healthy outcome responses. Feel proud of and confident of yourself that you are in the process of learning how to live life more consciously. You can also feel proud and confident about everyone in your family, even if their strategies for survival have not been ideal. The fact is, everyone always does the best they can do based on what they know. Your family has prevailed; otherwise you wouldn't have been born! Your personality is made up of a kaleidoscope of traits you have inherited genetically or through repeated interactions with your parents, siblings, cousins, and for generations you haven't even met. Your personality is even shaped when you were in utero! You therefore have the capacity to behave like any and all of your family. So if there is someone in your family whom you are ashamed of, or in conflict with, it's important to your own growth and development to start the process of new understanding why. Virginia Satir, internationally known therapist (1916 – 1988) suggested that we should always consider self, context, and other. Different aspects of our personalities show up depending on the situation we are in. We are an adaptive species. Therefore, there should never be a family member we can't love unconditionally if we come to understand their patterns with an empathic perspective. If you can do that, you will develop more resilience and a greater capacity for determining your own natural responses to relationship triggers. The less judgmental you are towards yourself, the more open you will be to feedback. The more open to feedback, the more long term your relationships will become. You absolutely need to hear your other. You absolutely need to express your upsets and points of confusion. You absolutely therefore well advised to understand the world through a 'whole' hearted lens. Compassion, empathy and a sense of loving discovery are the pillars of forever love.

Love is an action, seen your behavior and your behavior in turn is a predictable combination of nature and nurture. You are the complex sum of your mother's, father's, siblings', uncles', aunts', and grandparents', going back generations. Consider that thought! That's why it's so important to identify and develop the tools you need to accurately and honestly express and manage your feelings and needs. Good and bad traits and tendencies will show up in a recognizable historical pattern related to the context of a range of stressors. It's also why the less judgmental you are of others in your family, the more ready you will be for healthy self-love. To learn how to love, you need to be able to embrace the idea that you can get better at love every day. You need to be able to ask questions and to listen and be empathic when your partner 'bonk's you with his or her emotional upsets. If not, you will be on guard and increasingly defensive the more authentic the connection you dare to create. Developing your responses on the basis of compassion rather than defensive reactions will revolutionize your experience of other people's anger. It's also how you will stop yourself from a pattern of fixing your other.

Remember, therefore, that as you consider a partner, you will be taking on his or her 'whole' family. Granted some relationships are unresolvable. Sometimes it's best to accept and walk away from relationships that resonate with painful aspects of your family's history, especially when it comes to past experiences of abuse. But you also need to look deeper, beyond the obvious and ask yourself some important extended relationship questions. What do you think of your potential partner's parents and their style of expressing love? What are their relationship behaviors like? What is their style of play? Are they serious? Are they light hearted? Are they a version of the Bickersons or the Flintstones? What is your potential partner's relationship like with his or her mother and father?

If we don't ask these questions, these potentially unresolved experiences can 'project' on us as conflict in the present once the relationship moves forward. All those times your partner sank into deep silence, totally withdrawing, or exploded into volcanic rage over a misunderstanding; he/she may have been re-experiencing an unresolved issue in a prior relationship. The bigger the reaction of fight or flight, the more likely the trigger is to do with their past. For those reasons, it helps if both you and your partner have good relationships with most of your respective family members!

Don't disregard feedback from family members as it relates to their perception of your potential mate or your interaction with them. If someone in your family doesn't like your partner, pay attention. You are your own best wisdom in the end, so you are going to make the ultimate decision to love or withdraw. But just as you know you are a combination of personality traits of your whole family, it follows that if someone in your family feels negatively about your candidate for happily ever after, there may be a very valid reason that you are too blinded by the chemistry of passion to see. In addition, consider the future with children, large extended and blended family gatherings. The attendant and inevitable personality clashes can be quite stressful to deal with over time.

Love YOU

When I was growing up I loved the Stephen Sills song "Love the One you're with". At that time I thought it was about loving the person you were dating because you couldn't have the one you really wanted. As an adult, I realize that it's about loving the one you are with every morning and every day, all day long – and that's you! This was my theme song while I was getting my feet back on the ground. It's a fun way to start your morning. Try brushing your teeth to these lyrics!

Love the One You're with, Stephen Stills

If you're down and confused

And you don't remember who you're talking too

Concentration slips away

Cause your baby is so far away

CHORUS

Well there's a rose in the fisted glove

And eagle flies with the dove

And if you can't be with the one you love honey

Love the one you're with

Don't be angry - don't be sad

Don't sit crying over good times you've had

There's a girl right next to you

And she's just waiting for something to do

CHORUS

Turn your heartache right into joy

Cause she's a girl and you're a boy

Get it together come on make it nice

You ain't gonna need anymore advice

CHORUS

Who is This 'You' Waiting For Your Love?

Have you ever written a job resume and noticed that it is quite a mood booster? Writing out our strengths reminds you of your best assets. We are all taught the virtues of being humble and modest, but this, your time of transition after the end of a relationship! This is the time to rebuild! Don't be timid. You may tend to forget all the wonderful things you are and instead focus on beating yourself up over your flaws. This makes no sense at all. You should be thinking of your positives, your strengths, as you do when you are building a professional resume. What are your personality strengths? You're trying to sell yourself on a vision for a healthy future you, unencumbered yet informed and improved by the recent emotional wounds. Write your attributes and interpersonal skills out in a resume style snapshot of the past 10, 20, or 30 years depending on how old you are.

Consider your obvious traits that you identify with easily, and also consider the traits that you may recognize as coming from your Father and your Mother. If you were adopted, consider your adoptive parent's traits; they've probably been your strongest influencers. Consider your siblings' traits and how their strengths may be just like yours or how interaction with them has shaped your preferred traits and characteristics. Do this over a period of a week. Give yourself plenty of time so you don't forget anything. You may even have to do a little research with your family and friends to recall things you may have forgotten.

Take time to consider your pattern of social and community interactions outside of family. People, by the way, navigate through the 'tornedo' times, more successfully if they have a community of friends and like-minded people they can count on and share ideas with. This is just another reminder that if you've been working more than socializing and your friendships are a little scarce, now is a good time to get involved in a hobby or sport that you enjoy. As you enjoy the activity, you will naturally build deeper, more meaningful relationships outside of work.

But back to the resume. How have you helped others? How have you practiced patience with someone who really needed your time? How did your integrity show up when you might have cheated on a former partner, or your partner cheated on you? How true blue are you? How do you make others feel at a party; happy, angry, relevant, sad, threatened? How have you cared when others might have given up? How have you mentored or inspired someone in your life? What is important to you in your life, in your career, in your lifestyle? These are some resume building questions you can ask yourself as you recall your life at age 15, 20, 25, 30, 35, etc. They are also times when you may have connected with YUM universal. Some may call this God, Gaia, or a state of the Divine. There are so many types of religions. Though you may not know them all intimately, you know the feeling you have when you have the sense that there is something greater in this world that keeps you safe and feeling secure in your separateness.

I am reputed to be a little naive and have a healthy imagination. But I truly feel a sense of 'source' when I slow down, when I'm running in the woods, and when I'm feeling inspired. This being 'in-spirit' for me is connecting with a kind of super highway of good intention. Meditating, I imagine this universal super zone of love – it's so YUMmy! When I do, there is no space for fear, judgment, loneliness or lack of positive energy. A friend of mine taught me some basic principles of Chi-Gong, a Chinese practice of breath and movement (Chi, meaning energy, and Gong, meaning work). Try holding your hands facing each other but 6 inches apart. After a while you will start to be aware of a tingly energy between them. We are energetic beings and in the practice of moving our own loving energy and sourcing something greater in universal love, we can heal ourselves, and quite possibly aide in the healing of others. I know this sounds a little woo, woo. But just try it for yourself. You decide.

For many, going to Church, Synagogue, Mosque, or Temple, will be your source. I recall fondly when my Mother (who was Catholic) wanted to get my Father (who was an atheist Engineer) to go to Church with her. He challenged her that if she would convert to Protestant United, he would join her. So, my Mother converted and my Father joined us every Sunday... for about a year, after which he said "I'd really rather not". My Father was not a Church, group-oriented person. His spirituality was in his love for oil painting, growing vegetables at the side of our home, dancing in the living room with my Mom and ice-skating. I still recall his laughter and know he was a spiritual influence on me. Though he slipped out of my life in my teens, I would credit him with my love for stories (he was a great story teller), music, dance and play. Spirituality is very personal and we should all be afforded the grace of our individual and unique ways of accessing Source. My Father didn't need fixing or saving. He was one of the most inspired human beings I've ever known. YUM

Now, with your homework done, it is time to fall in love, deeply, enduringly and unconditionally with you. The next insight is that the more you know, accept and love yourself, and access universal love, the greater trust and capacity you will have to love others, whether it be the intimate love of a couple, love for a parent or child, or a universal love for humanity writ large, and life itself. This capacity to love is essential. It reduces conflict in all your relationships and increases your capacity to be intimate with that special someone. The more open and less defensive you are, the greater intimacy you will experience. The greater the capacity for intimacy, the stronger and more solid and enduring an attachment you can have with others. This may be the secret sauce to experiencing an enduring lifetime love.

CHAPTER 18

LEARNING FROM THE SCRIPTS OF YOUR PAST

This chapter will help you understand how your love story blueprint evolved. One of the most challenging reasons people keep going round and around the same experience is that they don't realize how much they are the dynamic that drives their repetitive relationship dances. I fondly recall a story in Winnie the Pooh. (Chapter III in which Pooh and Piglet go hunting and nearly catch a Woozle) Pooh is walking around and around the same tree looking for a Woozle.

"Hallo!" said Piglet, "what are you doing?"

"Hunting," said Pooh.

"Hunting what?"

"Tracking something," said Winnie-the-Pooh very mysteriously.

"Tracking what?" said Piglet, coming closer

"That's just what I ask myself. I ask myself, What?"

"What do you think you'll answer?"

"I shall have to wait until I catch up with it," said Winnie-the-Pooh. "Now, look there." He pointed to the ground in front of him. "What do you see there?"

"Tracks," said Piglet. "Paw-marks." He gave a little squeak of excitement. "Oh, Pooh! Do you think it's a—a—a Woozle?"

Pooh keeps tracking himself around the tree until he meets Christopher Robin who helps him see that it's his own footprints he's been tracking.

Christopher Robin came slowly down his tree.

"Silly old Bear," he said, "what were you doing? First you went round the spinney twice by yourself, and then Piglet ran after you and you went round again together, and then you were just going round a fourth time"

"Wait a moment," said Winnie-the-Pooh, holding up his paw.

He sat down and thought, in the most thoughtful way he could think. Then he fitted his paw into one of the Tracks … and then he scratched his nose twice, and stood up.

"Yes," said Winnie-the-Pooh.

"I see now," said Winnie-the-Pooh.

"I have been Foolish and Deluded," said he, "and I am a Bear of No Brain at All."

"You're the Best Bear in All the World," said Christopher Robin soothingly.

"Am I?" said Pooh hopefully. And then he brightened up suddenly.

We have all felt like the most foolish and deluded Pooh bears at times when it comes to love. Let me say also, however, that we can all get smarter at love as we recognize ways by which we can develop better love choices and relationship practices rather than continue to repeat the same patterns of pain. The more you understand your tendencies based on the 'family & friends blueprint', the more you can create new results in love in your future.

What maintains pain is staying in a story that offers you no opportunity for perspective. You need to be able to step back, to distinguish the forest from the trees. This is where everyone needs a Christopher Robin. A good friend or family member will tell you the truth if you ask questions such as: do you think I lost myself through my last relationship? Did you think he/she was the right partner for me? Will you be honest with me if you see me doing that again? If you don't have a friend or family member you trust to be your Christopher Robin, hire a psychotherapist or personal coach. When you think about all the negative impacts bad relationships can have on your careers, family, finances, and a healthy life path, you can't afford not to have someone who is 100% objective and on your side. And when they offer valid insights, have the strength and wisdom to listen. This is your life. How much do you want to love it?

The First Crush

As you reflect on your childhood, think about your first crush or first young love. What happened? How did you meet him/her? What attracted you to each other? Who was the most forthcoming in pursuing the attraction? I recall with fondness working with a thirty-year-old female client (let's call her 'Jennifer'). She was so frustrated at wanting to have a great love. Sadly she felt trapped in the desperate ruminations of the ending of her two-year relationship. It was this negative hopeless thinking that motivated her to seek therapy. As we began our work together, Jennifer told me that she had had a series of boyfriend experiences. Most of these had ended discouragingly, either with the other person cheating, or feeling distracted somehow. She came to see me with the goal of understanding why she was causing every relationship to fail. What 'Jennifer' came to understand, however, was that she was choosing the same type of man over and over again. 'Jennifer' chose men who were charismatic, handsome, alluringly withdrawn, and who challenged her. The more she felt challenged by their detached manners, the harder she'd try to win them. You maybe thinking, this has got to be about 'Jennifer's' lack of self-esteem. Why else would 'Jennifer' tolerate such passive, self-absorbed men?

As we explored her first impressions of relationships from her youth, she described the embarrassing story of a childhood crush. In her case, a boy in her elementary school felt the crush towards her. She recalled feeling overwhelmed by this boy (let's call him 'Jessie') in her grade that "obsessively" left presents for her on her desk. For weeks, she would arrive at school in the morning to find notes, flowers, and various homemade gifts he had crafted for her. What was so upsetting to 'Jennifer' was that even though she had not expressed any mutual feelings for 'Jessie', he continued leaving these gifts on her desk. Others in 'Jennifer's' class (who were probably jealous to some extent) mocked her and laughed at 'Jessie' obsession and demonstration of unrequited infatuation. Before long, 'Jennifer' recalled, "the whole school knew he had a crush on me. I was exasperated with embarrassment". These adoring notes, a rose on her desk one day, and hand-made gifts would be welcomed by any adult, but for 'Jennifer' recalling her eight-year-old self, the experience was torture. This was Jennifer's first experience of obsessive infatuation.

This single experience may have set 'Jennifer' on a path to resist love that is direct and clearly expressed because of the emotional feelings of embarrassment she attached to direct forms of attention (from boys at eight). At the time, the other children may have been envious but all she could recall was her feelings of "embarrassment" they had laughed. 'Jennifer' had felt so mortified in the expression of compelling childhood attraction by this eight year old innocent, that she had tended years later (as an adult) to be turned off by attentive men who were possibly otherwise healthy potential partners. It had taken her several challenging, hurtful experiences to realize that love should be as simple as it might have been at eight. As long as she was choosing unavailable and hard to get men, the chance of having a complicated love experience was high. Through new practices that included learning to choose a different, kinder, clear communicating style of partner, 'Jennifer' is beginning to experience men more positively.

'Jennifer's' openness to a fresh new style of love is evidence of her gaining confidence that love can be best expressed and shown in simple acts of spiritual generosity and caring. Love is not meant to be so challenging. Love is certainly not something to be embarrassed by. If you were embarrassed by an overtly expressed childhood attraction, do you tend to recoil as an adult when someone is forthcoming in his or her expression of attraction today?

****

Breakthrough Tips to receive love and re-wire the old anxious re-actions:

1. Practice saying thank you when someone gives you a compliment or a gift of any kind. Notice when you deflect and try to return to gratitude.
2. Challenge yourself to ask a question about the affectionate comment so you allow the compliment to land emotionally. (What made you say that just now? What inspired you to give me that gift?)
3. This makes more meaning of the exchange both for the giver and receiver.
4. Track positive things people say to you for a day. Make a list.
5. Track the positive things you say to others for a day. Make a list.

****

What this would mean for 'Jennifer', as an adult is that she may have tended to reject the constancy of healthy potential partners and, in contrast, go for the relationships that were more challenging and difficult. This would give her a repeated experience of high highs and low lows in a roller coaster style of relating that would set her up, over and over again, with complicated partners who don't write notes or express love in acts of kindness such as hand-made gifts! 'Jennifer' now has greater insight to this type of sequence and has begun to choose better partners to share her heart with. She realizes that the big thrill of the challenge was a competitive style of love with a 50/50 chance of "win or lose". With a different, other focused, caring partner, she will have a greater chance of long-term love. If you want to experience better love, know yourself and choose well.

In addition, and equally significant, 'Jessie', who expressed his eight-year-old 'love' and experienced rejection and embarrassment in return, may still struggle as an adult, with a pattern of pursue or withdraw, driven by an underlying fear of rejection. What that might mean for him would be an inability to feel good enough to choose 'his one and only,' resigned instead to wait to be chosen by someone else. Because he's not choosing his ideal, he will end up bored with partner after partner. Taking the risk at eight and encountering repeated rejection, 'Jessie' may continue to associate feelings of embarrassment and dread with the idea of expressing his true feelings of attraction for someone he honestly wants to get to know.

****

Breakthrough Tips to gain insight and brain change:

1. Make a time line of people you have been attracted to but afraid to initiate a date with.
2. On one side of the timeline write out what you told yourself with regards to rejection or fear of rejection.
3. On the other side of the timeline write out what might have been possible if you didn't have that fear?
4. Final step: write a note to your future self who doesn't have that fear of rejection.

****

Another example of learned childhood emotional sequences is well illustrated by a client I will call 'Max'. 'Max' grew up in an alcoholic family. His mother drank most nights, and he reported that when she drank, conflict and anxiety levels in their home elevated dramatically. 'Max', as a result, never invited friends home from school. He was embarrassed and afraid that others at school would find out that his Mother was an alcoholic. What this meant for 'Max' was that he became so self-conscious, shamed by his Mother's alcohol addiction, he developed social anxiety. 'Max' perceived his Mother's disease as a reflection of his own flawed identity and value as a high school student in comparison to his peers who "all seemed so normal" compared to him. Ultimately when 'Max' was fourteen, a girl in his school clearly expressed interest in him. 'Max' felt obliged to walk away just as fast as he could leave the encounter. He recalls sadly that he had actually been attracted to this young girl, but hadn't had the courage to return her attempts at conversation because it would risk her (and others) finding out how flawed he really was. Two salient internal negative self-concepts sabotaged him: "I'm not good enough." and "I can't trust." These core self-doubts lead to further considerations like "How could she like me?" and "How can I trust women when my mother is so unreliable?" Do you have a shoulder saboteur of your own, shaped by formative childhood encounters, who undermines your emotional freedom?

As an adult, when 'Max' initiated therapy with me, he was unable to form a long-term relationship. He wore too much of the family shame about his mother's drinking. As an adult in his 30's, 'Max' could initiate relationships but they would never last more than a few months. What he understood was that the slightest expression or hint of discord with a woman would cause him to withdraw and end the relationship. Reject before being rejected was his motto and coat of arms. There was no modeling of intimacy in his childhood home and he had survived this by learning to spend most of his life with his heart locked up and protected. Max was surviving an attraction, re-action roller coaster that was exhausting him. He was caught in a pattern of emotional withdrawal and his fear of others finding out he "wasn't good enough". This was childhood pattern that left him still single in his thirties and lonely, year after lonely, adult year.

Today 'Max' is finally happily married. Through emotionally focused, and family systems therapy, 'Max' practiced integrating the confidence he easily had felt in his professional role as an Engineer, but had not in his romantic life. Knowing what it feels like to be creatively engaged in a project, he practiced out the insecurities he felt and identified through his dating experiences. He also learned ways he could risk expressing his anxieties when they showed up, rather than continue to stuff them and run. He discovered that in sharing his feelings, his partner felt closer and more connected to his heart. At work, when he found himself stuck without the answers he'd had no problem asking for help and enlisting colleagues in finding solutions. In theory, this should not have been any different when it came to his romantic life.

We all feel stuck at times in our life. As human beings we are meant to access each other to collaborate to achieve greater goals than we could manage alone. The more you access others in your life, the greater capacity you will develop in every aspect of your life. Once you have had a positive experience asking and receiving, you can identify, recall and practice these feelings over and over again until they become a new style of being. The more humble you are in appreciating this idea that we need each other, the better your life will become. The difficulty is that the more wounded you are from relationships in the past; the more you may shy away from being as trusting as possible. You gain trust by reaching out and discovering 'we' are all there. The more you are guarded, the less love will be in your life and you are then back at the 'Wall'.

'Max' learned to risk his vulnerability and thereby re-storied his fear that he wasn't good enough, into a new self-appreciation as someone as good and loveable as anyone else. 'Max' is an attractive, intelligent, and highly successful professional person. He had every confidence when it came to who he was as an Engineer. What he learned was that he was the same 'Max' in his personal life as he was in his professional life. It was natural for him to have panicked at fourteen when (let's call her 'Julia') approached him. As a child, he was fearful. As an adult he learned to face his fears and express his worst dreads. Let's face it; if the person you are interested in doesn't welcome your vulnerable expression of affection, she's just not right for you. Being with someone who doesn't respond with caring is not a life you would love even if your efforts in courtship worked. Relationships should provide safe emotional landings, not pits of anxiety and self-doubt.

In 'Max's' example, children of alcoholics tend to either set up patterns of withdrawal, or to engulf their partners with a lack of boundaries and a tendency to be controlling because they are so afraid of not being good enough. The more over whelming they may become in catching and holding on to a partner, the more their potential partner may withdraw from them, feeling overwhelmed or smothered. Their relationship sequence then becomes catch and release. They may catch a potential partner but the hurt is in an early release when their partner feels overwhelmed after the first couple of weeks, months, or years. Don't ever lose yourself in someone else's life. Keep up your interests, prior friendships, and personal goals. It's tempting to spend more and more time in the interests, friendships and goals of the other. But sadly, the more you lean into their life without keeping a firm footing in your own, the more likely you are to fall into the destructive dynamics of co-dependence.

In a similar consideration, although I obviously never met the girl 'Max' described from his childhood, a sabotaging pattern may have been set up for 'Julia' at her young age of 14. As an adult, having been rejected by 'Max' for no apparent reason, 'Julia' may have had a relationship pattern introduced that led to an unhappy sequence of insecure self-judgment for years to come.

Many people have truly positive experiences with their first. Not everyone is tripped up in childhood relationships. However I guarantee that everyone will experience the bliss and agony of learning to love. There is a saying "Every cripple has their own way of walking". It is critical, when you are trying to achieve a positive breakthrough after a breakup, to recall your first experience and gain insight into how that may have impressed a relationship sequence fundamental to your adult life. Through self-knowledge, understanding and practice of new relationship patterns, you can be different. You can change old relationship habits and develop new patterns that lead you to happiness and more fulfilling interpersonal experiences.

Communication is everything. Once you recall your most powerful childhood attraction or first love and the underpinnings of your love blueprint, consider if you have been repeating the same mistakes over and over again. Are you most often a pleaser in the relationship? Do you tend to make everything easy for your partner and let your disappointments go unsaid? Is it time for more authenticity in your life? Or is it simply choosing a new style of partner that's key for you? Is it time to choose someone who is more generous of spirit; more stable and patient; more exciting and engaging? Think about who you really are, and what YOU really want.

How do you discover authenticity? Why is it so difficult to engage? From your school years, you were constantly observed and graded by your teachers. If you got an A in school, you are brilliant. If you got a D you are a failure. These subjective measures may be guiding your thinking into anxious choices based on other focused assessments for the rest of your life. From your peers at school, if you were popular, you were 'in' and accepted. If you were shy, or different, you may have been judged and subsequently come to judge yourself as 'geeky' or weird and be outcast. These subjective ways of thinking about who you are become imposed on yourself-perception and can condemn you to a roller coaster style of relationship, as an adult. If your partner values you and expresses positivity towards you, you may feel you are on top of the world. If your partner is dissatisfied with you and expresses their discontent, you risk feeling like a failure again. The latter shuts you down, makes you defensive and, over time, wears out love. A partner, no matter how loving, can only reaffirm their feelings so many times before they give up on breaking through your walls of self-rejection and seek a less demanding partner. Your work is to learn to be a love machine. Cultivate love, within and around you, rather than continue as an anxious, emotional chameleon doomed to failure in a series of complex, fabricated, unsustainable relationships.

Authenticity comes from thinking of your unique self in the context of all your good and not so good traits. You need to learn to think of yourself as being perfectly imperfect within the kaleidoscope of emotional perception. No judgment. Your feelings are just what they are. You feel several emotions every few minutes. Take some time to be inwardly reflective through journaling or meditating.

"The only tyrant I accept in this world is the still voice within" - *Mahatma Gandhi*

If you can take time to consider why you feel certain ways, you can then identify what you need from and have to offer your partner. When you know what you need, what you are prepared and able to give, you can simply express your needs to your love mate. If they don't want to meet those needs, it's a way of saying they are not able or willing to love you in a way that you can accept and return. Then you have a decision to make. Can you live without being loved in this way or not? It's that simple.

We tend to be quite complicated though. We often suppress our feelings and don't investigate what they tell us about our needs. This is unfair to ourselves (because we are feeling loved) and to our partner (because we aren't teaching them how to love us better). The same is true from the opposite perspective. Your partner needs to express his/her feelings and take time in to discover what he/she needs from you. Otherwise he/she is not being fairly engaged in evolving a balanced and healthy relationship of love and intimacy. Dr. Susan Johnson describes the science of loving secure attachment in her book "Hold me tight" (33). I heard Dr. Johnson speak at an International Family Therapy Conference in March 2012, and she gave a compelling argument that the leading element in any love relationship is safe attachment and effective dependency and conflict coming from too much enmeshment. Problems in relationships develop from too much emotional distance and a lack of empathy. From infancy we are designed for connection with others. There is a famous photo that made its way around the Internet. You may have seen it, and if not you can Google it. It shows a surgeon doing a C-section on a woman and the baby's hand reaching out of the incision to hold the surgeon's hand. We need each to know there is someone in our world that cares and is tuned in to our needs right from the start of life. This basic need doesn't change through life.

In her presentation, Dr. Johnson talked about her research, which studied the stages of coping with non-responsiveness between mothers and their infants. At the first stage of experimentation, the mother is smiling and engaged with their child (emotionally attuned). Then the mother is told to stop smiling and hold a blank face. The child at first is seen making gestures to gain connection with their mother. The mother is told to hold a blank stare. The child continues to attempt to gain the mother's attention, cajoling and being funny with no response from the mother. The child then returns with frustration and anger and the mother holds the non-expressive face. The child then bursts into tears. The mother holds no response and the child then looks away (hopelessness). In adult-to-adult relationships, we follow a similar sequence to seek physical emotional resonance. If we express our needs and feelings without gaining an empathic response from our significant partner, at the initial stages we may use humor or turn up the volume to gain connection. If there continues to be a lack of empathy, we may try to cope by distracting ourselves out of our feelings and needs. This may work for a while, until we get angry and more frustrated. If our emotional requests continue to be unheard, eventually there will be a rupture in the relationship where trust is broken—an attachment wound.

Partners tune into what they see in each other, not as much with what they say. Five minutes of face-to-face undistracted contact with each other can make a massive difference to integrate a more secure responsive relationship. I have had couples sit on the couch in my office and look at each other, without saying anything. I ask them to observe each other and to notice what they feel in their bodies as they do this. In this simple practice, I have observed amazing shifts from stonewalling (where they may have been stuck in a feast of blame) to a cathartic release of emotion. We all want to connect, and yet we can become so invested in a battle to 'win' that we lose everything. This is not to say, we don't need to talk. We do.

The practice of empathic communication where one person speaks and the other just listens can be a great way to ensure you stay attuned with your partner in the future. Start the practice being a better active listener with people at work, at home, and in your day. Choose a time in your day, every day to take turns sharing the things that matter to you and a friend using a modified dialogue. It's also important to take time for yourself to know what is going on for you. Meditation or journaling is a 'good house-keeping' lifelong habit to maintain. Dr. Dan Siegal describes the value of taking "time in" in his many books about emotional intelligence and how we can develop our mirror neurons (empathy centers) through a practice of meditation. In his book, Mindsight, Dr. Siegal explains the open limbic loop and that our ability to be in resonance with each other has a powerfully positive relationship to how connected we will feel in relationship to others (34). Through a practice of being more mindful of yourself and others, the more connected you will feel and the more resonance you will experience. Your brain is changing through your life and you can be dynamic in developing healthier brain states for yourself and for others. Dr. Siegal is an advocate for teaching mindfulness to children in elementary schools. Meditation and 'time in' should be as important to the developing brain as basic mathematics. To breakthrough feelings of grief, loneliness and isolation as you move through your rebuilding, meditate!

I have come to think love is a practice and not a state. Love is a verb, an action you take. We all need to practice to get better at loving behavior. Gary Chapman, in his book "The Five Love Languages" as referenced earlier, describes the ways we communicate love and how we can get better at understanding each other's learned style. Beyond knowing how to express love, you also need to know how to express yourself when you don't feel loved. You may need patience to sit with the frustrations and hurts of your former or future partner when he or she experiences pain due to something you have done. If he or she is feeling unloved, no matter what your intentions were/are, their experience is absolutely true for them. Let go of your resistance to hear how he or she feels you have failed. Listening and feeling their experience with them, can only help you both.

When you practice the pillars of love: patience, kindness, empathy, and constancy, you will create a new capacity to ask questions. "Am I defending my self or defining my self?" You need to practice recognizing and defining your needs and feelings. You also need to be open to hear and acknowledge your partner's needs and feelings.

As you think back to 'Jennifer' at eight, imagine if she'd been able to express her embarrassment to the boy who overwhelmed her. At eight we are not taught to express authenticity. We are taught to not hurt each other's feelings; the value of the golden rule! But this kind of formative teaching can conflict with honest expressions of affection and intimacy and that is not golden! Sometimes, when you avoid saying anything hurtful in the short term, you can cause even greater long term confusion and hurt. Perhaps in elementary school we should instead be taught how to honestly navigate those difficult conversations that are loaded with emotion.

Imagine young 'Jennifer' at eight if we taught this more informative communication skill in elementary schools. She might have said, "I can see you are a thoughtful boy 'Jessie' and that you really want me to know that you like me. But when you bring me gifts and leave them on my desk, I feel embarrassed. I really want you to stop giving me presents."

This is a useful formula: saying a positive first tells the other person that they are unconditionally 'ok'. This sets them up to be able to hear you without defensive reaction. The second step is to say what aspect of their behavior is upsetting and why. The third step is to say what you need from them.

This type of dialogue creates an authentic exchange of feelings and needs with kindness and without shame. The more you practice this type of communication, the more emotional safety can grow within you and in the between of inter personal relationships.

Don't spend your life boxing in the dark, fighting imagined demons of the past. We are all in a process of learning to love better. We have all had our points of confusion; our soft spots that need caring for. If you discover you are a little like 'Max' (from the second scenario), you might say to your partner, "I want to have a great relationship with you... and I know that I can tend to close up when I'm upset or feeling vulnerable. I'm going to try hard not going to let myself do that with you, but can you help me and let me know if you sense me withdrawing from you at times?" When you find yourself in a new practice of expressing your feelings (vulnerability) and needs (to get better at love) it will be a sign you are ready to love.

You can't love anyone else unconditionally until you can love yourself unconditionally. There should never, therefore, be anything too embarrassing or shameful to talk about. When you love all of you, then you are ready to love all of someone else.

****

Breakthrough Tips to build your EQ emotional intelligence:

1. In a conversation today, try holding the space without talking. Let the other person talk and try to keep your responses to a minimum. Notice what you feel in your body as you listen.
2. Tune in to what the other person is expressing visually while they talk. What do you see? What might their body language suggest? Does what they are saying with words, match what their body suggests?
3. At every doorway, take a second to notice how you feel in your body. Do a quick head to toe check.
4. When you notice a primary feeling, locate it specifically (in your chest, shoulders, hands, or stomach).
5. Ask yourself what your feelings may be telling you?
6. Share your feelings and thinking with one trusted person later in the day sometime before you go to sleep tonight. Or, if that feels risky...
7. Journal.
8. Sweet dreams... You will sleep better tonight – I guarantee it.

****

CHAPTER 19

THE IMPACT OF BIRTH ORDER

It may be hard to believe, but your birth order really may impact how you interact in relationships with others when it comes to stress and handling change. Frank Sulloway (1996) conducted an enormous meta-analysis of birth order affects in personality development and learned interpersonal and intra-personal behaviors. In contrast, Harris (1998), and Pinker (2002) suggest that birth order does not affect personality outside of the family of origin home. The difficulty in researching birth order effects has been in dealing with research confounds of socio-economic status, family size, and methodology, Hartshorne (2007).

What Hartshorne did report from his research was that birth order was a reliable factor when it came to long-term platonic and romantic relationships of the same birth order (35). The bottom line is that we don't have sound empirical evidence to give us an empirical yes or no on long-term impacts in styles of relating. Adlerian developmental psychology maintains birth order provides needed framework to consider patterns of communication and relating.

I have some observations in working with individuals in my counseling practice, which have given me an impression of resilience patterns based on birth order. (My apologies to the scholars among you, as these are solely observations and not empirically founded). I think they may be helpful to consider because we all need to take responsibility for who we become when we are anxious. Our coping through stress may not bring out the best version of who we are. With some insight you can train yourself to gain access to a more balanced way of communicating your feelings and needs.

First Born

If you are an eldest you may tend to have a well-developed community because you learned how to make friends when you were growing up. No one was holding your hand or watching out for you on the playground in your elementary years, so you are practiced at connecting with others. You are used to the leadership position of being the child who cared for his/her younger siblings. However you may not be someone who is as practiced at intimacy and letting others help you. For this reason moving forward from a deep loss can be more of a struggle as an eldest, because you tend to be an internal processor. Your work is learning to ask for help more. Allow others in on your pain. You may tend to over function when you are anxious, rather than express your feelings of fear, loss or despair. My advice is to take stock of people you trust most and choose one person who you can practice sharing your gut wrenching feelings with. As you share your 'dark tunnel' fears and vulnerabilities, you will develop stronger attachments generally and regain an emotional homeostasis. Otherwise you may develop a kind of maniac style of connecting with people around you, which lands you a big social network but less true soft landings of deep friendship you feel supported in.

If you are an eldest, you may find yourself being somewhat controlling of middle's or youngest. You also tend to take on more responsibility and have a difficult time saying what you need. This pattern of over functioning can lead to burn out and patterns of anger and resentment. Your emotional work is to learn to allow yourself to be cared for. You can rescript your life from a scarcity, victim experience, to developed loving abundance. Your future partners otherwise may experience you as emotionally unavailable and erratic. You may tend to assume you know what others are thinking and your relationships can then become paternal or maternal. Chances are, your potential partner may love your caring ways at first, but may come to resent them as what felt good in loves first bloom, soon feels like control.

Only Child

All things being equal, if you are an only, you have grown up knowing that you are the center of your parent's universe. You haven't grown up with the competition of siblings to find your place in the family. Although in anxious times of change, you may have learned the pattern of **triangulation** with either parent to gain autonomy. When one parent says no to their child, the child may go to the other parent to divide and conquer. If that sounds like you, you may want to learn more effective ways you can talk through difficult conversations to resolution with the person you are having trouble with. An example is to say "I felt___(whatever the feeling was), when you ___(whatever the behavior was)". Clear direct communication is easy once you put this new two-step into your emotional dance.

As an only, you may have a greater level of differentiation than children who grow up with siblings because you haven't been shaped into strategies of over functioning, under functioning or invisibility. If there was something to be done in your family, you were likely responsible, practiced and accountable to the result. You probably have an easy time communicating your needs because it was probably easy to get your parents attention when you were young. Some of the challenges may be in learning how to cohabitate. You are used to your own space and so bathroom etiquette or styles for living may take some learned negotiation.

Middle Child

If you are a middle child, you tend to fit in everywhere but no one will have a clue when you are struggling. As a middle child, you are typically the one who feels invisible in the relationship. Often middle children feel unappreciated and may resort to passive aggressive underground ways to gain attention. If you are a middle child, you can be a little plotting of revenge (if you've been left). You can also be a little complicated as you may gravitate to develop emotional triangles with friends to win sides against your former partner as you regain ego strength. Practice healthier patterns as you reintegrate into your social community as a solo person. These reactive strategies of punishment only hurt you. Your work as a middle child is to become a better communicator, letting yourself be heard so that you avoid building an overwhelming case against your partner over time.

As a middle child, you may also tend to build thesis about others. Try to practice being the person who doesn't know the answer. Ask powerful questions. Take up space in your relationships. Say to yourself "Here I am...here I am". When you feel others are not listening, make body contact to get their attention. You can put a hand on the other person's shoulder or knee. Check in with people you are talking to by asking, "how did I just come across to you? ...What did you hear me say?" These are clarifying and probing tools that will really help you outgrow the invisible child syndrome.

The Youngest

As a youngest, you are typically pretty easy going. You are used to adapting to other people. You have become adept at pleasing because you needed to adapt in order to be included in the play of your older siblings. You are the baby of the family so you will find others who show up to provide you support. You tend to move through this grief process a little more easily for these reasons. You tend to observe body language in others and you can be great at negotiating. If there is a division of assets or friends, you are resilient. You have a capacity for generosity of spirit and can see the 'big picture' because you have grown up observing the rest of your birth order. Your emotional challenge is to avoid pleasing yourself out of true happiness. Take the risk to say what you need. Rock the boat a little. You can tend to go along with everyone else's needs until one day you reach a breaking point. It's not fair to people around you if you don't let them know what you are actually feeling. If you don't share your needs, how can they love you back? You may find yourself taking on a martyr style of being in the world after a relationship ends. Your need to please may feel safe for a while, but you will be prone to loneliness. Be brave. Ask for help. Communicate what matters and what you need.

Ideally you will partner up with someone who is the same in birth order as you are. A youngest does well with another youngest because you both will need to practice leadership and intention in the relationship. In this way, you won't fall into complimentary relationship patterns where one person over functions and one-person under-functions. If you are a youngest and you connect with an eldest, you may feel safe and cared for at the outset, but over time this status quo, may dwarf your spirit because you are not challenged to grow independence. If you choose to be with someone who shares your own tendencies you may be more motivated to learn how to develop traits of an eldest, middle and youngest. Growing up may be a matter of growing into a one size fits all pattern. You have observed all three-birth orders and all three styles of being are within you. Developing the ease to move from one style, one part of your personality to another, may be a sign that you have become fully adult, no longer the 'baby of the family', 'the eldest' or 'the middle'.

As a youngest, I was pretty able to get along with most people. My former husband, Michael was an eldest child growing up in his family. Our relationship was complimentary. In the early stages of our relationship, I felt comfortable to have Michael be my primary guide in our life together. Sadly, later that loving guidance felt more an evolution of control and dismissiveness. The more controlling he became, the more my anxiety notched up. In the first ten years of our lives together, Michael made most of our big picture decisions and I felt safe and secure in the knowledge that he was flying the plane so to speak. This worked perfectly for me in the earlier years of our marriage. As I grew up, however, I felt constricted and our dance of life showed up in symptoms of misplaced anger. I use this as an example to show how your birth order can impact the way you will partner in your own relationship. It can be easy to fall into these complimentary relationship styles, which feel comfortable because they resemble our childhood experiences. However, over time you may find yourself frustrated in the limitations of holding that static role.

When you have an understanding of your own birth order and how your own positioning may influence your choices to be over responsible, slightly dependent, or to some extent invisible, practice other styles. You might be explicit about your intention with your friends or you might just subtly start acting differently when opportunities arise. It helps you build more compassion for others when you are conscious about their birth order too. For example, if you experience a controlling friend, consider that he or she may be an eldest. As you speak up more and take a leadership position, you will be helping him or her grow. You also won't feel as resentful that you are always doing something he or she wants to do.

****

Breakthrough ways to outgrow your birth order:

1. Write a list of your strengths and weaknesses.
2. Write a list of each of your siblings' strengths and weaknesses.
3. If you are an only, do this with your closest long-term friends.
4. Notice ways you can celebrate your strengths and develop your weaknesses.
5. What relationship in your life today best polarizes birth order effects for you?
6. Have a conversation with that person to partner in mutual growth.
7. Challenge yourself to go to your next social event practicing a new perspective in birth order. For example, if you tend to choose the restaurant and you are an eldest, let someone else choose the venue. If you are a youngest and you tend to order what everyone else orders, be the first to choose something unique. You'll think of lots of creative ways you can have fun trying on new styles of being.

****

CHAPTER 20

PARENTS

I can't impress upon you enough how important it is to be current with your parents and talk through those relationships until you feel truly adult and autonomous. Your parents are a massive resource in your own growth and process while you are learning to love better. How do you feel about how your Mother lived her life? Are there things you wish she had done differently? How about your Father? Is/was he fulfilled through his life? Have those conversations with your parents while they are still alive. If they have already passed on, you might do some research with your siblings on these topics. It's truly remarkable how often we can repeat our parents' life experiences in both good and bad ways.

Additionally if your parents are alive, do you feel like an adult when you are with them? Or do you feel controlled or 'parented' by them still? I recall working with a client who I will refer to as 'Debbie' in the Dumps. She was discouraged because, although she could easily connect with potential partners, none of her relationships seemed to endure. Looking back at her history with men, she found she either felt overwhelmed by them, or she became totally controlling of them (which didn't work very well either). As we explored what exactly happened that led to these disappointed dating patterns for 'Debbie', we discovered that this polarization could best be understood in what I call 'the masculine – feminine relationship paradigm'.

We all have both male and female styles of relating. If you are a woman, your feminine side is nurturing, curious, open and ready to be loved. Your male side is clear, well boundaried, structured and initiating. Depending on whom 'Debbie' was with, she tended to either feel intimidated (with confident men) or frustrated (with passive men). Essentially 'Debbie' was shaping her personality according to the man she started dating. If she was in her male side (with a man who seemed less sure of himself), she was keeping track of time, cutting off conversation, and being directive about the details of where, when and how their time together should shape up. Her defended masculine side was intuiting the insecurities of her date and essentially communicating "Shape up or ship out" with all the dismissive behaviors mentioned above… and so her dates, time and time again feeling a little overwhelmed by her abrupt style, shipped out. If she were in her feminine side (when she felt somewhat intimidated by the man) she couldn't decide what to order in a restaurant, she would struggle about what to wear when she saw him, and adapted her schedule to meet his every need. In this process she was so indecisive, her potential mate never had a chance to actually know who she truly was. Dating an invisible woman, he would lose interest and again, ship out.

If this pattern sounds like something you have experienced, you may want to see a counselor or psychotherapist to explore your childhood relationship with your Father. This type of polarized patterning can sometimes suggest you may have locked in some grief or feelings of abandonment because an interruption or lost relationship with your Father. Sure enough, in 'Debbie's' family of origin, Debbie had lost contact with her Father after her parents divorced at her age of ten. She had seen him once or twice a year since her parents' divorce, but with her parents' contentious separation and divorce, 'Debbie' had paid the price. The grief and politics from her family morphing had left her with a life wounding and deep confusion about men. "My Father left my Mother but he also left me. Maybe all men will leave me." Sadly 'Debbie' had lost trust that she was enough. She never really developed a true sense of who she was in relationship with men. Instead she developed an anxious attachment style, which is high on intuition and reaction. As a result, she never had two feet on the ground with a solid footing in both her male and female self. She was afraid to love with her whole self because she hadn't healed from the loss of her father at age ten. If your Father is alive, it can be so helpful to get in touch with him. Ask your Father why he left your Mother? If you lost contact with your Father for any reason, talk to him so you can start to understand his truth. Without challenging your knowledge of your Father and the ways you have been relating to men, you are guaranteed to repeat the same patterns over and over again. If you want to gain new results, you will need to do something differently.

In a process of reconnecting with her Father and exploring his experience of the divorce, she came to realize that her Father and Mother were simply a poor fit. The confusion that her Father had abandoned her childhood family came to be understood in the lens parental alienation. These anxieties and conflicts undermine many parental relationships in the wake of family morphing through divorce.

Twenty years ago, there was not a lot of information with regards to parental alienation and how important it is to keep politics away from children. If you've forgotten, you may want to re-read the earlier chapter on family morphing. Happily, 'Debbie' was able to complete some amazing Father – Daughter therapy and today they enjoy a loving and connected relationship. The good news for 'Debbie' is that she is now able to be her self with any man. She no longer worries that men will leave her. In fact she has found that this new practice, to engage her male and female self, gives her a new confidence in all her relationships (at home and work). With new understanding of her Father and by re-assessing the challenges she experienced with her Mother's volatility, she has come to see that her Father had "bravely left a toxic stuck relationship with my Mom". Today her Father enjoys a loving and enduring relationship with his new wife of twenty years. Debbie's father is actually coaching Debbie in the now, as she explores her dating options with a whole new optimism and bag of tools drawn from her masculine and feminine self! I love this family of origin work! It's so rewarding to see these paradigm shifts in families who learn to think in more connected, authentic, loving styles. Our own families can be enormous emotional resources as we develop through life.

****

Breakthrough Tips:

1. As you think of your Mother or your Father, how could their lives have been more fulfilled? How is that information for your life today?

2. Do your best to heal any emotional cut-offs you have with your parents, so that the confusion of the past doesn't limit your capacity in the present. Otherwise you may fall into pleasing patterns that polarize your masculine and feminine behaviors when it comes to relating.

3. If you are a woman, your feminine patterns may be: nurturing but lacking boundaries so you tend to burn out. Some may see you as 'dizzy' around men. You tend to dumb down in order to fit into what you imagine your man would perceive as attractive. This is a big trap!

4. If you are a woman, your masculine patterns may be: controlling and directive. You have strong boundaries, but they may be so strong that you are unavailable. Men may be a little frightened by you. Certainly you are writing them out of a role because you are so capable!

5. If you are a man, your feminine patterns may be: nurturing but lacking boundaries. It's hard for you to make a decision and you wind up letting the woman decide where and when your dates will occur. This may work for a while, but your own lack of clarity may totally frustrate the women and you also may get tired of never doing what you actually want to do.

6. If you are a man, your masculine patterns may be: controlling and directive. You have strong boundaries, but you may find yourself doing all the talking or coming up with all the ideas… which is a little boring after a while, no? Practice doing things that exercise both parts of your psyche: For the masculine: make decisions, suggest where to go for your dates, open or close doors, make the reservations, buy flowers for your date. Write a list of other ways your masculine self shows up. For the feminine: take photos, write notes, do nurturing things, notice how your other seems to feel, let the grocery man carry your groceries to your car. Write a list of other ways your feminine self shows up!

****

Age Differences

Talking about age differences can be so emotional because falling in love doesn't always happen in conscious ways. You don't always know what it is that draws you into a relationship that has a big age gap. You just fall in love because trust, emotional safety, attraction, compatibility and unconscious recognition of family features all occur. We then flip the 'fall in love' switch to on. If love was a completely pragmatic process, considering aging, common interests and power dynamics, you should choose a partner who is within five years of your own age. With the common ground that follows, you are more likely to develop an equal partnership over time and avoid the power struggles that come with age differences some times.

As you imagine your life in latter years, if you are partnered with someone a lot older than you, there may be a good chance of him or her passing away due to mental or physical decline before you. You may be on your own when it comes to your own aging years. If you have maintained close friendships and developed your supports this may be less of a concern. Still, 60% of seniors today report they are lonely (36).

If you have lost contact with either of your parents, often a wide age gap can suggest an unconscious desire or longing to be cared for unconditionally, in a way you missed out with your parent(s). If you had an unavailable or controlling Father, and you are a woman, you may be attracted to an older partner in an unconscious need to heal your unmet needs with your Father. If you are a man and you had an unavailable mother, you may be attracted to an older partner for similar reasons. With awareness, you can practice 'your voice' and express your needs and feelings in a way that keeps the partnership in balance. If you are a man and you grew up with an older sister, you may also be attracted to older women since it feels congruent with feeling happy in childhood.

It is not a bad thing if you find yourself choosing a partner much older than you. It's just good to be conscious of what is driving your attraction, and it may be worth re-reading the previous section on parents. If you are a man who has been dumped by your former partner, you may look for a much younger female to have more emotional control as you regain ego strength. The difference in your age may provide you a temporary confidence. You may however be setting yourself up for a future loss as the gap in your age shows up with the inability to participate in mutually stimulating activities (body, mind and spirit).

Having addressed all these factors, there are also times when love just happens and refuses to follow a well thought out, rational path. These pieces of insight are simply guidelines and not intended as rules for living. They are insights from one student of the heart to another. In real life, real time, keep some of these things in mind and when you feel love happening, flip that switch to on.

CHAPTER 21

LEARNING OUTCOMES FROM PART TWO

You are your own vehicle of change. You have all the wisdom you need right inside of you and in the reflections you have gained from your family, friends and colleagues. The more your awareness grows about who you have been in your birth order, modeling after your caregiver relationships, and as you practice new positive internal and external loops, the more capacity you now have to transform your life. You may start to notice a lot more in your every moment. My clients say to me "it's as if the sky feels fuller, and life has become more Technicolor". Your perceptions and ability to engage with others is starting to go way up because you have more calm. You are starting to see it's not the problems that have occurred in your past that matter most. It's what you have thought about those problems that have mattered most. All the subtle information you formed in your right, emotional brain is healing. And you now have new connections forming in your left-brain where you are integrating new stories about your past, present and what you want to anticipate in your future. Your brain is growing. As your internal patterns shift from fear and anger to loving curiosity, you will notice you gain more overall ease and connection. How you have thought about your past relationship, and how you will choose to think in the future, truly sets you up in how you will experience new challenges in the future.

Relax into your curiosity and celebrate all the ways you can continue to grow, love, communicate, play, exercise, and develop. Try doing new things. Try speaking up more. Try on asking for help when you need it. When you do, you will be growing new neural connections in your brain which give you the sense of being more and more at home in your body, mind and spirit no matter who you are with. This will bring your overall stress down and your overall experience of love way up every day. You will be defining yourself, not avoiding conflict or defending your stake. Take care of yourself. Eat well. Exercise. Be social. Sleep well. Try to *feel* one new feeling every day. *learn* one new thing every day. Try to *do* one thing new every day. Enjoy your life and look for things you are grateful for. Life is beautiful. Here's a quick review of Part Two:

Choose Well

1. You can choose a more suited partner once you step out of old habits of attraction.
2. Know your old relationship blueprint so you can make a positive change in the next one, as well as reinforce positive components of past relationships.
3. It's easy to fall in love, but you need to ask yourself if you will love the life you will live with your new partner.
4. We need each other to get better at love. Wholeheartedness comes with embracing our 'whole self' and loving the 'whole' of another human being without the need to fix him or her. As you change the internal story about yourself, your external experience will shift too!
5. We are in this world together and if we trust our experiences in the world as being part of a collective learning, anxiety is reduced and creativity and love evolves. In this case, we should all be open to new experiences as breakup breakthroughs not breakup breakdowns.
6. Confidence comes from taking a healthy risk to say what you need & what you are feeling.
7. Who you are at work is the same as who you are in love.
8. Birth order matters. Know your birth order and work to integrate your learning as a youngest, middle and eldest.
9. Stay current with your parents. If you have any cut-offs try to heal your past rifts (unless they are irreconcilable, or in cases of abuse have put you at personal physical or emotional risk).

10. Are you balanced in your masculine and feminine patterns? Keep a footing in both.

The Heart and the head

1. There is a balance between thinking and feeling yourself into the right relationship.
2. BE yourself in a 'wholehearted' way. One of the biggest traps is trying to present what you imagine might be your most presentable self. This takes a lot of work to keep up and you will probably resent yourself or your partner over time (when it becomes exhaustive to maintain an inauthentic you). Being all pleasing, you are likely to wake up one day and realize that you have become a chameleon, taking on the culture and style of who ever you are with.
3. Accept and appreciate who YOU are. The Desiderata or the Dalai Lama rules for living are timeless inspirations to keep posted in your home. As a student of the head and heart you are learning to be whole.
4. Practice compassion for your truly flawed human self. We are all spiritual beings learning to love in varying degrees and in varying ways. The more whole and transparent you are about what you feel and need, the less inner demon dialogues will possess you.
5. The less self-critical you are, the more non-judgmental, empathic and loving you will be for others. The more open you are the more capacity you will have with others.

Commit to New Practices for Life

1. When you get up, check in with yourself. How you are feeling?
2. You morning mood may be expressed in the clothes you choose to wear today. Or you may want to intentionally shift your morning mood. Are you feeling conservative, playful, outgoing, sexy, and demure? Is that what you want to feel? What clothes express those qualities best for you today? Wear that! In Part Three you will learn how to have fun with your style as you operationalize wholeheartedness and you open a new door.

PART 3

INTEGRATION, ALL OF YOU OPENING YOUR NEW DOOR

CHAPTER 22

BRING ON YOUR MOJO!

This is the door to your own Olympics - Faster, Stronger, Higher! Are you Game? You are playing with 'all' of you now because you are no longer distracted by the failings of the past. Of course those events happened, and now you can focus on what is going to be relevant to your future. Think of this as a time to participate in your own personal Olympics. Let your most trained self, work in perfect symmetry of body, mind and spirit 'be'ing. You aren't forcing or competing in your life but you are trained, like an athlete, to live in your best awareness zone. What have you dreamed about? Fantasy or reality, when is the last time you felt really alive? What do you look like when you feel you are most alive? Sitting in this exact moment (because reading, you are probably sitting) are your shoulders down, your arms open…is your head up, down, or are you reading standing? Is there a bounce in your step? What will it take for you to feel in your zone right now in this moment? Is there some part of you still needing more space, more breath, and more bandwidth? Is there an expression you have in your body that you can choose with intention?

Let your imagination discover who you are. What is most important to you right now? Are you a Blue Heron - peaceful? Are you holding your arms wide and open to the air – exhilarated? Are you a tree – planted strong and grounded? Are you a Buddha – all loving? Are you the Sun – warm and whole? Are you the Ocean – inspired? (That is mine because I love the fresh clean tingle of swimming in salt water). I imagine that waves are full of fresh possibility. My personal work is to practice not over thinking. As I imagine the ocean I let my thoughts wash through me like waves. I imagine myself surfing my anxieties or doubts and release to the source – the ocean. I work towards my calm under the surface.

Who are you? Why are you here? Feel the feelings you associate with being in your highest self and choose a body expression that fits for you. Do it now. When you wake up tomorrow morning, commit to stand for one minute in this imagined pose and say out loud what you want to be more often – "I'm peaceful". "I'm exhilarated". "I am strong and grounded". "I am loving". This simple practice has an amazing effect on your brain pathways and puts an intention in your day that will lead you to miracles.

I'm aware that we all have our roadblocks or shoulder saboteurs that tell us NOOOO... "I am small", "I can't do this", "who do I think I am?" "I can't write", "I can't play", and "I have no time". "My children are my first priority", "my job is pressing", "I'm broke", "I can't afford running shoes", and "I am not ready". "I'll just hide in my cave another month". These are natural aspects of your current reality and symptoms of your life in change. When I was at my yoga retreat in Sayulita, for part of our practice we were in the middle of a jungle. Around us were these Cucaracha birds, which would make the most hideous sounds... "Screech squawk screech". No matter how much our Yogi would shoo them away, they would continue to garble and squawk beside our yoga Palapa. The saboteur is like that. We are bound to have internal noise showing up to activate our fears and judgments at times. Be at peace with them. Feel the fear and do it anyways!! When this happens, redirect yourself and focus your thoughts to the positive. (We found out later, by the way, it is mating season in February for the Cucaracha birds. Apparently they celebrate Valentines month too).

If you truly want to feel good again, you will find a way to overcome saboteur distractions. If you are time pressured, you may decide to get up an hour earlier. If you have a difficulty with concentration at work and your responsibilities are falling behind, take a full mental break in time blocks going to work, at lunch or at the end of the day. Renew and de-stress you so you become work ready. Cutting back on the quantity of time spent at your work will help you regain your quality outputs. You are in an evolu-

tion, not a revolution. Just make one commitment you can be true to...
One day at a time can mean try one new thing every day.

One Step at a Time

The better you feel about yourself, the more can contribute in your day-to-day. The healthier you feel, the more capacity you will have: parenting your children, collaborating at work, enjoying your friends, and your community. The more mindful you are, the more others will be drawn to you. The more connected you start to *be*, the sooner you will feel good about your whole life.

Step by step, you are totally leaving the insecurities of your past thinking and grieving behind. There is nothing you can't say, hear or challenge yourself with. Can you talk to that attractive someone in the groceries store now? No problem! Now that you see yourself in a context of 'we', you are never alone. Even at the grocery store, you are not alone.

Have you noticed that the sky seems bluer lately and that the people around you are so much friendlier? It's not them. It's you! You are friendlier because you aren't living in an inner war with fear and pain anymore. After doing your relationship timeline and understanding family learning, you are now able to see your past in a perspective of your 'whole life'. Every new step every day, you are powerfully faster, stronger and living in higher consciousness.

One of the amazing things about the process of coming alive after a breakup is how you get a suddenly clearer vision on the world. You will notice this new aliveness gives you more courage socially. You become less 'you' focused and more 'other' focused. You will start to be more aware of what is going on for other people because you are not feeling so overwhelmed by yourself anymore. You are no longer surviving in a war with pain but in the discovery of your creation. You've probably started noticing other people's body language more, hearing cues about their life that you may have been missing during the more intense earlier stages of your own grief in Part One and Two.

This is an exciting phase you are in. You will gain insight as to how much have been your own worst enemy in the past few months. Oh my gosh! Life has been happening all along and you may wonder what took you so long to come alive. Just remember how you are feeling right now, so you can remind yourself on days your saboteur starts bogging you down. The thing that really starts to change is an insight that you can embrace all the things that happen in your life. In a sense it's an awareness that what is, just is. Your relationship ended. It just did. You will have new relationships. You just will. Change is painful. Change is also rewarding. It just is.

Listen deeply to what others say to you. You may find yourself more able to truly stand in other people's perspective. Your myopic bias so common in the 'survival' stages referred to earlier, is forever broadened because you are relaxed. You have more working memory because you are not so stressed out all the time. You may realize now that a few months back you were only hearing and seeing the things that were congruent with 'my world has fallen apart'. Jon Kabot-Zinn, founding Executive Director of the Center for Mindfulness in Medicine, conducted a research project whereby he had a group of students watch a video of a basketball game. The students were asked to count the number of basketball hoops the players scored in a short video clip of a game. The students all came up with a range of scores, noticing only the basketball players and the number of shots on the baskets. He then played the same footage they had just watched and asked the students to look at the right side of the video where a man in a gorilla suit would come out and taunt the players. There was laughter and great surprise as he found none of the students noticed this funny mascot in their first viewing because they were so focused on counting the number of shots on goal. The research showed that we can have a narrow field of focus and whatever we are looking for is generally what we will see. This research reminds us of how important it is to observe and listen with a child's mind of unknowing. Psychologists at the University of Utah replicated this research in a similar project, this time with the students themselves passing a basketball while a person in a gorilla suit walked past. They found that only 40% of the students noticed the person in the gorilla suit, results they attribute to 'inattention blindness' and varying capacity of working memory (Seegmiller, 2010).

The bottom line is, welcome back to your full life and all the wonderful little details you may have been missing for the past while. It's a good world that your acorn fell into and there are a lot of details in it that you can now enjoy.

****

Breakthrough Tips:

1. Recall your carefree, most creative self in elementary, middle, high school, university or post-graduate school?
2. When in your life have you felt you're happiest?
3. What activities did you like doing at the time?
4. Were you happiest with your friends or alone?
5. How would your best friend describe you then?
6. Who did you most admire (in your family or social networks, on television or at the movies)?
7. What did you value most at that time of your life: adventure, learning, companionship, family, music, sports, the arts, creativity, challenges, spiritual learning? Any others?
8. Circle five values that matter the most to you.
9. How do those values show up in your life today, at home, at work, with your friends, with your family?
10. If you notice your values are missing in an aspect of your life, what can you do differently starting today to be more in line with what you value?

****

Hire a Professional Stylist

This may be a time to be more conscious of your style of dressing. It can be helpful and fun to employ someone to help you update and coordinate your wardrobe. What is uniquely expressed about you in your wardrobe style? If hiring a professional stylist sounds expensive or too self-indulgent, invite a long-time friend who knows you, body, mind and spirit to give you feedback. Does the 'you' on the outside speak congruently for the 'you' on the inside? Our wardrobes are like rose bushes, they thrive with a good pruning each season! Often it's hard to do our own pruning and it takes an expert to assess the best ways trim and balance a wardrobe. Were you hiding parts of your personality during your previous relationship? Is there a more carefree or sexy you waiting to be reborn now that you are single again? Taking a creative action such defining your unique image really helps in the process of building confidence. You are worth it after all!

Too often we hold on to our 'fat clothes' or wait to wear our 'thin clothes'. This type of thinking will clutter your closets and your feelings about your body. While you wait to wear your thin clothes, you are putting yourself in waiting. Holding on to your fat clothes… says what about yourself-image? If you don't have things you feel good in at the weight you are currently, buy yourself some new clothes that fit you today. If your finances are tight, check out a second hand clothing store—treasure troves of style.

Clear out the self-doubt and feel good today, as you are, right now! Make peace with your body and start to enjoy it as it is. I recall getting a panicked email from a client who signed up on an on-line dating site. She had her first invitation for a date and the panic was her fear that she should put off going on the date until she lost ten pounds. She described her feelings of shame that without losing the additional weight, she would surely be rejected by the potential suitor. I asked her why she had so many conditions on her best friend, her body.

It was as if she was saying she wouldn't go out with her unless she lost weight. That sounds like conditional love to me. "I will only love you, body, when you are ten pounds lighter". Wow, would anyone say that to his or her best friend? I doubt it. Would she have said that to her children? "We aren't going to the playground today kids, unless you lose weight". This sounds crazy, but that is essentially what she was saying to her body, her faithful friend who needs to carry her spirit through her whole entire life!

As we see our bodies and observe ourselves in relationship with self, we have a primary opportunity to develop unconditional love and care. Celebrate the body you live in. Play, dance, and move it! Don't starve it or stuff it with crap. Forget the trendy new fad diets. Eat food that you know is good fuel. Refocus your attention to things you love to do. The sooner you engage new playful habits, the sooner you will naturally shift to your most ideal body weight.

In the process of dating, you may feel overcome with the worry that he (or she) may not like you or find your body attractive. What would you say to someone new if he (or she) criticized a very dear friend of yours? Be at least as loyal to your own body (your true friend for life) as you are to your friends. Stand by who you are and what you look like. The most amazing thing is that the love and gratitude you engage for yourself, lights you up. Appreciating all of you (flaws included) makes you more beautiful than you've ever imagined yourself to be. Looking beautiful is all about what's going on inside of you. You may think this advice is a huge contradiction to the recommendation to hire a professional stylist. I think not. If we are grateful for our bodies, we also want to put care into the way we dress them up. Enjoy, be playful with your best friend ever. She will thank you.

Stylists typically come to your home to check out your wardrobe, weeding out the things that are not current or flattering to your body type, skin tone, age and lifestyle. They will then go with you to the store to help you shop, working within your budget, lifestyle, and color scheme. They are professionals who know where to shop and how to get the best value and can help you put your best foot forward. With the right things in mind, you will start to have more fun living in the beautiful body your spirit calls 'home'. Time and time again, we can be so hard on ourselves, unhappy with various aspects of our shape. This is a sad trap to get stuck in because the worse you feel about yourselves, the less inclined you will be to take care of yourselves. The clothes you wear should make you smile. In your right clothes, you set your spirit free to express your most authentic self.

Feel good about who you are today, and embrace all of your parts. Be grateful for your health, your spirit, and all of the privilege around you. Thank you, thank you, and thank you. There is a stylist that is just right for you. Check on line for professionals in your area or ask for recommendations at your favorite clothing store. You might even twitter or send a Facebook request out for someone others might recommend. If not, call a good friend and invite her to be 100% honest in a reassessment of what your style currently says about you.

When you are done with your wardrobe and style makeover, you may want to hire a professional photographer, or your friend, to take some new headshots of you which you can put up on various dating sites or your Facebook home page. It's not that you are jumping 'headshot' first into a new rebound relationship. It wouldn't hurt though to connect with other people like you who could do with some new company. Think of on line dating as a support group. Meeting new people who have gone (or are going) through their own transition will normalize your fears of being alone. And, you may offer a new optimism to someone else who is not as far along in the process as you are. Helping someone else is a great way to feel more at peace within yourself. It also reminds you of how far you've come as you crystalize the wisdom you have gained thus far. All the things you can do to bring your stresses down, remember, brings love up in your life. The more separate you feel, the more anxiety you will experience. You might even have fun when you have coffee with someone you get to choose to meet. Remember this moving forward process involves doing a little bit of this and a little bit of that. The more you participate in any or all of these ideas, the faster you will get back into your game of life. It's time to have fun again.

This may be a time to be more conscious of your style of dressing. It can be helpful and fun to employ someone to help you update and coordinate your wardrobe. What is uniquely expressed about you in your wardrobe style? If hiring a professional stylist sounds expensive or too self-indulgent, invite a long-time friend who knows you, body, mind and spirit to give you feedback. Does the 'you' on the outside speak congruently for the 'you' on the inside? Our wardrobes are like rose bushes, they thrive with a good pruning each season! Often it's hard to do our own pruning and it takes an expert to assess the best ways trim and balance a wardrobe. Were you hiding parts of your personality during your previous relationship? Is there a more carefree or sexy you waiting to be reborn now that you are single again? Taking a creative action such defining your unique image really helps in the process of building confidence. You are worth it after all!

Too often we hold on to our 'fat clothes' or wait to wear our 'thin clothes'. This type of thinking will clutter your closets and your feelings about your body. While you wait to wear your thin clothes, you are putting yourself in waiting. Holding on to your fat clothes… says what about yourself-image? If you don't have things you feel good in at the weight you are currently, buy yourself some new clothes that fit you today. If your finances are tight, check out a second hand clothing store—treasure troves of style.

Clear out the self-doubt and feel good today, as you are, right now! Make peace with your body and start to enjoy it as it is. I recall getting a panicked email from a client who signed up on an on-line dating site. She had her first invitation for a date and the panic was her fear that she should put off going on the date until she lost ten pounds. She described her feelings of shame that without losing the additional weight, she would surely be rejected by the potential suitor. I asked her why she had so many conditions on her best friend, her body.

It was as if she was saying she wouldn't go out with her unless she lost weight. That sounds like conditional love to me. "I will only love you, body, when you are ten pounds lighter". Wow, would anyone say that to his or her best friend? I doubt it. Would she have said that to her children? "We aren't going to the playground today kids, unless you lose weight". This sounds crazy, but that is essentially what she was saying to her body, her faithful friend who needs to carry her spirit through her whole entire life!

As we see our bodies and observe ourselves in relationship with self, we have a primary opportunity to develop unconditional love and care. Celebrate the body you live in. Play, dance, and move it! Don't starve it or stuff it with crap. Forget the trendy new fad diets. Eat food that you know is good fuel. Refocus your attention to things you love to do. The sooner you engage new playful habits, the sooner you will naturally shift to your most ideal body weight.

In the process of dating, you may feel overcome with the worry that he (or she) may not like you or find your body attractive. What would you say to someone new if he (or she) criticized a very dear friend of yours? Be at least as loyal to your own body (your true friend for life) as you are to your friends. Stand by who you are and what you look like. The most amazing thing is that the love and gratitude you engage for yourself, lights you up. Appreciating all of you (flaws included) makes you more beautiful than you've ever imagined yourself to be. Looking beautiful is all about what's going on inside of you. You may think this advice is a huge contradiction to the recommendation to hire a professional stylist. I think not. If we are grateful for our bodies, we also want to put care into the way we dress them up. Enjoy, be playful with your best friend ever. She will thank you.

Stylists typically come to your home to check out your wardrobe, weeding out the things that are not current or flattering to your body type, skin tone, age and lifestyle. They will then go with you to the store to help you shop, working within your budget, lifestyle, and color scheme. They are professionals who know where to shop and how to get the best value and can help you put your best foot forward. With the right things in mind, you will start to have more fun living in the beautiful body your spirit calls 'home'. Time and time again, we can be so hard on ourselves, unhappy with various aspects of our shape. This is a sad trap to get stuck in because the worse you feel about yourselves, the less inclined you will be to take care of yourselves. The clothes you wear should make you smile. In your right clothes, you set your spirit free to express your most authentic self.

Feel good about who you are today, and embrace all of your parts. Be grateful for your health, your spirit, and all of the privilege around you. Thank you, thank you, and thank you. There is a stylist that is just right for you. Check on line for professionals in your area or ask for recommendations at your favorite clothing store. You might even twitter or send a Facebook request out for someone others might recommend. If not, call a good friend and invite her to be 100% honest in a reassessment of what your style currently says about you.

When you are done with your wardrobe and style makeover, you may want to hire a professional photographer, or your friend, to take some new headshots of you which you can put up on various dating sites or your Facebook home page. It's not that you are jumping 'headshot' first into a new rebound relationship. It wouldn't hurt though to connect with other people like you who could do with some new company. Think of on line dating as a support group. Meeting new people who have gone (or are going) through their own transition will normalize your fears of being alone. And, you may offer a new optimism to someone else who is not as far along in the process as you are. Helping someone else is a great way to feel more at peace within yourself. It also reminds you of how far you've come as you crystalize the wisdom you have gained thus far. All the things you can do to bring your stresses down, remember, brings love up in your life. The more separate you feel, the more anxiety you will experience. You might even have fun when you have coffee with someone you get to choose to meet. Remember this moving forward process involves doing a little bit of this and a little bit of that. The more you participate in any or all of these ideas, the faster you will get back into your game of life. It's time to have fun again.

****

When you did your resume, what stood out for you about your most positive traits? Write out your five favorites and keep the list with you in your wallet as a kind of talisman of your commitment to love. I love myself because I am:

1, _____,

2, _____,

3, _____,

4, _____, and

5, _____.

Next, go through your photo albums prior to your last relationship. Choose a photo of yourself where you see those five traits most vividly and shrink the photo to a wallet size. Visual reminders have been found to be more effective than written words.

Every time you open your wallet to pay for something, you will be reminded of your happiest most confident self. You will also be reminded of your life habits, which fed your bliss when the photo was taken. These habits, when engaged, will guarantee to give you a similar return in happiness and confidence today. What were you doing at the time the photo was taken? Broaden your scope. Recall your prior activities: job, social connections, which you maintained in that stage of your life. The great thing about doing this exercise is that it helps you recall things that are natural for you. It helps your brain bounce your thinking back into healthy life scripts...from victim, scarcity scripts to possibility scripts— your winning formula.

****

CHAPTER 23

LOOK WHO'S TAKING THE FIRST STEP NOW

This chapter is your 'kick in the butt' to develop your social life as a single person. Having lived life as a "couple", it can be a social challenge to re-introduce you as a solo flyer. Exercise your inner Amelia Earhart (the first female pilot to fly solo) or Charles Lindbergh (nick named Lucky Lindy, American Aviator, inventor, author, social activist), spread your wings and plan an "I am single" party. You might even suggest a BYOS "Bring your own Single". It's a fun way to create a social event that first identifies you as ready to date, and secondly sets an opportunity for others (including you) to be in a setting with other single people.

Many of your friends will have a friend who is single and who may appreciate this pay it forward initiative. There is a good chance that you will also enjoy the company of your friends' friends. Having a party can feel like a daunting proposition. Even attending a party solo can feel overwhelming. But seriously, if you look back at your social calendar and recall how you and your former partner attended social events, were you joined at the hip? Probably not. Is it really all that daunting to think about launching your solo social self? When you think about it, isn't it more liberating than terrifying? You don't have to worry if your partner wants to leave, isn't having a great time, or whether he or she feels happy. So why do we sweat about the idea of enjoying the freedom of being uniquely individual at a party? Just imagine yourself flying Amelia or Lucky Lindy style across the Atlantic Ocean for the first time. Throw caution to the wind and just do it.

One of the things that I hear most from clients is the loneliness they feel in being on their own. I generally respond to say: "This is probably the ONLY time in the rest of your life that you will get to be on your own. Why not take it all in and enjoy it?" I know, you worry, that's why. I know those worries you have: "What if I'm on my own forever?" "What do people think?" "What if I make a mistake?" "What do they say about me, my family, my breakup?" You worry when people in your community pin 'failure', 'weakness' or 'brokenness' on you. Worse, you may cringe to think 'they' feel sorry for you! They may judge you as self-absorbed, weak, flawed, and avoid you like a bad social virus?

Or they may be jealous. They may wish they had your courage and see you as a 'success' that you (possibly unlike them) are living honestly. The truth is you can't be certain of the potential impact of a judgmental rumor mill or even the promise of kind support. You can only be certain that in every moment of your transition you can count on yourself. You are the judge and champion of your own life and it's yourself that you face in the mirror every day. Yours are the inner voices you can count on and never escape. Let your life be the incontrovertible evidence of your worth and growth, as a human being, as a parent, as a life partner, and as a friend. The world needs more honesty. Honesty starts within. It's who you are, whom you allow to manifest in your life, every moment of every day. Own your learning.

This brings me back to the value of having a wingman. I recently heard a story at one of my book club meetings about a woman who went dancing with her newly single friend. On this occasion, the single friend ended up in a titillating flirtation with a man who was young enough to be her own son! This is when your wingman should glide right in to rescue you from making a huge mistake in integrity and spirit. Sadly, this is not what happened that particular evening and the friend let the flirtation take hold. What should have been a brief flirtation landed her in a tryst she may regret today. In the strange stages of newly single, for many, the solid structures of integrity can be forgotten. You will thank your wingman one day. He/she is the one who saves you from making poor judgment calls you can't take back. If your confidence is down, chances are your judgment may be too. In social situations such as that, who is your wingman? One of the only things you can take with you wherever you go is your integrity. When you are a newly single, it really helps to have someone who loves you enough to rein you in when your impulses take over. They help you to say no.

Enjoy being single and learning about yourself by meeting new people. But, with the help of careful reflection and a good wingman, hold on to your compass! Go get your hair done, join a favorite boot camp, put on your favorite music, re-decorate your home space, call your old friends, and let the world know you are back.

Two of the most helpful practices I had during my adjustment years of being on my own after divorce, were to commit to a daily practice of running, and to indulge in a regular therapeutic massage. When you return to a life on your own, it can be so healing to get a massage. The body produces oxytocin when you are hugged, touched, and massaged. It may be a while before you can expect this kind of physical contact on a regular basis, much less engage in sex (a primary way to access the attachment hormone oxytocin which gives you feelings of security and calm). In the meantime, massage can be very healing.

I'm a firm believer in paying for support when support is not available. Babysitters, housecleaning services, a life coach, and a good massage therapist, are all great investments if you can afford them. If not access your friends and family to help out. You might even share babysitters, or clean each of your homes in succession together. In buddying up, your friends can provide a safe holding for anxieties. The more supported you feel, the more you are able to care for yourself, and your children, and be attentive and productive at work. This in turn allows you to move forward through the grief of loss towards healing and a new life.

Start doing the things you love to do. Are there any childhood hobbies you have let go of in the past ten years? Is there a bucket list waiting to be discovered? Are you a budding rock star, photographer, athlete, or artist? As you start doing some of these activities, you will naturally discover a whole new circle of friends who are like-minded. Start having fun.

****

Breakthrough tips:

1. Cherish your old friendships that are anchors to your past, present and future, but at the same time, develop new friendships with others who are also single. The perspective of fresh relationships can give you a break from dwelling in the past.

2. Have a house / apartment warming party, to re-establish you are your own identity and ready to start socializing again even with others who are coupled.

3. Thank your friends for the support and encouragement they have given. This is so important! Don't take your friends for granted. Be grateful and appreciate everything. This positivity is good for your brain and prevents you from burning out your friends' gracious spirits.

4. Who is your wingman? Consider all your dearest friends. Is there one person who's wisdom and caring you feel confident has your best interests in mind? Check in with him/her regularly as a mentor and values anchor. Give him/ her permission to be honest with you; to help you with your blind spots.

5. How do you define fun? (Dancing, gardening, running, skiing, knitting, rock climbing, singing or learning to play a musical instrument?) Start doing it today!

****

CHAPTER 24

YOU GUESSED IT, NO REBOUNDS

Please! No rebound relationships! Quick fixes delay you from getting to know who you are and discovering what you really want. This chapter reminds you not to leap into dating after a breakup or divorce. If your first forays showed signs of bad relationship patterns, take time out of the dating scene and learn to be you again.

Otherwise you will tend to want to fill the emotional void, rather than heal and start a relationship when you are fully whole. We have evolved from our Neanderthal ancestors who swung from tree to tree mating for procreation and moving on when offspring were old enough to be self-sufficient (the proverbial Seven Year Itch relates to this). Don't jump into a new relationship expecting true love until you have had enough time to be able to say

"I LOVE WHO I AM. I AM WHOLE. I FEEL GOOD. I AM GRATEFUL FOR MY LAST RELATIONSHIP AND FOR ITS EVOLUTION."

If you say this without meaning it, trust me, you are not ready to start a healthy romantic love for someone else. Remember, when you are ready, you should choose a potential partner based on what you now know about yourself through the first insight. You already know your love blueprint (from Part Two) based on the amalgam of your first love experience, the models and stories of your family and friends.

Food, shelter, water and the need to belong drive us all. This past year, my husband & I travelled through some European countries. In Austria, we learned about early Renaissance civilizations. In those eras, kingdoms were ruled through dynasties of arranged marriages. Children were often married by the time they were twelve or fourteen. Love was by design to develop heirs and cultivate blood based political alliances that would maximize power, kingdom to kingdom. In this competition for power and prestige, people lives tended to be short lived. With the constancy of scarcity, and drive to simply survive, people may have lived in a near perpetual state of high stress and fear. Certainly these were survival cultures. We have advanced a long way in scientific knowledge as it relates to longevity factors like healthy food, shelter, hygiene, and clean water. On a tour in Switzerland, visiting a castle, we discovered that in the 1400's noblemen ate only white flour as it was thought, because of the color, to be divine. Peasants ate whole wheat and foods grown from the ground such as vegetables. Noblemen were only to eat things that flew – or were closer to heaven (white in color). We know now, that we should eat a diet primarily of vegetables and fruit, complex carbohydrates and just about everything opposite to the thinking of those times. Think for yourself when it comes to your 'heart' health. You know your relationship learning, your love story blueprint, your relationship coping style, and what type of person you are looking forward to sharing your life with. Reference your notes regularly and remember the art of conscious choosing if you want to live with heart health.

Choose a partner you feel safe and at ease with, not because of their position in life and who they are, but what kind of person they are. Making the 'right' choice for you will allow you to be creative in other aspects of your life. Keep your stresses down and love up in your life, and chances are you will live longer and avoid brain and neurological diseases such as Alzheimer's, and Multiple Sclerosis, or stress related illnesses like cancer and heart disease.

Today we know our brain (second to our heart) is our greatest asset in health and longevity. Choosing a partner who naturally feeds your spirit rather than drives your adrenals with stress inducing demands or rejection, means you will live longer. The results of a thoughtful choice in future life partnership means you will be more creatively engaged at work and at play. The results of a poor choice may show up in stress symptoms such as: forgetfulness, lack of concentration, poor short-term memory, impatience, irritability, anxiety, frustration, aggression, isolation, and negativity. Poor choices may lead to feelings of emptiness, sadness, a lack of energy. You may see yourself making a lot of mistakes, and generally have trouble meeting the demands of life. Physically, signs of stress can show up as headaches, physical pains in the back or shoulders, frequent illness, and an overall attack to your immune system, and trouble sleeping. You might even find yourself gaining or losing weight. When you don't get enough sleep, your body produces a hormones grelin and leptin, which are linked to weight gain. There are a lot of reasons you can take your time in the process of choosing the next 'right fit' for you.

Stats Canada reported that 43% of all Canadian suffer from stress, and 75 – 95% of all doctor visits are stress related ailments and complaints. The U.S. stress statistics show 77% of all Americans regularly experience physical symptoms caused by stress. 33% feel they are living with extreme stress and 48% feel their stress has increased over the past five years (37). This doesn't mean that all stress comes from miss-matched relationships. Yet this may speak to the need to slow life down generally. We should get intentional about the foundations of our life. We should make sure that we take care of our self and feed our relationships. Our own sense of power in today's world comes, more and more, from living our best life— healthy body, mind, and spirit. This trifecta of bliss is a symptom of health by design and relationship choices well made.

If you are wondering how you are doing with regards to stress, try journaling to track yourself-talk and what others are saying to you. When you do this, you will start to gain insight about things you need to change or things you may need to get more boundaries about. Live intentionally, addressing dynamics within your control and choice. Don't live passively until things fall apart. Miguel Ruiz's book "The Four Agreements" reminds us to do our best, knowing our best may change every day. His book offers guidance when you feel overwhelmed and or when you find yourself over functioning, controlling or fearful. Mr. Ruiz reminds the reader to use words impeccably, to not take things personally, to not make assumptions, and to always do one's best. So, take the pressure off and refocus on love.

****

You may set up strategic changes in your weekday schedule, which give you better transitions from home to work, or work to home. An example of these might be:

1. Wake up and go for a walk or run first thing in the morning. If you are not a runner, a simple walk around the block before you go into the office will give you time to reflect on your 'big picture'. Anything that gets you breathing deeply and slowly – yoga breathing for example, even for five or ten minutes is a great way to start the day. On inhale, welcome breath into your body, open your heart to what this day will bring. On exhale, focus on the release of tension that will serve you well during whatever stress this day will bring. Remind yourself that a deep breath can help you diffuse stress as it comes up, and with each time this happens you get more grounded.

2. Manage your inputs through the day. Check your emails at a defined time so you aren't always 'on call' for everyone and you can get your own things done.

3. At every bathroom break, take two minutes and breathe deeply into your belly to release stress. Drink a glass of water when you are back at your desk (which flushes the cortisol stress hormone out your kidneys).

4. Keep note of one goal for the day. Write it down on your 'notes' app on a sticky at the back of your cell phone or inside your wallet. At the end of your day, put it in the trash or press 'delete'. It feels great to complete one thing every day.

5. Transition out of work by going for a walk, a run, or go to the gym before you go home. Once you get home, there is less probability you will actually do your workout. Its otherwise, too easy to sit back in the comfort of being home.

6. Invite a friend in on your team to get better at any or all of these strategies. We are more inclined to change patterns when we commit to change with someone who can hold us accountable. Sharing your commitments with someone else also turns the project of becoming better into more of a fun game.

****

If you take your time, you will likely make a better choice. Jumping in too quickly to commitments is risky. Too often we let ourselves be chosen, or we continue to choose the same kind of partner over and over again. What you don't want is to end up with a complicated and destructive life pattern of separation and divorce. It's easier to not have to work through the hearty project of blending a family. It's sad to see the wake of mistrust and trails of broken hearts for generations when breakups cause breakdowns. Remember, your children and great grandchildren may very well base their own relationship patterns on your decision for self-love and agape healthy relationship behaviors today.

To make the right choice you may want to take time out from the dating game until you feel you have had enough experience dating you. It is possible to create a self-reflective pause in your life so you can figure out what you truly want? Or can you lighten up on your intentions and just have some social fun flying solo for a while? You can avoid the rebound patterns and meet people who (like you) are learning to be comfortable with them selves again. The next chapter will help you brainstorm 'your new social life 101'.

CHAPTER 25

LETS HEAR FROM YOUR SOCIAL COORDINATOR

This chapter is to help you branch out socially engaging the part of you that can get the party started. One of the benefits of developing new social circles is that they give you much needed relief from the constant reminders of the break up. Often your friends can love you 'too much'. Your friends may also still be grieving from the loss of your relationship break-up. Their sad feelings can be a type of contagion to your own grief. Just as you start to feel better, you may be reminded to feel sad again because your friend innocently asks about your former partner. These reminders to your past will feel easier and easier to handle as time goes by. After a while you may feel you are talking about an old family member like a sibling, not a past lover. It's so important to maintain a healthy connection with your past. Friends are emotional roots to your health and all the best memories you can continue to cherish for a lifetime. Your friends are the multi-colored threads in the fabric of your full strong heart. The more your friends are with you throughout your life, the more solidly you will feel in your day to day. Just the same, it's also important to develop new friends who may bring a welcome breath of fresh air to your life with new activities and social ideas that are not steeped in the past.

Now is a great time to reflect again on your favorite photo (chosen in the earlier chapters). What were you doing at that time? Were you part of a running or cycling group? Did you do a lot of hiking back then? Did you dance, go to the gym, skate, swim or go to concerts a lot?

If you used to have dinner parties, start having them again. One comment I often hear from clients is that they don't get invited out to social events because their friends are in relationships and they feel like 'the odd man out'. This thinking will hold you back. When you consider your old, part-nered/married self, holding or attending a party, did you tend to stay hip-to-hip, shoulder-to-shoulder with your former partner? I'm guessing not! Then why do you need a partner to hold a dinner party? You don't! Dust off your address book and start calling a few friends for this Saturday night. Serve something easy to make or ask your invitees to bring some-thing in a potluck style. The central goal is to establish yourself back into familiar and new social networks. Keep it simple and your stresses down on this renewed venture. Your new entertaining experience is meant to be life enhancing not draining!

How Did It Go?

What made you most happy while having your dinner party? Write a list of all the positive outcomes. This helps your brain incorporate and associate positive feelings with taking the risk and following through with steps to engage new practices (like having a dinner party for the first time). You might call a friend who came to the party and talk about your favorite moments together. Or you could journal the best and worst of your experi-ence. Just try to make sure you always write a few positive things down. They might simply be: "everyone showed up, the food was great, the music really worked, I had a good time." Negatives might be, as in the movie Diary of Bridget Jones, "I made blue soup".

After having had your first party, chances are you will start to get invited to other peoples' events too. Try to say yes to as many invitations as possible. Even in those moments you really feel you'd rather not, be a yes person and fake it till you make it! You can always leave early if you need to. And again, each next morning, take stock of how you feel. Hangovers not included, chances are you will have positive associations simply from having made the effort. A great way to practice rehearsing the positive is by posting photos from the night previous on your Facebook page or email. You might send a fun note to someone who you enjoyed talking to during the evening. Any of these activities hold your brain in the positive ideas and feelings that will motivate you to do it again!

CHAPTER 26

YOU CAN DANCE: DATING, INTIMACY AND SEX

What is life truly about? Let the last person you kiss in your last breath in this life be your collective ONE. My hope for you is that your one embodies the optimal combination of the best character traits of every person you have come to know well. He or she will represent everyone you have ever loved and everyone who has ever loved you. He or she will be within you and outside of you. You will see the ways you are similar and also the ways you both are so different. Your one will embody both the spiritual feeling of wholeness for you and represent love itself in your world.

In that way of thinking you will embrace every experience of love, past, present and future. All your experiences of the heart are part of your journey to arrive at agape, that other-focused, loving state that is the epitome of the human experience. I think this way of thinking allows you to embrace life's experiences rather than regret life's painful bumps. Life and love is a beautiful collective of everything and everyone we experience.

The biggest hurdle for many people who are ending a deep relationship is being truly open enough to let another person into their heart. No one wants to be hurt or to go through a painful breakup… again. Yet if you see loving as a verb, an action statement, like breathing, you will be able to practice it again. Love is like oxygen. So take a big breath, you are ready to try out dating again.

Putting all your tools into practice in a fresh new experience is the only way you will truly know that these tools can work! Trust me, they do work. Sharing your loveable self with another is the way you will grow into a fuller life experience. As you share your authentic self, with the right person, at the right pace, and with the right relationship habits, you will grow and heal your raw spots... and you may quite possibly be the catalyst of growth and healing of someone else too. Our world needs more love. So imagine yourself in a collective evolution of trust, care, and positive intention.

You may need to kiss a few frogs before you discover the alchemy of love that works for you. So relax into this voyage of loving. You are ready. Practice your boundaries, use your communication tools, follow your inner guide, but put on your wings, it's time to take off! You'll know when you have found him or her. He or she is looking for you too! Guard down, trust up within the boundaries and value systems that you have worked hard to define.

We work and wait and pray that our own shall know our face, but we shall have often to subdue the heart's lone cry, else our own shall find us with a foundling in its place.
- Muriel Strode 1912

Advice for Women

Men want to feel like men. Men want the opportunity to court you. It is in their DNA. Try to say yes to 'his' next invitation to hold the door for you, carry your groceries, treat you to a coffee, or possibly even a date. When he opens the door for you, smile and enjoy 'his' caring. When he asks to carry your heavy bags, say thank you. Enjoy being a woman. You can practice in small ways even in these routine daily living activities. If you haven't had your first date, start practicing when you are at the grocery store and someone asks if you'd like help to your car. Do you usually say, "No thank you, I've got it"? Is that you, fearlessly walking away...on your own... again? Or will you say, "Thank you, it's so kind of you. I'd love some help!" You are now less fearful and actually walking with someone. At elevators when a man says, "after you", just smile and say "thank you!" At entrance doors when a stranger holds the door for you, enjoy his chivalry! Practice, practice, practice being a woman! You'll get the hang of this and lots of opportunities will present throughout your day as you start to notice how this works. One of the biggest traps you can fall into during a post relationship phase is becoming a team of one. You were born a girl. You are now a woman. Enjoy the benefits and you just might actually make someone else happily the man they want to be!

Don't be so fearful that you block yourself from love. For many women, the fear you will be hurt becomes a hurdle that you must overcome in order for your dreams to come true. Your defense in 'devoted' self-reliance and self-containment makes you an island unto to yourself. Can I help you? No. Do you need a hand? No. Are you OK? I'm fine. Does this sound like you? This type of protective 'style of being' can write any man or woman right out of your future love story. This may be a pattern of control. The more your life feels out of control, the more your controlling behaviors ratchet up. The more you fear, the fewer the risks that you will take. You may start to engage your masculine assertiveness; you might become so clear in communicating and initiating that you become something of an emotional hermaphrodite! Your inner warrior stands guard at the gates to your heart in a way that your defensive self-reliance blocks a man or woman from having any role at all in your life.

You may have found yourself a little more controlling when it comes to men or women because you haven't wanted to be controlled, hurt, or betrayed. Of course you don't want to be hurt! No one does. You definitely don't want to feel exposed. Nothing risked though, nothing gained. If my words resonate with you, you are like many post-relationship women. If you want to be happy, you need to practice getting out of this guarded style of being and enter your new world. Believe it or not, we all need each other. When you take a risk to love again, you may actually heal the painful historical stories you have held on to, for example that you weren't 'loveable' or 'deserving' in the past.

As you become more and more self-aware, you might be shocked at the power of your knee jerk reactions, for example that you say no initially when a man or woman offers to help you in small or big ways. It's going to take some patience and communication for you to regain a higher level of trust with men or women again, (or for the first time). So tame your inner tiger that is keeping you locked in a cage! Let your love out. Otherwise, by being both woman and man, you may unwittingly write romance right out of your future. Although you have discovered that you love yourself again, it would be nice to share who you have become with someone who is whole like you! Otherwise it can feel pretty lonely living life on an emotional island or your own making.

Advice for Men

After a break up, you may feel so abandoned or hurt at the end of a significant relationship that you temporarily lose the confidence that women will ever see you as a strong and sexy male again. For you, your inner white knight may have gone a little underground. You may want to help a woman with that heavy load of groceries but you hold back rather than risk over-stepping. You might hold a door for a woman, but still avoid eye contact or dodge any potential opportunity for an appreciative return. If this sounds like you, one of the fastest ways to regain your footing as an attractive male is to step back into your 'Inner Gallant'. This takes practice. Take a risk and fake it till you make it. After a while, you will again notice the exhilaration and excitement of being a man. It's fun seeing the effect you can have on women when you step up to perform these types of caring behaviors. I often suggest to my clients that they look for an old photograph of themselves in which they are reminded of their confidence. You may want to carry this photo of you in your wallet. Photos are great ways to reactivate your feelings of positive personal regard.

Men, if you are having a difficult time re-engaging yourself-confidence, try thinking about the last time you chased someone that you had a crush on. As you do this, recall yourself in the courting process. Rewind your relationship videotapes so that you can recall these old courtship phases in your life. Recall the feelings you have in your body as the memories of those old fun experiences come to mind. You are the same innovative romantic you were back then (and will be again). Bring on your inner James Bond! Do you ever wonder why James Bond always ordered martinis shaken not stirred? Research suggests that people who take chances in life are happiest. Everyone might feel a little nervous and out of practice some of the time. Shake up your machismo and you just might stir a new flame into your life. Look for small ways you can practice. You might let "her" go first in the coffee shop line up. You might give her your bike at spin class. You could hold that door open for her when you see her rushing to catch the elevator at work. Even if she isn't your One, she may have a friend who is! Either way, just watch how the good feelings start to grow in your day. Isn't it fun being a man?! At work, at home, in your community, in your activities where ever you are, you'll be capturing the hearts of women all over town.

Both men and women have a precondition requisite to be date-ready. *You are date ready when you know your basic needs are fully met by you and you feel whole as a result.* Abraham Maslow, a developmental psychologist, identified core needs for living, starting with the physiological (food, shelter, water, basic body functioning), the need for safety (having employment, integrity, constancy and an ability to self-sustain), love and belonging (friendship, family, sexual intimacy), the need for esteem (personal and maintaining respect by others), self-actualization (problem-solving, creativity, morality) and self-transcendence. The more we move through these life stages with ease, the more we feel loved and connected.

From infancy to latter life the more loved and cared for that we are, the more we are free to explore in the dating world. When we are trying to break through the painful loss of an attachment to a loved one, our need for safety becomes more dominant than any other need. This may explain the patterns of defense described above, where we write ourselves out of a new partnership by being too guarded and too self-contained. Your fear of being hurt again will feed your anxiety and disconnect. If your boundaries have become so rigid that no one can penetrate your walls of steel, you are bound for isolation not recreation!

Moving on from being your version of James Bond, think of the comic book character Super Man (recently remade on the big screen as the Man of Steel) who has super human powers to heal, fly fearlessly, save the World and fall in love with Lois Lane too. This film sends the underlining message that behind the big "S" on his jersey this man is in fact the manifestation of Hope for humanity, not Super or Steel. Launched from Planet Krypton as an infant, he finds love, constancy, and meaning with his adoptive family on Planet Earth. If, while reading this chapter, you don't feel confident that you have solid support with own anchors yet, I suggest that you back up to the previous chapters to deepen your connection to family and friends first.

You are human and want to feel attached, loved and connected again. But the fear that you might potentially have another painful ending of an important relationship is hard to overcome. This is the dilemma. Herein lays the battle, and the assault on the castle of intimacy. You long to trust, belong and love again. Yet fears of inadequacy may block you from being intimate because you've been busy judging yourself (and others).

Advice for Men and Women

Trust me, when you are reintegrating your new, loveable self into the dating world, you will have to practice trust in order to get better at doing it. Everyone you meet is on the same learning curve you are. They are also learning to trust, belong and love again. Practice, practice, practice in small ways, and then in bigger and bigger ways. Maybe having someone carry your groceries (if you are a woman), or you carrying someone else's groceries (if you are a man) is the most intimate thing you can do at this stage. That's ok! Thank your temporary Prince, or give a smile to your temporary Princess, and then try it again in another similar way. Practice little, random acts of loving engagement as you work towards dating again. Before you know it, dating will become unconscious and fun again. Then, before you know it, you will have tripped upon your big love – the one you will choose as your 'last kiss'. So embrace this zany, crazy, fun, exhilarated time of dating.

Dating Websites

Dating sites are a great way to bring your anxieties down because they can help to relieve your fears that there are not many single people out there. You won't believe how many people are just waiting to meet YOU! Whether you find your future partner or use the dating site to just get back in the game, just sign up and try one out for a while. You may want to curb your enthusiasm from signing up for a bunch of dating sites. Just choose one or two at the most. Selecting potential partners from a dating site can be overwhelming and become more like a job if you have too many sites to keep up with. Meeting new people is not supposed to have the flavor of another full time job!

If you are looking for someone who is more of an executive type, you may want to choose a site with a fee associated to joining. This also rules out recreational visitors to the site. The price of membership selects out people who might not otherwise be very intentional. Most people don't want to pay for something they aren't taking seriously.

When you check out the profiles that match your criteria, you will see that there are a number of ways you can describe yourself and the type of person you are looking for. Remember, however, as I advised earlier, be honest. Don't sign in with a photo from years ago or ten pounds lighter or heavier. Take your time to describe yourself and your interests. Be honest, not pleasing. If you write things that aren't accurate, you will be wasting precious energy in a very depressing, self-defeating process. Just be you, so you can get on to meeting your right one. Narrow the gap in age preferences. Some choose to widen the net to catch more fish. It's up to you whether you want to make a job of this process or narrow the field of play so you can enjoy each new experience. Be choosey. You haven't gone through all this self-development to be with someone who isn't self-evolved.

Flirting

Flirting in a social setting is also a learned skill. If you've come out of a long-term relationship, you may be a little out of practice. Do a survey with your friends. Ask them how they get other peoples' attention. What do they notice about how others flirt? If they are already in a relationship, ask them how they met their partner. Go out with some friends and observe them flirting. Be yourself. Recall your body, your best friend, and what his/her best parts are – your eyes? Then walk into the room with your own fabulous eyes.

Operate from your strengths rather than feeling self-conscious in overcoming your weaknesses. What's the best part of your personality – your humor, your grace, your intelligence, and your athletic ability? Be yourself. Don't take on doing some sexy walk and talk thing if that isn't you. That would be self-defeating because it is insulting to the strengths of who you are. Keep your grace and self-confidence up front and center. If you aren't sure what your strengths are, ask your friends why they like being in your company and being your friend. Write a list of things you have participated in over the last five years. What books do you like to read? What types of music do you most love? These are questions to get you building conversation points from your strengths and authentic interests.

Joining In

You might do a body check before you walk into a venue. A grounding exercise can be to stand into your heels and feel your connection into the ground. Shift your weight to the balls of your feet and then back again. Roll your feet to the outer edges and then to the inside. And finally, focus your attention to the center of each of your feet. You also may want to practice ways you can 'join' in social settings. Steer conversation to develop ease finding common ground with people you meet. This is a skill you can observe in your friends too.

The first strategy in 'joining' is for you to listen more than talk. Many people find they talk faster when they are nervous. If you tend to do that, anchor your nerves while you practice listening. If you are 'self-conscious' in any one moment, practice being 'other conscious' while your nerves balance out. At the outset of your conversation focus on and appreciate the other person. By making the other person more at home, you will also relieve your own inner. Remember that everything you feel unpracticed at, and self-conscious about, reflects what every other person also probably feels to some extent! Listen for what he/she tells you about him/her.

A second tool in 'joining' is to try to use a few of the same words that you hear him/her say. These 'joining' techniques may sound a little awkward, but they are useful tips that will help calm you while you are becoming more relaxed in the process of learning to flirt and start dating again.

Human beings are a pair-bonding species. Like some birds, mammals, animals, there is a dance we all do in the early mate selection process. Eye contact and then a quick look away, another eye contact and maybe a smile? Recognizing some universal traits of humans in the dating phase is really helpful for getting back in the game.

✱✱✱✱✱✱✱✱✱✱✱

Breakthrough Tips for Flirting:

1. Stand and sit tall. This is your time to shine!
2. If you are feeling self-conscious, try switching the spotlight off you. Think about the others in the room. What might be going on in their lives? Who looks attractive to you?
3. Smile from your head to toe. (Yes, imagine you can even make your toes smile!) This impacts your brain state/mood in a positive way and makes you attractive to others.
4. If you notice someone who you think is attractive, send out an invitation: make eye contact, smile, look away, and then look back and smile again. He/she may take a moment to process the invitation.
5. When a conversation follows, if you are a little nervous, ask the other person a question. This gives you time to breathe and center.

6. Avoid any giggle presentation. This gives you a flighty, non-confident air and is distracting to the other person who might want to get to know you.
7. Remember the Tallulah Wisdom; sit back and enjoy the experience. Let others pursue you.

****

More Tips to Get Back in the Mating Game

Try utilizing open body language. For example, your feet should be standing parallel but slightly turned out, your arms open not crossed, with your shoulders back but not rigid. Smile, but not in a forced way. Think of your whole body smiling and feel the connection in your eyes. If you are nervous about flirting, or getting back into the social scene, you might go for a run or brisk walk before heading out. This kind of exercise will help put you in a less stressed, endorphin enriched brain state. Wear something you feel good in. Before you head out the door, you might spend a few minutes meditating. As I think of living examples of great human kindness and global caring, the first person who comes to mind for me is the Dalai Lama. When you see him speak, he stands with every part of his body open. It's as if he is literally generating loving energy out of his palms, chest and eyes. So bring on your inner Dalai. You can fill a room with your loving spirit. Just watch what happens when you do.

Here's a quick meditation to bring love and inner peace up

Breathe in, breathe out.

Repeat.

Imagine you can release stress out through your breath and breathe in loving-kindness.

Imagine you can breathe out loving-kindness and breathe in universal connection.

Imagine a pair of very loving hands gently held on your shoulders.

Breathe in, breathe out.

If you have been nervous about the prospect of dating again, just leave these worries behind sign up to a dating site tonight! After you've done that and said 'yes' to actually meet someone for the first time, here's a few tips on how to proceed:

1. Remember that you are both in the same boat – nervous and not sure what you are getting into! Make sure you meet somewhere open and public so you both feel safe. If you are really worried about meeting up with a stranger, give a good friend the phone number and name of whom you are meeting. This may be a totally unnecessary step, but anything that makes you feel more relaxed is going to lead to a better outcome.

2. When you greet him or her for the first time, say something right away aimed at putting the other person at ease. You might even acknowledge that you are nervous! Being honest paves the way for the other person to be open and honest with you too.

3. Try to match his/her language. If he or she says, "You look so much better in person than you did in your photo", you might return the compliment. You know that if he/she is thinking that about you, he/she probably is a little self-conscious about his/her own physical desirability. Be honest though. Don't say things you don't actually mean. There is always something you can say that positively regards the other person in some way. He/she has beautiful hands, smile, eyes, positive energy, etc.?? You may be surprised that they don't look much like their photo. But just take a breath and focus on enjoying the practice of getting to know someone.

4. If you find yourself being really nervous when you first meet, switch the spotlight off you and on to him/her by asking questions and then just

listen carefully and reframe what he/she says. This will give you some time to get your feet on the ground and feel more comfortable.

5. Every person you meet won't be your future 'One', so just relax and enjoy the experience. Think to yourself that if you walk away with a new acquaintance, you are so much the richer. This may be the start of a singles network within which you can hike, run, and play. Sit back wherever you are, and relax with whatever happens.

6. If you enjoyed meeting this new person, take the initiative to suggest a hike or a walk in the next week. I don't know how many times I have heard clients say they wanted to set something up but felt too awkward and didn't know if it was appropriate. Believe me, it is entirely appropriate. So just do it!

7. If you don't get a good vibe, be honest but be kind as well. "Thank you for meeting me today. It's been so fun anticipating our ...coffee date. I think you probably feel, as I do, that we aren't a great fit for each other, but I'm so glad I met you". You will find your own script and your own authentic way of 'exiting stage left'. Just do it with grace.

Still feeling some social anxiety? You are normal!

A great trick in bringing down social anxiety is what I call, 'switching the spotlight'. We feel self-conscious because we are trying out something new. You are a beginner flirter, a novice solo flyer, and you are like the hero in the movie Avatar, in a whole new beautiful world of possibilities. Start pushing the spotlight off you and redirect it onto this whole new world. Imagine what other people are thinking, doing, and loving about their lives. Switch the spotlight off you and onto someone you might really like to get to know. Who will that lucky person be tonight? And don't plan on 'getting lucky'. The relentless hunts for the new one is, remember, totally repelling. Think of my cat Tallulah wisdom. Once you get there, just sit back and enjoy without harboring any big intentions. ENJOY. Love being you in your body, mind, and spirit.

Should you text or...

should you avoid the text and go face to face?

This is definitely a hot new topic since mobile communications technology has facilitated such a new pastime these days. Texting can be a really fun way to breakthrough intimacy barriers. Without the visual distraction of an 'in-person encounter', you may find yourself more confident in being honest about yourself and expressing yourself more intimately. With a text, some people feel a little more focused because the visual cues are not there. By texting, people often are able to allow more authentic conversation to stream. Clients report they feel they can be wittier and let their humor out. The only trouble is that you may find that you breakthrough so many of the barriers by texting that when you actually get together face to face, it can be just a little awkward!

The interesting thing is that when you text you can start your curiosity going... what is he/she doing right now? As you ask these types of questions, you will find out what kind of things he/she likes to do naturally. On a date, people tend to do extraordinary activities. In the humdrum of daily life, we participate in activities that are natural to our character traits. Is he gardening right now? Is she on a hike? Is he reading or listening to music? Is she hanging out with her friends? A text is a great way to get a true snapshot of a person's life that will give you a better indication of 'good fit'.

But texts can also be the source of challenges often caused by miscommunications. One difficulty that may arise can be the misinterpretations that happen when the visual cue is not available to you and/or the other person. A space in your text, a capital or bolding, a delay in response time can be interpreted in a way you (or the other) did not intend. Texting is a relatively new phenomenon, so there is not a lot of research available about it yet. However I did find Amanda Klein's qualitative research which looked at university students twenty-three to thirty years old in various stages of relationship uncommitted and committed. Her research suggests that the phenomena of the text have put a strain on romance because of the lack of rules or guidelines available. Her thesis based on the interviews she conducted is that face-to-face communication is always best (38). But my suggestion is that you should just keep communicating in whichever way feels right for you. Monitor yourself though, so that you don't use the practice of texting so much that you develop a whole new pattern of addiction! We have all been witness to couples at restaurants where, sadly and remarkably, there seems to be more heat in the cell phone exchange, than in their face-to-face contact.

Addictive, anxious patterns of living show up in the relationship that we might have with our cell phone. We can worry so much that we will be alone in life that we engage desperate ways of staying in contact through technology such as posting on Facebook, texting, Tweeting, or Instagram'ing. You may have caught yourself sometimes in the habit of compulsive texting. If so, learn how to better manage your time on your cell phone! When you are with someone at lunch or coffee, leave your cell phone at the office or in your car. If you are on a first date, you may want to have your cell phone on you for safety reasons. But keep it out of sight. Meeting someone for the first time is anxiety invoking enough without the competition of a cell phone on the scene!

I often see clients who say they are 'on call' 24/7 because of work, family or social demands. If that sounds like you, it may be time to strengthen your boundaries. Being on call every moment of your day, distracts you from enjoying the present moment, conversation or activity. This sends a message to the person you are with that you don't value them. It also is very stressful for your brain to be chronically multi-tasking. Over time, if you continue the practice of (what I call) 'cell-tell', (being a prisoner to your phone), you will find yourself over time feeling lonely because your friends will likely lose interest in being with you.

Who wants to sit across the table from someone bent over their cell phone and barely listening much less actively participating in your conversation? What does that behavior say about you or the person you are with? Over time, your friends will not likely be willing to set aside their day to spend time with you because they know you will not be prioritizing them. Cell-tell is only one of the symptoms of addictive living. Other symptoms of a life unmanaged may be over-spending, drinking to excess, or over-eating. Are you cutting off from your feelings, your fears, your anxieties, and your loneliness with these kinds of addictive temporary escape habits? Is it time to get back to what is really YUM—love? There is no shame in feeling shy, intimidated, anxious, insecure, or sad sometimes. Share your feelings and you will develop a stronger loving relationship both with yourself and your significant other(s).

"It is our light, not our darkness that most frightens us... as we let our light shine, we unconsciously give others permission to do the same. Liberated from our fear, our presence automatically liberates others." - Marianne Williamson, A Return to Love

In the early stages of being solo you will probably feel hungry to be touched and held. Given the end of your former relationship, it's probably been a while since your body, mind and spirit felt cherished by another. Anxiety about being on your own also drives a chemical need for oxytocin (the attachment hormone referred to earlier). You need to be hugged, touched, or have an orgasm to trigger your brain to respond to release this calming chemistry. In fact, our innate need for oxytocin may be one of the primary drivers in our 'hunt' for a new partner. Again, enlist your wingman to help manage your decision-making in mate selection when you out on the town or need a second opinion in a social setting. If you worry your chemical hunger may over-ride your good decision, you may want to start getting therapeutic massages from time to time. A gem of nickel knowledge is that therapeutic massage works to release dopamine, serotonin and oxytocin. The more oxytocin you have in your system, the more calm and connected you will feel in your world. In the first months or years of separation, if you can afford it, get yourself a weekly or monthly massage.

There seems to be a trend of compulsive casual 'hooking up' these days. In some ways, this may speak to the cultural pressures of high stress living, which may have turned love -making into a sporting activity. This can also reflect a reaction to having 'survived' a lack-luster, starved sex life with your previous significant partnership and give rise to a renewed hunger to feel alive, sexy, and delicious again. In addition, whereas previous generations may have calmed themselves after a hectic day with a glass of scotch or wine, today it seems that casual sex often fills the gap. Perhaps you might best understand these incidents of casual 'hooking up' are just like any other addiction that is caused by your inner ongoing unhappy feelings. They can be the results of your anxieties that are submerged, loneliness hidden under ground, your inadequacies or anxieties, or are part of a grand cover-up of your inner deep sadness.

Over-functioning, or hiding out, you may be trying to avoid simply claiming your pain. A best way out of your dark cloud cover-up is always to simply talk to someone. You might also decide to journal your experiences in order to gain a fresh perspective. Overall, your goal should be to start to feel more connected to your spiritual, global WE. Just say, "I am in pain." Getting into patterns of avoidance or denial through temporary 'fixes' with multiple sex partners can be risky business. Even if you are using condoms, if you are sharing your body, mind, and spirit in a casual way, this can lead to a form of soul sickness in you. When you share yourself physically with someone, before actually knowing who they are, you may become less motivated to build deeper spiritual or emotional attachments. These casual 'hook ups' can be a rehearsal of the story that you 'aren't worth it', you can't trust or be trusted, you don't deserve to be loved, you are on your own. Are those the kind of stories that describe you? Do these stories serve your best interests?

I recall a client 'Booker', who started seeing me after his ten-year relationship had ended. Trying to feel better, 'Booker' immediately started his hunt for a new woman, any woman, who would fill the gap in his heart. There began a revolving door of juicy experiences for him. Sadly, one day 'Booker' realized he had fallen into a deep depression. The symptoms of this state of depression were his over-riding sadness, irritability, loss of enjoyment in things he otherwise used to love, difficulty concentrating, trouble sleeping, and weight loss. He started experiencing erectile dysfunction and that became the trigger to seek help. Other signs he was depressed were seen in his social withdrawal. 'Booker' had lost his motivation to exercise, or even get out of bed to go to work in the morning. His libido had taken a hike as he began cocooning himself more and more. When 'Booker' showed up in my office, he presented with a general lack of affect and reported his feelings were clouded with a pervasive and deep-seated shame of who he was and who he had become.

Shame is a base driver for all addictions, whether shame is displayed in an abuse of alcohol, drugs, shopping, or sex. The self-defeating cycle starts with sad feelings (of loss, anxiety, or pain) that the person has not faced. Caught in the addictive behavior of choice, he/she tends to look for some way to find temporary relief out of this state of misery. These are learned patterns, and are often modeled through one's family of origin or even genetically inherited. The user finds a temporary lift out of loss or pain with the addictive behavior of choice, but then experiences a resurging tsunami of despair coming off the brief high derived from drugs, alcohol, sex etc. A route out of this addiction cycle is first to admit, "I am in pain". Then ask for help. Then talk about what drives your sad feelings. Identify what you need. Then begin a process to strengthen your core and ego identity through a course of therapy treatment. Take steps to build supportive community connections. Develop your emotional intelligence. You are human and we all go through these kinds of dark tunnels in our life. You are not alone if you ask for help. Caring- in, caring-out. We all need love in our life.

In the case of 'Booker', he saw a nutritionist and hired a physical trainer to get his body back in homeostasis. He joined a local running group to develop a new healthy community that helped him to concentrate on the two things that he most needed to strengthen—his physical and spiritual center. Booker made a commitment that he would not date for six months. During this time he dedicated his passions to rebuild from within. He began dating himself!

We worked together during this time to move through the stages of grief model, first coined by Kubler-Ross:

Denial,

Anger,

Bargaining,

Depression, and

Acceptance (39).

I know I have drummed home earlier the need for you to commit to move forward in your life. I also want to clarify the importance for you that you access, process and address your own healing. 'Booker' had never accessed or addressed his grief when his ten-year relationship had ended. His pain had been so overwhelming that he couldn't recall having actually cried. His manic hunt for sexual partners was an expression of denial. "I don't feel sad that she left me and our relationship ended. There are plenty of fish in the sea. The ending of our relationship wasn't my fault". As you can see, 'Booker' was focused not on moving on from his relationship but rather whether he or his former wife was to blame for its failure.

As long as you keep stuck in the blame game, you will never get out of the emotional sand trap. As long as you are whacking away at the same old story of fault finding, you feel terrible. In 'Booker's' case the cycle of addiction was to blame, feel terrible, and then have temporary relief with a sexual conquest. Then the cycle would start all over. He'd wake up feeling angry that his marriage fell apart, blame whoever or whatever he could think of, feel terrible, and so on and so on. This is the cycle of a sex addict.

In therapy we explored 'Booker's' relationship with women, and his fear that he was not good enough. We started by exploring 'Booker's' relationship with his mother. We also considered what he felt was his identity as a man, starting with an inquiry about how 'Booker' understood his father as a male role model. We looked at the ways that loving communication was expressed between his parents. 'Booker' practiced to communicate with more honesty in all of his relationships, in particular with his parents and with his work colleagues. He started to value himself more by setting up greater work-life balance that provided him with more time to attend to his personal care. On reflection, he came to understand that his sex addiction, as displayed in serial sexual relationships with women, was an expression of a cycle of anger within him. He used women as sex partners but would leave them before he could get close or risk being hurt within these relationships.

'Booker' continued to see me for weekly therapy for three months, and then progressed to a schedule of coming once per month for another three months. I am happy to say that two years later, he returned to my office to introduce the 'love of his life'. He reported that during the six month 'no dating celibacy commitment', he had learned to trust himself and his own value as a loveable human being because he discovered intimacy rewards in pre-sexual connection. His capacity to commit to love behaviors correspondingly went up. These kinds of outcomes verify to me that I have the best job in the world as I witness these types of evolutions in my clients who come to know and embrace love as an evolution of body, mind and spirit.

A healthy and fulfilling sexual relationship is key indicator of a life in balance. Within a loving relationship, this is a life to be cherished. There is no doubt that our sexual passions are best expressed in the context of a loving and committed relationship. In contrast, if we just follow our sexual compulsions outside such a committed relationship, we are likely to end up exploiting others and also damaging our own spiritual and physical self. *And in case you are wondering, it is just not true that men have sexual thoughts every seven seconds. A research project conducted out of Ohio State University followed students aged eighteen to twenty-five over a one-week period. The students had to keep track of the frequency of thoughts of sex, food and sleep in a twenty-four hour period. They added up the seven daily reports and then divided by seven. What they found was that the tally of sexual thoughts showed a huge variation between one to 388 for men and between one to fourteen for women. On average, men thought about sex between one to two times per hour, no more or less than they thought of food or sleep (40).*

In the case of 'Booker', when he started coming for therapy, we identified his fear of loving again because he was afraid, (as we all are), of being hurt. The loss of his relationship had left him unable to trust women and in having superficial relationships, he had prevented himself from getting too close. The symptoms of his lack of trust and fear showed up in his body as erectile dysfunction, which is what motivated him to seek help. When our body starts to show physical symptoms we tend to pay attention. Thank you body! Why is it we listen to our physical pain more than our emotional pain? New mantra: I love my body. She/he is my guide.

Women (and some men) feel pressure to 'put out' in offering sex in the early stages of dating because they fear that their potential mate will not continue to be interested in the partnership with them if they don't. This may come from a deep-rooted insecurity in the self as well. I have also witnessed a type of competitive sibling rivalry amongst some women who seek to attract the same man in a club or a coffee shop. It's the stuff of what some reality television series are built on. These television shows colorfully highlight a fear of rejection, of being voted off the island (Survivor) or not getting the rose (The Bachelor). These shows can be a great education if you are looking to set up a new movie series. But not if you want an enduring, meaningful relationship with a safe relationship pod in which to grow, relax and enjoy who you are

My advice to you is to take all the time you need to learn about your potential love mate and who you are with him/her. Most of us already know that our bodies are healthy and responsive. You don't need to prove this to anyone. So take your time to discover the alchemy and joy of doing activities together. Explore how you both think, how you feel in various contexts of life, and practice expressing what you need along the way. This is what courtship is all about. Don't skip this stage of your relationship because it is a key foundation for how you will set up an enduring attachment.

The safer you feel emotionally, the more mind-blowing your sexual contact, expressed as lovemaking, will be. And if you are dedicated to your faith, you may want to choose someone of like mind. Many of the dating sites such as "Plenty of Fish", "Just Lunch", "E-Harmony" or "Lava Life" (there are so many today) have a checklist for faith. There is a good reason for this. So check this item off! The more specific you can be in selecting in who you are, the more successful you will be in finding your true love. Setting a wide net can be exhausting and fruitless in the end. There are even specialized dating sites for example "J-Date" which is a Jewish Dating Site.

I recall working with a client 'Mary'. 'Mary' is a devout Roman Catholic who believes that an important tenet of her faith is to be a virgin when she marries. This presented a massive roadblock for her, as there are not many men who hold this type of commitment to abstention. 'Mary' reported that she had experienced two deep relationships since leaving her parents' home. Either of these men she would have potentially married in a heartbeat. Sadly, neither of them was willing to commit without exploring their sexual fit. 'Mary', like 'Booker', came to me reporting a kind of soul sickness. She was devastated and depressed. She agreed to take some time out to regroup and rebuild within her spiritual community. Her commitment to her faith was undeniable; she simply needed to meet her match through God. For 'Mary', her breakthrough was to realize she could narrow her field of search to select men of the same religious denomination. You may not be religious like 'Mary'. For you it may be that your potential mate has a commitment to fitness, or some other non-negotiable defining practice. Select out and select in as you set yourself up for success!

The take home message here is that you should just take your time. Organize your life and your heart. You need to be smart to get really lucky! Some things may be random, but the Right One for you is Divine.

A Little Insider Information

People have similar characteristics at work and at home. So if you want to know how another person's values are expressed in their lives, just ask them about how things are at work. According to a World Wide Gallup Poll report released in October 2013, only 13% of employees like what they are doing and are engaged in their work. This was a 142-country study on the State of the Global Workplace. So one in eight workers are happy at work and are psychologically committed to their jobs and feel they are making positive contributions (41). So asking a potential partner how they feel about their work, can be a powerful question that gives you information about how engaged they are likely to be as a partner in life. If he or she just works to get the day done, he or she may not be someone who puts a lot of energy into personal relationships either. If a person describes their work life with passion because their work fulfills a need to contribute and give back, chances are they are caring in all aspects of their life. If they are routinely immersed in conflict situations at work, chances are they will be involved in tempests in family dynamics as well. It is fair to say that people generally talk more freely about their careers than their personal lives. What your potential beloved one says about his/her work can be revealing of values and integrity in a style of living. Also, if he/she has jumped around from job to job, he/she may do the same with romantic relationships. So pay attention to what is going on in your potential partners work life because this can be a great way to discover who he or she truly is. This is also something to footnote about yourself. If you are unhappy with your career, consider talking to a career coach to get a fresh perspective.

Ask questions about your dear one's family of origin too. If you want to know about a person's true character in good and bad times, just ask them about their parents and siblings. Every person in your family is a part of your whole self. In the early stages of new relationship, darker characteristics may not reveal themselves. But I guarantee that as the stresses of life go up, those darker characteristics are likely to show up, unless your significant other has participated in some self-discovery, personal growth or psychotherapy that has helped him/her overcome past difficulties in getting along well with others in their family. If he thinks his father was controlling when he grew up, there is a good chance that he may become more controlling when he becomes a father too. With the judgment he holds towards his father, he may not reveal himself in these similar characteristics until he feels the pressures of more complex stages.

If she describes her mother as over-bearing, she may ratchet up her attempts to control you as a way to cope with her stress when her life becomes more complex. We are mother, father, sister, brother, grandmother, grandfather, and even great grandfather and grandmother. So the next time your date asks you to join him or her at a family dinner, be there in spades with your antennae on full alert. The same can be said about the community of friends we attract. Each friend often reveals a part of our own personality. If you like her friends, no surprise, you will likely love her too over time.

Making Love

I have come to think that the first kiss says a lot about who is a 'good fit' in a partner. What do you notice about the kiss? Is there just the right connection for you? Or is there too much pressure, so your teeth click awkwardly? Or is there not enough pressure or connection, so you're not even sure it happened? Did the kiss take you by surprise, or were you waiting for days or weeks for that first kiss to happen?

Think about it. Our emotional patterns may show up in the way we kiss. Did you tend to control the kiss? Did your partner? Did he/she talk too much or not enough? Did the first kiss happen in a context of private space or was it a racy, out in the open, moment of passion? Are you a spontaneous lover or quiet private lover?

How do your lover's lips feel? Does he take care of himself? Does she wear lip-gloss? Does he shave or groom his facial hair? Does she? Ha! Just trying to see if you're alert. If any of these things feel misaligned with you, do you feel comfortable to talk through your differences?

To be a great lover, you need be a great communicator to. The more differentiated you are, the more you are able to relax in your body, mind and spirit. Now is when all the work you've done on yourself will start to pay dividends. The more whole you feel, the less self-conscious and more free your connections will be. And, guess what...the less your shoulder saboteur will show up with negative distractive chatter. Once again, my mantra for you is keep your 'stress down, love up'!

Rather than endure performance pressure to be a god or goddess with your new object of pursuit, why don't you just try pursing a godlike experience of falling in love and making love? When you are so worried and caught up in the stories about what 'sexy' looks like, plays like, feels like, you might forget that to make love is actually that. It is being and doing sexy in real time. It's the experience of the energy of love in the indescribable mix of physical-spiritual body fusion. Too often we are tripped up on techniques to reach a climax instead of simply trusting you can release into heart, mind and body. All it takes is for you to follow your own gentle inner guide and to have sublime confidence in yourself. You need to be an unconditional lover of your own wonderful, imperfect self. You also need to have a sense of unconditional love for your other. This is why love-making is so much better when you engage the spirit of love. Otherwise you may find yourself constrained and anxious in the need to perform at your best. Your shoulder saboteur has no place in your bedroom!

But the shoulder saboteur will be a third party to your sexual experience if you are worried about your body parts and moving them in perfection, 'just the right ways'! Think back, for example, to my client who was holding off on dating until she could get her weight to an ideal state. Are you holding back on enjoying the amazing experience of sex until you lose or gain ten pounds? Have fun in your body and your weight will probably reset to its ideal state naturally. (When you are happy, you probably notice you eat better food and generally take better care of yourself). I wish there was a book like 'Strengths Finder 2.0' that focuses on loving your own body. We need a book that focuses our attention on being grateful for and maximizing our body assets, as is. Instead we tend to dwell and fixate to improve our perceived weaknesses.

In April 2013, Dove released a touching commercial called "We are Beautiful". Dove relied on research that showed that people tend to focus on and report on imagined physical deficits, entirely distorting what they actually look like. The research showed that others can see our beautiful selves more readily than we can. This blocks us from the ability to be grateful for the blessings of our beautiful body, mind and spirit. It turns out that we should appreciate ourselves a whole lot more than we do!

Have you ever worried about favorable 'looking good' love making positions? For example, which way you are facing when you are having sex? Is your stomach hanging out (often a concern for many women)? Are your arms looking strong (a concern for some men)? Is there shrinkage in my penis (an episode from Seinfeld)? If this type of chatter is going on in your head, just as you consider whether it's time to take it to the mattress, think again. Take your time to move into the stage of physical intimacy. When you are ready, you won't be as tripped up by these fears. When you feel secure in your relationship, and confident that you have developed a soft landing of unconditional regard for each other, then it's the right time for lovemaking. When you love someone, these details will no longer haunt you because you are more connected in the spiritual sharing of love as an energy and expression. When you are in performance mode, you can easily be tripped up by the ego discrimination of 'perfection'. Try to think of your body as a holder of your spirit. Your eyes are the windows of your soul. Your hands are the means by which you reach into your special other's space.

Take time to be in rhythm with your dear one. The breath can be your Geiger counter. Take time to get in rhythm. Our lives can be so rushed. Transitioning from 'work mind' to a 'lovemaking mind' takes intention on your part. Did you know that sex releases a series of hormones that also relieve pain and stave off cardiovascular disease? Research has reported that having sex three times per week can make you look nearly a decade younger (42).

There are many tantric love books available which give you hands on practice for breath and body exercise. David Schnarch in his book "Passionate Marriage" describes a beautiful tantric exercise in which you lay with your lover, chest-to-chest, pelvis-to-pelvis and breathe together. As your lover breathes out, you breathe in, and as your lover breathes in, you breathe out (43). This is a delicious way to share spiritual space and the feelings that arise with the touch of your skin. The titillating electricity that you will feel between the two of you is quite ecstatic! Have fun in your bodies together.

Sex should be playful and unencumbered by judgment. You can't do it wrong if you have a smile in your heart. Your practice of sex also brings balance to your body, mind and spirit. There is an amazingly healthy elixir of chemistry that is whipped up and released in your system after orgasm. When you activate your sexual brain you produce oxytocin (the attachment hormone), serotonin (the feel good hormone), dopamine (which helps you sleep), along with other health inducing responses in the brain and body. Men need two to three times more touching than women for their oxytocin to release. But most men are embarrassed to even so much as ask to be touched. If you have had a stressful day, send out some 'SOS', skin on skin! Any kind of skin on skin contact helps your parasympathetic system to kick in (44).

Your sexual histories write the scripts that you bring with you to bed. Were you aware that your parents were sexual? As a child, did you hear giggles coming from your parents' bedroom? Did you ever innocently walk in on them mid-act, possibly in front of the living room fireplace? What are the stories you have told yourself from these histories? We learn more by what our parents do than we realize. If they had healthy scripts of sexual play, then chances are you will see sex as a natural activity engaged in a loving relationship. We all know that our parents had sex at least once, but for some it's still an awkward conversation. For example, if you walked in on your parents in the act and they reprimanded you for being so reckless, you may feel a sense of shame or embarrassment around sexual feelings as an adult today. Another example might be that if you were in your bedroom masturbating as a child and someone walked in on you, you may feel somewhat anxious about your sexual feelings today. Even watching a television show, which has sexual content, can be excruciatingly embarrassing for many.

Being comfortable with the topic of sex may start with being comfortable asking your parents some simple questions about their sex life. How old were they when they first had sex? When did they first have sex? Was it with each other? What do your siblings recall of your parents sexual relationship? Do your siblings think that your family of origin may have influenced their sexual confidence today? For you, all these inquiries can be helpful because some of the messages, (whether buttoned down or enjoyably shared), give you rich information about the sexual culture that you grew up within. These conversations are also ways through which you will become more comfortable talking about similar topics with your future partner.

When was your first sexual experience? Was it in a car, on a field, or in a bed? Some of the physical cues you had in your first sexual experience will continue to be the catalyst of sexual sequence for you today. Was your original sexual experience planned or did it happen in a stolen moment? These are the cues that form sequences in your brain even today. When you had sex for the first time, did you initiate sex or did your partner? If you were an initiator, you may feel more relaxed when you are the one take that the lead today. Or vice versa. Here's where the idea, 'you have to be smart to be lucky' really is true! Learn as much as you can about your scripts, context and your body.

For many, starting a new sexual relationship can be really exciting. For others starting a new sexual relationship can be terrifying. If you are in the latter category, talk about these feelings with your lover. The timing, the context, the care you take, all form a healthy balance of love between the two of you. The more you share the closer and more attached you will become. Help your body to get in tune, to be ready for love, one-step at a time. From the time you shower, shave, and put on your favorite under-wear, you are setting up.

Setting up for Success

The brain responds acutely to smells, so give some real thought to your choice of after-shave, cologne or perfume. Consider what your particular needs are in that context. If you want to calm yourself down, put on a little lavender. To feel more sexual, dab a little vanilla on. Or if you just want to feel more feminine, try lilac or gardenia. To feel manlier, try something spicy. Ask at your favorite store. If you have been in a long relationship, changing colognes can be a great way to set up a fresh start sexually. The sense of smell goes right to the limbic system (your stress centers) in your brain, bi-passing your upper cortical brain (where you think). So, smells do matter!

Another thing to consider is music. You may want to develop a music library for love. Tunes and other mood creators that relax you, turn you on, and make you feel sensual, will make a difference. Candles can be a great way to create romance and trigger your brain to feel more meaning-fully engaged with your other because you are relaxed. Remember to keep your stress down, and love up!

Our cultures have become so hectic. We hurry to get to work, we race to get home, we rush to meet a social deadline … no wonder there are so many people with chronic sleep difficulties! If that sounds like you, you should set up a transition exercise that you can do before you go to work, before you get home, or before you go to a social event. These kinds of transition exercises are especially important to practice before you head out for a romantic evening. Some activities that will relieve your stressors include a twenty-minute jog, a mindful walk around the block where you pay attention to your five senses. Try meditation. You might even do a few push-ups or planks in your living room. Work with your body and your body will return with its best efforts to support you.

That First Night

Your first sleepover can be exciting for some, but for others it can be really anxiety provoking. The worries clients report to me most often include: I might snore. She might snore. He might see me drool, fart, look horrible in the morning! I can't sleep in the spoon position! I like to wear a nightshirt/ no nightshirt. I can't sleep without the windows open; or with the windows open.

There are bound to be so many things you will need to talk about. Think back to the pacing chapter: take your time. If you are having a difficult time adjusting to a nighttime tango, work it in on a graduated schedule. The more you talk, the better your life will be. If you are not sleeping well, you can develop a full-blown psychosis! So you and your partner should arrive at some game plan so that you both get your sleep no matter what it takes.

Often your first experience in love making may not go as well as you hoped. The anxieties of being with someone new can cause your body to not respond as well as it usually has in the past. On a first experience, many men can't maintain an erection or ejaculate too soon. If that's you, know that you're normal. No worries! If you and your partner can laugh it off, the shared emotional safety builds a more secure attachment between you.

Generally the problem goes away if you try again in an hour or so, or wait until your next date. Don't sweat it, especially if this is a first for you.

Your first love making experience probably did not go well. You are learning about your body and your partner's body. It's normal to feel a little anxiety on that learning curve and with that, you may discover that your body and/or your partner's body may not be relaxed and responding. Think of your body having a voice to tell you to slow down your pace of engagement. You may not be entirely over your past relationship. You may need to get to know your new partner more intimately and/or spiritually, before your body will let you be as intimate physically.

For many women when they have sex with a new partner for the first time, penetration can be a challenge and it feels like you own the Gobi Desert of all vaginas. Don't worry. Again, you should see this as your body's voice saying that you are going too fast. Slow the pace of engagement down. For some women, vaginal dryness can also be the result of hormone changes and age effects. You may have been out of practice for a while and your arousal needs re-sequencing! In the meantime, keep a vaginal lubricant on hand to help your own love juices along. Take a trip down to your local love shop to see about purchasing Astro-Glide or JO H2O (a water-based vaginal lubricant). There are many such products available today. Ask questions at your choice of love shop. Ask your friends what works for them. Every conversation you have will lead you to your more confident sexual self.

There is always a learning curve to being a good lover with someone new. What worked for you in the past may be totally different for you with your new partner. Remember how complex your verbal communication can be when you project your feelings on another. It's so easy to misunderstand one another, even when you are well intentioned. To discover each other's sexual history takes time. Enjoy the new journey. Try to be curious and open when it comes to your emotional, physical, and sexual learning. This will not be easy because we usually think confidence comes from knowing a lot. But the opposite is the case when it comes to relationships. The more you don't know, the more you can discover. The more you are open to discover, the more intimately connected you become emotionally and physically.

Learning all about your partner's body will take time and practice. But how fun will that be! But start by first getting to know your own body really well in the same way that you have come to know your emotional scripts. Otherwise you will end up complicating your other. If you have been on your own for a while, you may have been a 'private partner' to your sexual life. Masturbating, you are obviously on your own. However, you might share the experience of masturbating with your partner so that they learn how you bring your to orgasm. You will also learn how they bring themselves to orgasm too. There is no one more expert at your own equipment than you! The same is true for your partner. If historically, you have had trouble coming to orgasm; it may be helpful to return to the Love Shop to get yourself a small vibrator! In the early stages of re-orientation to sharing body, mind and spirit, you may need a little assistance. It is entirely normal for you to have some anxieties. So set yourself up for success. Hopefully your partner is comfortable with you bringing a vibrator to the bedroom. Some partners though may be intimidated. He or she may see this as a deficit within them. Obviously this is not true. We all need a little help some of the time. Just talk it through.

If all of these ideas are feeling way too much of a challenge for you right now, you should just back up to basics. Try having a shower together. Feel each other's body with soapy hands. Enjoy your skin — your biggest organ. No men, it's not your penis! Feel the texture of your skin as it varies from the hidden spaces under your arms, between your fingers, behind your ears. You might wash each other's face – a very intimate exercise for sure. Enjoy your bodies and use all the toys you come equipped with.

Know your love button, the G-Spot. It's a trigger spot on your body that, when gently massaged, will bring about an intense orgasm. For women it is about one to three inches up the front (anterior) part of the vaginal wall. For men, the G-Spot is the prostate gland, about two inches up the anterior anal wall. Other sensitive areas of the body are the nipples for both women and men. For some women, touching the nipples alone is enough to bring an orgasm. Enjoy the discovery and wonder of your amazing bodies together. It's fun to be playful! Engage conversations between your toes, your backs, or your knees. The more you give your body a voice, the more you engage this idea that making love is a conversation in care, not a performance in results.

Your sexual life together will bring you closer and create a more intimate and secure attachment. In an ideal world, your lover's arms would be your safe landings at the end of your every day. That may be an overwhelming thought for many. Every day!? Yes, every day. Why not bring our body, mind and spirit into alignment and optimal chemistry every day?

Having said that, I realize that every day is not practical or ideal for many. Your life is busy and depending which stage of life you are in, this is not always possible. Have a conversation with your partner to decide on a schedule that feels mutually satisfying. For one person it may be that having sex once per week is enough. For the other it might be that an ideal is to have sex seven days a week. You would then negotiate a middle ground – how about three times per week?

Don't let your sex life be an area of control! Many partners will withhold sex if anything was miss-said or didn't happen to their satisfaction during the day. This makes your practice seem so complicated. Of course if you have been arguing all day, there is probably little chance you will want to express love or play in the night! Rejection of a partner's initiation of sex play can be painful. Don't end up as the gatekeeper in a power play. When sex becomes part of a power struggle, it's as if you are saying "all these chores need to be done before I will consider loving you". Keep chores and life's other tasks out of the bedroom.

Another obstacle that some couples grapple with can be to see sex as "another command performance after a draining day". Sex can be a great way to relieve your anxieties after a challenging day. Research from Brigham Young University suggests sex lowers your blood pressure. If you aren't having sex, it helps to have a strong social network. But sex may be your best way to keep your blood pressure down and your heart health up (45). Sex has been researched as a way to boost your immunity (46). It raises your levels of immunoglobulin A (IgA), an antibody that can prevent you from getting the cold and flu.

If that hasn't already motivated you to become a lover, read on! Sex is also a preventative influence when it comes to fighting off depression. In a study out of the University of Albany, women who had sex without condoms are less depressed than women who use them (47). A 1997 study of nearly 1,000 middle aged men showed a 50% drop in mortality in the men "with high orgasmic frequency". This suggests there is support for the thesis that sex is also going to help you live longer (48). I could go on and on in reciting the virtues of having sex to your physical, mental and spiritual health, quite apart from the emotional side of your being. But research also tells us that none of these positive outcomes from having sex will happen unless you find a great fit with your new partner. Your sexual life can be your safe landing. Your sexual life will keep you healthier and living longer, even when everything and everyone else in your day has been letting you down. So get down and keep it up!

✱✱✱✱✱✱✱✱✱✱✱✱

Breakthrough Tips:

1. If kissing has been a roadblock for you or your partner, communicate from the positive perspective (what you like) versus a critical one ("you're a terrible kisser"). For example "I love it when our lips touch softly and I can taste your breath…"
2. Communicate what feels best to you from an "I" statement. If the communication starts with a "you", it sounds critical and will tend to produce a defensive resistance, or expression of hurt, not understanding aimed at getting better being together.
3. Discover your bodies together. This 'not knowing' state makes the shared experience alive and in the present. Your sexual experience will be different with each partner. Cultivating the mindset to approach each relationship, as an exciting new discovery will allow you to leave old baggage behind and will add to the thrill of mystery and adventure that lies ahead for both of you.

4. Keep stresses down, and keep love and responsiveness up. Transition into lovemaking time with exercise, meditation, or music if you have had a challenging day at work.

5. Practice, practice, practice! Learning about your body and your lover's body takes time, curiosity, confidence and communication. The more you practice, the better it gets. The better it gets, the more intentional (and satisfied) you both will be.

****

CHAPTER 27

GETTING THAT CALL FROM YOUR PAST: NOT HOME...DON'T ANSWER!

Just about the time you feel great again because you have fully closed the door to the past and you are starting to experience the joyful freedom and wonder of you, you may get that call from him or her of your past to say "I miss you". Or someone lets you know your former boyfriend, girlfriend, husband, or wife is dating someone new...and your heart sinks. Don't tell yourself stories around these events. It just is what it is.

Practice generosity of spirit and be happy that your former partner is engaged in a new discovery of their heart, even if they are missing you right now. You could suggest they do their own work to move on and give them a copy of this book! If the call is about your former dating again, it's tempting to dwell and ruminate on what the new partner looks like, acts like and feels like compared to you. You may have a twinge of pain that tells you that you have been replaced. This is a path to misery. It's so tempting to rehearse these negative brain pathways; manage yourself! You have come so far in your own journey. Hold on to your grace and let the negative thoughts go. If you need to, revisit your three 'R's exercise. If your heart is sliding in and out of grief, know that the process is a little like the board game "Snakes and Ladders". It's normal to feel sad or longing for the past from time to time, and especially with new information that your former partner has a new love in his or her life.

When you are triggered like this, journal or talk the feelings through with a trusted friend. Then close that old door. Remember, you out grew him/her for a reason. Hopefully his/her new partnership will bring him/her the happiness yours didn't. Fixating, you may be tempted to ask friends questions, check out their Facebook postings, or even swing by their home to check out whose car is in the driveway. These obsessive, possessive thoughts and behaviors can be so toxic.

****

Here are some tips if you've got that kind of scratch happening:

1. Ask a friend or family member for support.
2. Book a therapeutic massage to up your oxytocin hormones.
3. Make sure you are eating, sleeping and exercising.
4. Choose your music carefully – listen to up-beat stations versus ones with heart break stories.
5. Invite a friend for coffee or meet for a drink after work.
6. Take time dressing in the morning.
7. Practice your smile through the day! (There is so much research to suggest that the simple act of smiling improves your mood). You might keep some funny object on your desk that reminds you to smile.
8. Get out of Dodge for the weekend with a friend or by yourself. A change of perspective can help remind you of your big picture.
9. Ask yourself, how important will these feelings of loss and longing for my former, be to me in five years?
10. Don't call or email your former him/her. To do so, would be feeding the grief and loss.
11. Go to a yoga class. Go for an evening walk. Read a page-turner novel.
12. If the obsessive thoughts persist, seek the help of a therapist or life coach.

****

If you can keep your focus, your earlier slip backwards will abate in a few weeks. Your own big love is just around the corner waiting to meet you!

Get back to celebrating the strides you have made since your break-up. You may want to read your personal resume again. You might invite some friends over for dinner to remind yourself of the love you have in your current and newly developed social circles. This might be a great time to write yourself a personal mission statement.

****

Still scratching?

1. Keep your goals front and center
2. Invite a friend to partner with you to hold you accountable to meet your goals. He or she may have their own goals that you can help them be accountable to as well.
3. Assess your time spent in focusing on your relationship (to family, friends, career, community or health).
4. One really great exercise is to build a life by design. Draw a 'pie of time' that illustrates how you spend your time in a typical day. As you look at your pie, you will have a quick snapshot of where your attention has been focused. Your time pie will also show you where you are getting good results! If you like certain things that you paid proper attention to, you can reward yourself for a time well spent. If you don't like what you see, re-assess a new design for your day, emphasizing where your intentions need to go.

****

Getting That Call That He or She Wants to Reconcile

One of the toughest experiences can be when your former partner has an impulsive habit of trying to resurrect the dead because their new life is feeling stuck. In those times you may get that call from him or her to say he or she misses you. This is can be so crippling to all the good work you have done. Re-read the boundaries chapter. It can be so upsetting to hear that the one you have loved is in pain and (possibly because he or she has not done any personal work of their own), returns to you with a get out of jail free card.

Reconciliation may be what you want to consider (especially if you have children in the mix), but revisit your 3 "R"'s before you embark on this path because it's not without its risks. Remember that you are the one who has been changing. If your former partner hasn't also worked through some of their own issues and grown, there is probably a good chance you are going to have another crash of your hearts.

This dance through the past is a common experience. We are generally an impulsive culture that wants fast fixes and has low pain tolerance. If you are identifying with this on and off relationship cycle, you are not alone in the experience. Recall the movie "It's Complicated" where Alec Baldwin plays the role of the malcontent, who raises havoc in Meryl Streep (who plays his former wife)'s life as she is starting her own process of rebuilding. It is complicated to embark on reconciliation. However if you have children, you may find the process of couples therapy is a helpful solution to the confusion. Whether a therapy process rekindles and realigns your old relationship, or whether it doesn't, your breakthrough may be to break this complicated rehearsal of idealizing and then realizing you are (once again) ill fitted! The following story is a painful example of why it's important to be clear.

Fit to be Tied

I recall working with a client "Fit to be Tied" Tyler who was a victim of his former wife 'Amanda' who regretted her decision to leave their marriage. Together 'Tyler' and 'Amanda' had built a family, complete with three children, a dog, a beautiful home and a fifteen-year life together. Sadly, 'Amanda' had fallen in love with 'Tyler's' best friend. This event had catapulted their marriage into a fast separation and divorce, and 'Amanda' moved in with 'Tyler's' best friend. Over a period of the two years, the bloom fell off the rose, so to speak. 'Amanda' started reaching out to 'Tyler' saying she regretted leaving him. 'Amanda' was, at that point still living with the new boyfriend.

This was un-nerving for 'Tyler' who started feeling depressed, unmotivated at work and at home. The possibility of reconciliation possessed him. Over the next few months he waited for her to be certain about ending her relationship with her new boyfriend. Being controlled by her in this way, he was distracted from his work and eventually, one year later, was let go because of his poor performance on the job. Being captive in this emotional bind with 'Amanda', 'Tyler' had sunk into a passive victim mode, which eventually undermined every aspect of his life. To this day, 'Amanda' continues to live with her boyfriend and shares stories with 'Tyler' about her ambivalence for the boyfriend and regret for giving up 'Tyler'. Talk about being screwed, blued and tattooed!

How can 'Tyler' be released from his own jail? 'Tyler's' job one is to consider his relationship with women generally. Coincidentally it was also a woman boss who fired him from his executive career. As he gains insight about how he is controlled by women, women will begin to respect him. His second consideration will be to assess his pattern of victimization as he considers how he could be more present and confident regarding his needs and feelings. One of the core motivators for 'Tyler' to reconcile with 'Amanda' was to do anything possible to keep his family together. However the cost of the "on again off again" and the emotional turbulence of reconciliation needs to weigh in on the decision too! Being an on again, off again couple can have negative impacts on your children. It can be difficult to not share the possibility thinking with your children because you love them and you know that in most situations children hope their parents will reconcile. When they get a hint something is up, their magical minds will be swept into a multitude of feelings that confuse and depress them over time. Remember how important constancy is for children going through family change. If you are working through all the considerations of reconciliation, make sure those preliminary conversations with your former partner and with your friends, happen outside of your homes and not when your children are around. First, be clear that you want to reconcile. Choose a period of established time that you both have maintained that fresh commitment. Then after a reasonable period of constancy, share the happy news with your whole family with everyone in the room at once. This pragmatic process is so protective of your children who shouldn't be riding the up and down waves of indecision; the results of which can be depression, anxiety and trouble concentrating at school.

****

Breakthrough tips to gain insight and confidence if you are at this cross-roads:

1. Ask yourself; is reconciliation in **your** best interests?
2. What has changed since you were together before?
3. How will the changes you have made and the insights you have gained help you to have a different outcome this time?
4. What behavior patterns has your former partner changed in their growing since you were together before?
5. If you didn't have children, would you still be motivated towards reconciliation; rebuilding a life you can love with your former partner today?
6. Rather than dwell on reconciliation with your former partner, you can go back to your time pie. Re-jig your day to focus on other things and reward yourself once you have accomplished that.
7. Could you re-focus on your work, or on getting fit? Choose another focus to give you a regained feeling of control and inner peace. The time you put in to these aspects of your life, you will gain certain benefits from.
8. Get back to your gratitude exercise! Every morning and evening, write down one thing that is going well.

****

I have worked with many clients who moved happily through this reconciliation process and they remain happily married today. Couples therapy really can work! Guiding couples back on to a loving path is one of the most rewarding experiences in clinical practice. When there are children involved, they are the big reasons you may want to take the leap of faith. Just don't leap blindly off cliffs!

CHAPTER 28

WHAT DO YOU WANT TO MANIFEST?

Now that you have your own 'love zone' going on within you most of the time, you are ready to share your life again. Take a moment of quiet either at your desk or in some natural space where you won't be interrupted. Try to imagine the qualities of the person you want to attract to your life.

What will it feel like when you are with your new partner?

What kind of activities will you do together?

What personality traits will he have?

Is she sensual?

Does he have a great sense of humor?

Is she philosophical, intellectual, sporty, athletic, spontaneous, romantic, adoring, self-accomplished, altruistic, spiritual, atheistic, interested in science, politics, sports, or gardening?

Ideally the qualities you have identified in defining yourself will be the ones you are looking for in your other. The more aligned you are, the less friction and stress you may experience. It may be true in many cases that opposites attract, particularly if there is part of your psyche still needing to develop. But after developing your 'whole' self by putting into action what is suggested in this book, it may be the right time to look for 'another one' just like you, who is also whole and ready to boogie.

If you look for someone just like you, there may be an ease of fit. More stress down, and love up! Does he like the outdoors or is she a homebody? What can you picture the two of you doing: an exotic climb to the top of Kilimanjaro, a hike to Machu Picchu, or a helicopter ski in the Rockies? Or are you happy going dancing or just staying home to play cards in the warmth of the fireplace?

Often I see clients who get hung up on the specifics of what their ideal mate should look like physically (not too tall, not too short, not too thin, not too fat, not too many wrinkles). In many ways, thinking like this can be a big trap. Looks fade. It's the time you will spend together with your new partner in activities you both love that will feed your hearts. If you imagine yourself in a room the last two weeks of your life, who might you want sharing your last breath with—a rock solid beautiful statue or a loving spirit with whom you have danced through life?

Joe and I recently watched a made for TV movie called 'Jack', the story of a prominent Canadian political leader and head of the New Democratic Party named Jack Layton. The movie told the story of the last year of Mr. Layton's life which he spent campaigning in a federal election which in his view was part of fulfilling his father's call to action *"Jack, if you have the chance to help others, do it."*

In a very poignant last scene of the movie, Mr. Layton's daughter and granddaughter embrace the ailing grandfather in a tearful, long, last embrace. Jack's wife Olivia is seen in the last scene, flickering SOS's with her flashlight to Jack from the hallway of their home. Jack's final letter to Canada, he called 'A Life in Legacy, I believe that we should all pay attention to the message in this letter, because it contains an important life lesson and powerful call to action for all of us (abbreviated):

August 20, 2011

Toronto, Ontario

Dear Friends,

Tens of thousands of Canadians have written to me in recent weeks to wish me well. I want to thank each and every one of you for your thoughtful, inspiring and often-beautiful notes, cards and gifts. Your spirit and love have lit up my home, my spirit, and my determination.

Unfortunately my treatment has not worked out as I hoped. So I am giving this letter to my partner Olivia to share with you in the circumstance in which I cannot continue...

To other Canadians who are on journeys to defeat cancer and to live their lives, I say this: please don't be discouraged that my own journey hasn't gone as well as I had hoped. You must not lose your own hope. Treatments and therapies have never been better in the face of this disease. You have every reason to be optimistic, determined, and focused on the future. My only other advice is to cherish every moment with those you love at every stage of your journey, as I have done this summer.

...All my life I have worked to make things better. Hope and optimism have defined my political career, and I continue to be hopeful and optimistic about Canada. Young people have been a great source of inspiration for me. I have met and talked with so many of you about your dreams, your frustrations, and your ideas for change... Canada. I believe in you. Your energy, your vision, your passion for justice are exactly what this country needs today. You need to be at the heart of our economy, our political life, and our plans for the present and the future.

... We can be a better one – a country of greater equality, justice, and opportunity. We can build a prosperous economy and a society that shares its benefits more fairly. We can look after our seniors. We can offer better futures for our children. We can do our part to save the world's environment. We can restore our good name in the world...

My friends, love is better than anger. Hope is better than fear. Optimism is better than despair. So let us be loving, hopeful and optimistic. And we'll change the world.

All my very best, Jack Layton

Besides being a heroic figure, what a loving human Mr. Layton was. At the same time, how tragic that he did not have more time to spend with the big loves in his life. It's a very clarifying exercise to write your own 'last letter' to determine what is important to you (i.e., your values for living and relating). When you do this type of exercise you engage yourself in a powerful question:

- "Why am I here?" and
- "What is important to me?" and
- "Who will be the ones who I want with me sharing my last breathes of life?"

If you can answer these questions you will likely find yourself getting much clearer about the qualities of the person you want to attract to your big life partnership.

And your legacy is really defined by all the small things you do when no one is looking. It's the thousands of small actions you do every day. Life legacies are created through the generosity of spirit that you show when you help a friend out, or when you leave work early to attend your child's concert. Who we are is defined in our actions through our adult life. Most of us won't have a chance to write a "last letter", because death often arrives unexpected or in circumstances where our cognitive capacity has dramatically declined. But it can be so revealing if, at this very moment you were to imagine yourself at your last stages of life. What do you think is important about your life?

Be mindful. At the beginning of each day when you breathe, open your heart... and at the end of the day breathe, and reflect on the day. Pull in all the good thoughts about the things you did for others and yourself too that are your own legacy. Breathe out knowing you did something to make the world a little better, for someone, in that moment. In this way, your legacy is written by the way you live your life every day.

And this includes forgiving yourself and moving on from the inevitable bad days – and this helps in developing understanding, patience and compassion for others when they lose it too.

In his touching movie "Big", Tom Hanks reminds us that it's so important to know your values. We see his character discover the values of humility, fun, lessons learned, and the assertion that no matter who you are at whatever age, always try to deliver your best.

Look for the qualities in the partner of your future that you cherish the most. They may show up in simple gestures like how she pours you a cup of tea, whether he opens a door for others, or whether she is moved to donate money to a street person. You may have a sense of his authenticity in the way he discloses his raw feelings or her state of 'unknowing'. He may have an expression of love that shows up in creative cooking. Behavior, more than words, tells us who we are. Love is seen more in the behaviors we exemplify than in the words we say, (although those are important too!)

When we are young, we choose to trust and connect with people who have familiar features to our immediate family members and ourselves. Current research suggests these mechanisms may be in place at birth. A leading research study reports that even before they can walk children trust those who have similar features to them (49). It would be interesting to know if this is why, as human beings we tend to make decisions of attraction based on what people look like versus whether they are kind, caring, or healthy. Is this why we tend to follow an attraction sequence of physical features, then spirit (how do we feel with the other), and finally their intellect (how stimulated to I feel with them?)?

It would be much more productive to re-sequence our inquiry by focusing on spiritual attraction first, followed by intellectual attraction before we get to physical features. I believe that this would lead us on a path to more positive and enduring relationships over time. In making the biggest decision of your life, you may be selecting partners based on unconscious criteria that are pre-programmed into us because of our natural selection drive that looks based on health, stability, as indicators of the ideal baby maker potential. Better to leave this search until after you have found a partner who is mentally and spiritually compatible with you and therefore a better partner in a relationship from which you can make good babies.

****

Breakthrough Exercise:

1. Write your own 'Last Letter' sometime this month. This requires a quiet uninterrupted space at your desk. Pour yourself a cup of tea and turn your phone off. Check in with your letter once a year to get you out of the trenches and back in line with your values.
2. Ask yourself "why am I here?" (The Oprah Question) This is a great way to become even clearer about your life purpose, who you are, because living a life you will love starts with you.
3. Ask yourself "what is important to me?" (What are my values, what would I put into my personal mission statement)
4. Who will you want to have with you sharing your last breaths of life?
5. Imagine him right now. What does her heart feel like next to yours?
6. What qualities describe the love of your life? Is that the person who will be standing beside you at the end of your life?
7. Write a list of all your friends in one column and in the next column write out their values, as you would perceive them to be based on their behaviors that you have witnessed.
8. Next, look at your time spent with each of these friends and adjust your attention to each friendship (allocating more or less time) according to the relative alignment in values held by you and these friends.
9. Start a journal. Your Last Letter could be the start of it. It helps you acquire a deeper understanding when you write, because the information at play becomes more distinctive in your memory systems. We know from research that tracking your thoughts and behaviors helps foster desired change in both your mental construct and your course of action. Programs like Weight Watchers utilize this approach and are testaments to the benefits of this type of tracking.

****

CHAPTER 29

YOU ARE THE MASTER OF YOUR LIFE AND LOVE IN BALANCE

With all the deep personal work you have now done, you now know how your childhood has shaped your present feelings and thinking. You also know what new life strategies will help you to shape a more fulfilling life and love experience. You now know you can live more expansively if you broaden your habits with new patterns of behavior. You now know you can over-ride your old emotional habits of avoiding, withdrawing, pursuing, or projecting. You are now more aware of your personal stress habits and how they have blocked your heart in the past; or caused damage to another's heart in the process. How will you maintain your commitment to life-long change? How will you cherish yourself and your new true love when he or she shows up in your life? What in your life will you do that will keep you accountable to your growth? Who could you invite to hold you accountable to a maintenance plan for authentic expression and loving behaviors?

Defining a mission statement for life is a creative way to ensure that you keep top of mind your core values and integrity. Your commitment to living your life in balance by paying attention to mind, body, and spirit health is your insurance policy for life-long joy and creativity. I recall my yoga retreat in Sayulita and the discovery of a YUM that's within. My life purpose at the age of 55 is expressed a little differently than it was when I was 25, and yet my purpose has been to inspire better love in our communities. At 25 I was having babies and leading my prenatal exercise classes. At 55 I am still dedicated to building supportive systems in our communities. Inspiration comes from the ways we engage together. Our ideas and behaviors shape each other. Hopefully each generation will become more loving, and more inspired. I think quite possibly we can all get better at being more supportive to each other.

One of the reasons I feel renewed by the ocean is that each wave represents to me the surprise of something new, fresh, clean and constant. The ocean is full of life. It's where life on Earth began. The ocean clears the remnants we would otherwise trip on. Fresh start... fresh start... Don't live in the past... Live your best life you can in your 'today'. As I look back at my career path, I have always held a belief that our communities, like our oceans, are our key resource to enhance global health and caring. If we care for our oceans, our communities, and our selves, I believe that our world will assuredly get better. When you embrace yourself as 'love' in your own life, our Universe becomes more loving.

Between each ocean wave there is a pause. It is in these pauses in our lives, that we will find time for better balance and better love. Take advantage of these pauses every day in your life to enhance your health, and to care for your family, and for your most meaningful relationships. Be current with the ones who matter to you. It is in those relationships from where renewal will flow. God, Elohim (Hebrew name for God), Gaia (Earth God), Shiva (Hindu God), Mithra (Iranian God of Light), Ganesh (Asian God), Ngai (African God) or our universal 'Godly' state might be otherwise understood as 'love'. Being in a loving state, you are God. Everything you choose in your life from today onward should support you to be more loving and therefore more powerful than you have ever been before. When I speak of power, I am really saying at peace. I'd suggest those words could be considered synonymous. If you choose the fabric of your life, you will do amazing things in your lifetime. I'm not suggesting a grandiose project or that you become an egoist, but truly in your own way, you can make our world better. We all can.

So, now...what is your life purpose? Would you define it differently today, than you did a year ago? This is a huge question and one that will shift and change for you through time. But you should be able to answer it on an ongoing basis because it will guide the way you design each next stage in your life and love relationships. When you think of your parents, are there qualities in either of them that you wish they had more consciously developed? Are these qualities you might develop in you? Confidence? Personal Care? Athleticism? My mother never finished high school. She grew up in a small town in New Zealand and gave up her opportunity for education to support her family. She left New Zealand when she was nineteen and found a job at a bank in Vancouver during the Great Depression. Although she was really smart, her role models were Jacqueline Kennedy, Marilyn Munroe, and Doris Day – beautiful women who aspired to live in a man's world. For my Mother, marrying my Father an Engineer made her life a success. My role models are (the late) Katherine Hepburn, Jane Fonda, and Oprah; all women who inspire me to come alive in a partnered world. I was the first woman in our family who got two University degrees. Learning and upgrading education is a value I try to inspire in my practice and it was important to me that our daughter went to University for those reasons. What do you wish your parents had done differently? What potential in them was unfulfilled?

In the pauses of life, I know how important it is for me to have a day-to-day strategy of meditation (for my mind), exercise (for my body), and love connection with my husband Joe (for my spirit). I continue to covet Sunday for family time with my adult children, to either go for a run or play tennis together (for body, mind and spirit). How about you? Depending on your own stage of life, these social outlets can be naturally occurring or needing more intentional design. I was with a client last week whose son has recently moved to a different city for his work. In his twenties, his life is fully his own and for my client who has been solo parenting for much of his life, there remains a hollow gap of time. She reminds me to highlight the importance of developing your career, home, personal, health, hobbies, friendships and your romantic life. If you have any doubt about how valuable it can be to maintain balance in all parts of your life, just ask yourself what you want your children to learn from you about living their lives in balance? What would you feel if your children grew up to be just like you? Hopefully positive thoughts come to mind. And is there an area of your development you could improve on?

I also know how important it is for me to feel connected with my girl-friends and my community, so I participate in a book club. Once and a while we have a girls weekend away. I am training in a running group towards another half marathon. I try to commit to participate in one vol-unteer focus with our community each year. My husband has a group of men he gets together with to watch sports. He also has a breakfast group to discuss ...whatever comes to mind/heart. Whatever is said on the trail, stays on the trail. Omerta! Having your own social supports is healthy.

Are you someone who tends to shop to feel better? That can be problem-atic to your wallet and to your spirit. In any case, keeping track of your spending can really help you. Notice if you tend to shop for those extras at times when you are struggling emotionally. Instead of shopping, go to a yoga class or fitness class. The spend trend to feel better may be short lived, for there now seems to be a growing global shift of care and towards sim-plicity. I'm not Catholic but we see this trend even with the election of the new Pope Francis, whose coat of arms, motto and ring provide a message to live simply. Think for yourself; could your life be simplified in any way? What kind of difference would that make for you? You don't need to join an ashram or walk naked in the street like St. Francis of Assisi a thousand years ago. But what if you walked or rode your bike to work today instead of using your car?

Be more heart centered the way you live your life rather than being so results-oriented that you become lost in your hustle to achieve. Don't set your goals so narrowly towards the 'results' of your chosen focus that you miss being in 'the process' of your day. Being too goal oriented can take the most joyful activity and turn it into another work project. For most of us, the point of learning to play tennis is to have fun and to get some exercise, not to become a Wimbledon challenger (unless you are dedicating your life to become a tennis legend Roger Federer or Andre Agassi).

I was reminded of this 'process versus results' idea on a Sunday run recently with my daughter. We ran together in a beautiful bird sanctuary called Burnaby Lake. It's a soft surface trail that meanders around a stun-ning lake, with many offshoot streams that in March are filled with lily pads. It's a ten-mile run, which is no small feat. We were lost in conversation before too long. We moved through the miles of spongy sawdust distance. My daughter described the stage of her career (it had been six months since a previous breakup) and how difficult it was to meet perspective romantic partners. She works long hours and most nights is happy to just relax in her apartment. Between work and friends who are already in relationships, she described the life of most young professionals today. I stopped her mid-sentence to say "Look up right now". We had jogged over a little bridge and to the right and to the left were breathtaking views of nature. We both smiled, as we recognized we had been so focused on completing the task of the run, that we almost missed the beauty of the single moment.

The message is to keep your head up and to get out of the trenches once and awhile. This suggestion is five to two times more salient in your workweek (which is five days long), than it is in your weekend (which is only two days long). Your quality of life is best experienced in your present, no matter where you are. It resides in those special moments that take your breath away: when you see a sunrise or sunset, or simply meet someone who works in that cubicle at the other end of your office! Look around you no matter where you are. When you keep your head up, you will notice so many amazing things. Lift up your spirit up from the repetitive and often dreaded route way of living. By the way, one year later, Ashley has a new boyfriend she met indirectly through work!

Walk slower. Take time to connect with people around you, at coffee, at lunch, and in the elevator. Have a conversation you have never had before. If you do, you will discover, (as we did on the bridge), those moments that take your breath away. So look up! In our case, we were almost too busy to notice the ripples of water, the buzz of life in the marsh, the way the light dances on the water. But when we gave ourselves a moment on the bridge, presto, our lives were more beautiful.

If you think you can't meet a potential partner because you work such long hours, make sure you build small bridges into your day. Did you know that statistically most people meet their life partners at work? One fifth of Canadians and Americans meet their mates in their work settings. Surveys show that one quarter to one half of office romances lead to marriage. The reasons for this, as explained in a 2012 study, are firstly because of proximity, because you have more daytime contact with people at work. In the fullness of a 24-hour day, our most energetic time is during the mid-day. After a 40 to 50 hour workweek, you may not have the energy to put into dating. People tend to be selected for workplaces based on similar characteristics such as empathy, caring, and intelligence. You also have a preselected similarity in values and interests because the people you work with are focused on similar pursuits as you. The workplace is also where you get to see the fitness of a potential mate, in how he or she handles stress and how creative he or she is day to day. You can also access a lot of data about another person based on their reputation from colleagues (50). Heads up boys and girls!

But it's hard to slow down and look around because we are so busy *making* money so that we can *spend* even more money. Without self-management to curb your appetite to spend more, your body raises its volume to say: "hey you…you are off balance… stop your addictive spending". You shake and quake or shake and **bake into burnout**. That is when symptoms of anxiety and emotional reactivity show up. Feelings of isolation and loneliness will likely follow, and all the symptoms of stress show up. Remember the 'love up, stress down' principal for life. Don't lose the mission statement for your life that you developed in the past few weeks. Keep it in your wallet or at your desk. Slow down and you will probably notice you are spending less. Impulsive over-spending can also be an indicator of anxiety and depression.

✱✱✱✱✱✱✱✱✱✱✱✱

Breakthrough questions:

1. What in your day makes you happy?
2. What in your day yesterday made you smile?
3. How did you make someone else smile yesterday?
4. What is one positive lifestyle change you can make today that you will continue to do every day from this day forward?
5. What do you notice when you look up right now?

✱✱✱✱✱✱✱✱✱✱✱✱

If you choose love in all aspects of your life when it shows up in self, career, partnership(s), family, and friendship, what kind of person is going to be your big love this time? What defines wealth to you in this context? Is it a financial accumulation or an intimate room full of people who you love and love you? What are you more interested in? Financial wealth or wellness? These are some of the questions that will shape your choices and will influence the way you spend your most precious commodity in your life. That is, the way you spend your time. Anything you focus on, you will get good at. So focus on love and exploring the adventures this wonderful world has in it. Do you want to see the annual Tomantina tomato fight in Spain? Do you want to watch the sunset over the Pyramids? Do you see you and your loved one swimming with dolphins in Costa Rica? Do you want to create a secret garden in your back yard?

When you consider your ideal partner in life, are they interested in developing in body, mind, and spirit like you? Your ideal soul mate should be someone who is also doing his or her best to live an authentic, balanced life. If you choose well, it will be easy to keep the momentum and personal commitments you have made to yourself through this book.

Love After Love

The time will come

When, with elation

You will greet yourself arriving

At your own door, in your own mirror

And each will smile at the other's welcome,

And say, sit here. Eat.

You will love again the stranger who was yourself.

Give wine. Give bread. Give back your heart

To itself, to the stranger who has loved you

All your life, whom you ignored

For another who knows you by heart

Take down the love letters from the bookshelf,

The photographs, the desperate notes,

Peel your own image from the mirror.

Sit. Feast on your life.

(Derek Walcott)

CHAPTER 30

LEARNING OUTCOMES FROM PART 3: YOU ARE STRONGER THAN YOU THINK!

You now know for sure, it's great being you. Like Dorothy in the Wizard of Oz, all you needed to do all along was click your ruby shoes together three times and know you are home in yourself after all. This review embraces your learning from all three parts of this book. The door to the past is firmly closed and you have now stepped through a new door to a new life you can love. You know as well as I do that there will always be tornedos in your life because we can't control for forces of nature or what other people do and say. Generally though, I'm sure you agree, it's a pretty wonderful world.

Relax, you can handle whatever life brings your way because you have tools to help you gain perspective, empower you, and guide you. You now know your emotional patterns based on your family learning. You know how to spot your emotional habits to pursue, withdraw or avoid. You know, like all of us, you have gotten stuck at times in these recursive emotional loops that emit stories that you are disempowered, rejected, abandoned, or not good enough. These internal stories are antecedents from past historical hurts. You are now standing in a fresh perspective, which invites the adorable, whole imperfect you to come into the light. Enjoy the ride. Life is long and you have a whole lot of loving to do.

What a soul-saving practice journaling can be to enhance your life. In your journal, you share your life, with all its daily ups and downs. When you have a dip, ask yourself "which negative cycle am I living in now? What story am I telling myself that takes me into this painful spiral?" Love lives inside you wherever you go because you make the choice to step into your experience and work through the confusion or withdraw and avoid it. When you choose the latter, you end up in a disconnect with your body, mind and spirit. No more proving yourself. You are enough. With anyone you meet, as long as you have the courage to ask questions and share your feelings, no matter what they are, you will grow and potentially so will the other person. After you journal, reframe your negative internal stories and speak up.

As you have these courageous conversations with yourself (in your journal) and then with others, you will be able to relax into your life more. Your experience with others will change because you will start noticing more positive things and less negative. This gives you more internal and external emotional security. Less drama and stress means more love and capacity in your life. A sign of health that you should watch for will be noticing your own inner ease at being able to laugh at yourself and with others. You are sleeping better, communicating easily, and enjoying the company of those around you. With your new two-step, you will have greater internal capacity to be intimate through all your emotions in the spectrum from love to anger.

So go on and do the two-step: (1) Feel it. (2) Talk about it! You are also more able to safely and courageously identify with other peoples' emotions now. You have a two-step approach for dealing with other peoples' upsets: (1) Listen for his/her story. (2) Be empathic to his/her feelings. With your two-step, you are fully ready to dance into love again.

The energy and strength of love inside you is constant and enduring. Can you see conflict now as a transient condition like changing weather patterns? Conflict is just confusion, it no longer calls you to pursue, withdraw or avoid. Anger invites you to an intimate world of judgment or fear that you hold deeply under the surface. It is through an awareness and understanding those feelings, that you come to recognize that you may have attachment wounds from childhood that need healing. Anger is a feeling that you will surely experience from time to time. So you must gain mastery over your anger, and develop your capacity to have empathy for other's anger. This ability may be the ultimate key to achieving intimacy and success in the loving relationships in your future.

Managing anger is not a desired emotional space in which to live your life. But neither should you be afraid of it. Rather, anger is useful information that you can now walk curiously towards. So feel it and heal it! Otherwise you will set yourself up for anxiety.

While on a hike with my husband Joe, my stepdaughter Berkley and her fiance Sean, Berkley drew my attention to a tree that had been split in two by lightning. The tree lay in blackened splinters. I told her that when lightning strikes a field, it puts electricity in the soil. This injection of lightning actually makes crops grow in fields. Maybe anger is a little like lightening. It can split us or wake us to our roots. It's all in the delivery, the location, and the cultivating. We all have our own life lessons gained from gut wrench, heart shred, and the life-altering process of moving forward. One of my many take-aways from the loss of my twenty-year marriage is that I should never be afraid of anger. I should always feel accountable to my authentic feelings. I should live honestly and do my best to continue my own personal process of lifetime learning.

Anchor in a strategy to communicate your feelings and needs, no matter what they are. Anxiety is a human experience that even Canadian Astronaut Chris Hadfield disclosed recently that he too experiences! Sometimes you may feel like you are free falling in space. And then, as if the universe has a common pulse, you will be reminded of the things that help you get your bearings in life: your life partner, your family, friends, and all the little things in life that make up the constructs of your day to day living. It's you and all the anchors of your life that you are now fully able to count on and resource yourself with. Even just thinking of your body, your best friend, and every time you breathe out...you know you are whole, safe and good.

Whatever you need now to be able to be more in your natural state of love, just do it. Self-care has just got to come first. When you have a pile of work in front of you and its time for your yoga class, you may flinch and think you should do your work. Wrong…Just go for your yoga class. I know it's hard to put yourself first sometimes because your inner saboteur squawks "don't be so selfish". You deserve to be happy. If you burn out because you have not been taking time for yourself, you will not be able to contribute to anything. So commit to your new health habits for your whole life.

With your revitalized energy and newfound ability to calm yourself, you are better able to maintain the gains you've already achieved. You now have all the tools and capacity to feel your 'zone' whenever you want to engage it. One of my clients came into her session recently to say she totally gets this idea that she is "enough". She smiled and continued, "its actually really fun to be self-aware and curious about my life now. I'm noticing so much more going on in every moment. People are hilarious some times. I am totally hilarious some times!" We shared a great belly laugh together.

Speaking of great bellies, some say when you see the Buddha (a symbol of enlightenment) you should stomp on him because you should never stop growing. We are never done learning or developing. Life presents opportunity to be inspired and be inspiring. We are all a little flawed and doing our best to develop depending on our unique situations and histories. After Part Three, you have developed your own unique style and lifestyles. It can be fun to return to some of the chapters in Part Three from time to time to remind yourself to try on creative new styles of living. You may currently have a Miley Cyrus or Bruno Mars mentor that may shift into Lady Gaga or Justin Timberlake next month. Isn't it time to have fun with your newly-found style and better way of being in the world?

You are always your own best guide to discover relationships that are healthy or not healthy. Remember that happiness, self-assessment scale of 0 – 10 from Chapter One? What number will you give yourself today? How much has yourself-assessment scale changed for you? What is it like to know you have created that change for yourself? What new practice started your biggest shift to breakthrough from your breakup?

I was on a run in the Capilano River Canyon recently with Heidi Gravel, a good friend of mine. We ran past a woman who was on a hike with her Golden Lab. We laughed to see her dog with great fortitude and strength carry a massive 'log sized' piece of wood, which was probably equal to its own weight. I thought to myself, isn't that what I have done at times? I have carried my own dead wood, the emotional weight of distress from my past, when I could have set it aside long ago? Maybe we are like faithful determined dogs, naturally attracted to pick up more than our share of what is comfortable to carry. You can live your best life. And you know you will live it with greater capacity now that you have truly let the weight of your past painful ending(s) go.

Relationships cause your heart to squeeze, pound, and even to break at times. These are all the symptoms of a live heart. You are alive in this present moment and you have stepped into your magic and the wonder of life again. You have everything to risk, but also everything to gain. You always have the choice about whether you will carry your past in a way that will weigh you down, (that dog's stick was as wide as the path and about two feet in depth). Or you can move forward towards your own lightness of being by leaving the past in the past. Live in your present. The tornedo of your breakup was over as soon as you chose it to be over. The click of your own ruby shoes to know you are at home with the real you, is also the click of your right and left-brain connection! Dance your whole heart and whole brain into love with you and everyone you meet every day. Live your best life with a new ease of being, capacity of self-expression, other focused caring, and sense of the unique contribution that you bring to your world. You are well on your way to living your most inspired, energized, and resounded healthy life. Jump over all large obstacles. Don't carry them.

You are the only one who can actually bust through the walls of your inner battles with vulnerability. When you reflect, you will now be better able to appreciate that the struggles that you went through in your break up have now given you a new sense of abundance and vitality that you otherwise might never have experienced. You know more now. Actually you are more Be-You-Ti-Ful than you've even been before. Forgiveness and freedom are the frameworks of your new open door. No pain, no gain. Your body, mind and soul are now much more resilient, abundant, and beautiful. You now know profoundly that love lives within you. These joyful feelings of possibility are inside you where ever you go. There is pain sometimes and there is joy sometimes. And 'Its All Good' because you are now able to actively manage a life-long process of personal growth. You are stronger than you think.

So say that out loud "I am growing". You now know that your relationships with all significant others in your life are laboratories for personal growth. And when these relationships feel the most challenging for you, you can also view them as the most fertile sources of future research about how to live your best life. You are now so much more curious about learning from your own soft spots, and able to tap into your ability to manage these areas of vulnerability. All this life experience provides you with new insights that help to continue to learn how to love better.

We are all born with an innate sense of trust. We are born with a primordial scream and we know instinctively that our cries will be held, nourished, and honored. Trust IS your natural state. The never-ceasing challenge that you will face in your life is to commit to being in that natural internal state as often and as well as you can. But to get there, you will need to give up your resistance to change.

Change is bound to happen every day for the rest of your life. Change occurs within you, as you validate and frame your feelings and your needs by saying them out loud. As you come to trust yourself and to experience the safety of sharing your deepest fears and vulnerabilities, you can provide yourself and others with a powerful source of healing. Your brain is an inherently social organ and it will continue to grow ever healthier throughout your life when you view change from a perspective of awakening and lifetime learning.

By now, you have discovered many new things about yourself, including a new license on life that you will enjoy as you learn ways you can get better at looking for love. The more you are curious about who you have been with your partner(s) through life, the more capacity you will have not to not to fall back into those power struggles that define love by rigid rules. There is never any useful purpose in trying to convince anyone else of how to behave in a relationship with you. So my advice to you is to just focus on who you are, what you are learning, and how you can get better at love. The power struggles that many couples remain franticly stuck in, are almost always about the colliding of egos and the need to be right. You know not to fall back into that trap of self-righteousness. What you have learned should forever liberate you from that dismal self-righteous struggle in which there are really no winners but sadly so many losers.

In contrast, love is an energy that is other-focused and unconditional. Love is the miracle agent, that secret sauce that inoculates our hearts against the assault from our insecurities. Love provides a soft landing at the end of a challenging day. So be gentle with yourself and with those who you have loved or who you will choose to love in the future.

Continue to work on your need to control what happens in your relationships. When you sense that you want someone to think your way or do things according to your plan, check in with yourself on what you are afraid of. Sit back and notice when these dynamics of control show up in your life. The more controlling you are, the less loving your behavior will likely be. Likewise, the more controlling the behavior of your other, the less loving he or she is being. New and informed experiences of healthy loving relationships every day will help you to overcome your old beliefs if you commit to staying flexible and curious about yourself.

As you look back now at your most significant relationships and the transformations that you have gone through with each one of them, have you noticed in yourself a new-found joy, pain, exhilaration, disappointment, caring, abandonment, strength, or weakness? Whatever other experiences this transformation from then to now has provided you, would you change anything? Every close relationship that you have been involved in has developed you in some particular way and has also had impact on your other. From what you have read above, you should now know that your success in navigating within these important relationships is directly influenced by how skillfully you receive information and the way you choose to interpret and apply that information.

But a dose of reality is warranted here. You will likely experience times going forward when your old instincts may take over and cause you to regress and to repeat those old negative stories from the past when you regurgitate and reapply that information from your important relationships. But you now know how to climb out of this emotional ditch and how to immediately do a reframe! This ability to renew yourself requires practice so that you are able to process every such reminiscence in a more positive and skillful way so that you can get back to enjoying your life. Your brain and heart and everyone who loves you are counting on you to do this!

Love is magical, enduring, and transforming. All the stories of your past experience of love are the web, strength and resilience that shapes your capacity to initiate new love going forward. I can assure you that in both big and small ways, love has touched my life from the day I was born to my ripe middle age of fifty-something. I wouldn't change anything. Everyone I have ever loved is in the mix of my 'lub/dub' (the systolic/diastolic) blood flow of my heart. The pauses between intake and outflow have sometimes been painful. I am grateful just the same.

My hope for you is that you are more curious about yourself than you were before you started reading this book. Curiosity is the alchemy that can create magic in your life. If you unleash your curiosity, you will open yourself to experiencing a new and enriched quality of life that is more vital than any life pathway you could have ever dreamed before. There is freshness in curiosity—an abundant unknown-ness. So try always to be curious. You can start by developing a sense of confidence and trust that everything you have gone through and will go through in your life is leading you to exactly the right place for you.

The things you learned in the last year are all part of a plan to prepare you for what is in store for you next year. If you don't believe me, I suggest that you go back to the relationship timeline exercise you did earlier. If you do this, you should be able to see more clearly the ways that each of your important relationships has developed you. I bet you will also see how you have influenced the development of your significant other(s).

****

Learning Outcomes from Part Three:

1. Love is inside you. Start having some fun fine-tuning your unique style.
2. Enjoy the dating stage. It may be the only time for the rest of your life that you will get to have this kind of freedom!
3. Choose your best life with habits that keep your body, mind and spirit stimulated.
4. Choose your best life partner who naturally enjoys similar life habits as you.
5. Live in your "now", not in your "then".
6. Balance your life with a two-step of 'feel it and talk about it', so that you don't become emotionally unavailable 'avoiding' through your work or by compulsive 'do'ing'.
7. Keep your values front and center, because they will be your guides about how to live meaningfully.
8. Love the one you are with – You!

****

Gratitude

Take love in with a massive big breath of gratitude. Don't take anyone or anything for granted. Focus your thinking on the positive take-aways in your life experience because this will help you to build positive new brain pathways for your better life. Try to live with the attitude of giving more than you receive. If you can do this, I can assure you that you will be happier. Our world needs more people guided by this other-focused attitude of giving.

My hope for you is that after you have put into practice the life skills that I advocate, that you will have regained both confidence and trust in yourself. With trust, you will be better equipped to choose all the elements of your new and amazing life. You will be able to choose your home team that will work better for you. You will choose friends that will love you unconditionally through time. They will enrich and challenge you. Sometimes your friends will hold your feet to the fire and at other times cheer you on. So accept them just as they are, without the need to change or fix them. BE There for them too. Practice mindfulness. Let...go.

Love is a verb. Love is also an action statement of an activity that is unconditional and accepting. Love takes time. Trust that you have what it takes. If you sit back and enjoy the ride, if you can put the perspectives and skills that are in this book into play, you will discover your true self in all its original fullness. Congratulations. You know how to love again because you now have the requisite knowledge and the insights about yourself to be good at love. Have you noticed a new bounce in your step already? Can you sense a break-through? Look in the mirror to see your body, mind and spirit smile back at you.

My hope for you is that you are now deeply committed to a life of balance. Stress down, love up. So stay tuned. That is the subject of my next book in the Better Love Series! I'd like to leave you with a poem from a yoga class I recently attended while on vacation on Salt Spring Island, located off the coast from my home in West Vancouver. The author is unknown. Perhaps it resonates from a voice within us all.

GLOSSARY OF TERMS

Differentiation: a stage in our human development where we see our selves, our ideas and our values as unique and separate from the pressures of those around us.

Dream journal: when you wake up from a dream, write your dream down. Keeping a dream journal is a great way to gain insight into what is going on in your unconscious inner world. Everything you dream about is a part of your own psyche. So everyone in the dream and every 'thing' in the dream are all parts of your own psychological process. Dream journal can be great tools for processing emotions and a huge help to you get back to sleep if you have sleep interruptions. Don't let anyone but you do the interpreting! Dream journals can be helpful tools to bring to therapy or share with a friend. Remember its your unconscious not someone else's that you want to gain insight from!

Emotional Fusion: when your thoughts and feelings are 'the same as your partner' and you don't share anything that might challenge your partner. This is the basic tenant of the pleasing personality, when maintain peace becomes more important than being honest. The underlying fear is loss of the relationship, and a consequence is a loss of the true self. If your partner is upset with you, you feel devastated. The greater the emotional fusion, the more roller coaster ride in the relationship. Murray Bowen coined this term. See Bowen Family Systems Theory.

Extrovert: someone who resources themselves by spending time with others. An extrovert loves going to social events and time with others. In these settings he or she feels energetic and inspired. He or she likes to process thinking with others. Ideas develop in the mix of the group. An extrovert wants to talk ideas through with you as he or she is thinking of them.

External Processor: someone who processes thoughts in the sharing of information. This person tends to figure things out with others.

Internal Processor: someone who tends to figure out things out inside his or her own head before sharing his or her thoughts with the person he or she is relating to.

Introvert: someone who resources themselves by spending time on his or her own. An introvert loves quiet time and refuels spiritually in activities such as reading, and participating in activities that are more solitary. An introvert likes to think things through internally using the things already in his or her head. Generally an introvert will talk, once he or she has figured out the problem and the solution. The Myers & Briggs Personality Inventory describes this in more detail.

Insecure attachment style: when there has been a loss of care due to parental neglect or childhood attachment wounds between parent and child, due to illness, loss, or family addiction. People with insecure attachment styles are highly reactive in relationship. Secure attachments tend to have greater levels of intimacy and emotional safety. For this reason, the relationship may be more enduring.

Limbic Resonance: when you share deep emotional experiences with someone else, you are in 'resonance'. It can be thought of as a mood contagion when you and another are in feeling of empathic connection. Limbic resonance includes all feelings—love, anger, and fear.

Mirror Neurons: the start of emotional regulation. Your capacity for empathy is experienced through your mirror neurons. You feel other people's emotion through this function of your brain. Mirror neurons are the start of emotional regulation. (see below for emotional regulation).

Projection: When a person attributes his or her own deficit feelings or failings on another.

Scripts: the stories or details that fulfill schemas. They are the expectation of things that occur within a given situation or structure. We all have scripts about what people do when they are in a relationship. Scripts help us organize our memories.

Schema: organizing your expectation around a situation. It's the way your memory organizes the way you come to think about structures; like what a relationship is.

Self regulate: manage your feelings—calm yourself when you are upset, and pick yourself up when you are feeling low. It is the ability to self soothe so that you can communicate in a way that preserves emotional safety between you and the receiver.

Triangulation: distracting off conflict with one person, by seeking to reinforce with a third person. In doing so, the conflict is unresolved and the 'issue' develops a political strong hold. The more positional one is in the process of conflict, the more this pattern will show up. This is a term defined in Bowen Family Systems.

Withdraw-withdraw: a relationship pattern whereby the individuals in the couple partnership, go inside and stop talking to their partner. Their body language then is closed and the relationship is consequently under risk of dissolution. Other combinations are Pursue-withdraw (where one person is reaching to connect and the other person withdraws), Pursue-pursue (a highly emotional relationship sometimes with high reactivity. In this case, both people are actively trying to connect emotional with each other.

May the Long Time Sun Shine Upon You

All Love Surround You

And the Pure Light Within You

Guide Your Way On

Sat Nam (Truth Identified, or True Identity)

ENDNOTES OF WORKS CITED

1. B.C. Vital Statistics, 140th Edition of its annual report. Life expectancy climbed, women 35 and older are having more babies than in previous years since 2002 an increase of 30.8 percent.
2. Dr. Kalman Heller, The Myth of the High Rate of Divorce, APA, Psych Central, May 10, 2013.
3. Daniel Siegel, MD., Mindsight, The New Science of Personal Transformation, (2010).
4. Josine Verhoeven, Journal of Molecular Psychology, Major Depressive Disorder and Accelaerated Cellular Aging, November, 2013. Study found that people with clinical depression had shorter telomeres than that of their healthy peers.
5. Harvill Hendrix, PhD., Helen Hunt, Receiving Love (2005).
6. Why Humans, Like Ants, Need a Tribe, Biologist E.O. Wilson, April 2, 2012 In Newsweek Magazine.
7. Aromatherapy Benefits: Scents for stress relief, by Elizabeth Scott, M.S., About.com Guide, May 14, 2011.
8. Tots Who Sleep Less Have More Behavior Problems, Journal of Developmental & Behavioral Pediatrics, July 10, 2013.
9. Judith Wallerstein, The Unexpected Legacy of Divorce: The 25-Year Landmark Study (Hyperion, 2000). For fuller discussion of how to help children of divorce move into adulthood see Judith Wallerstein and Sandra Blakeslee's, What about the Kids? Raising Your Children Before, During and After Divorce (Hyperion, 2003).

10. John Bransford, Marcia K. Johnson, State University New York, Contextual prerequisites for understanding: Some investigations of comprehension and recall, Elsvier, Volume 11, Issue 6, (December 1972), Pg. 717-726.

11. Mahatma Ghandi, Indian spiritual leader (1869 – 1948).

12. Dr. Brene Brown, The Power of Vulnerability: Teachings of Authenticity, Connection, and Courage (2013).

13. Male and Female Brains: Similarities and Differences, Education and Science (30, 567), Medicine and Health Science (1,159), Neurology (45).

14. The Male Brain, Louann Brizendine, M.D., (2010).

15. Dr. Christine Northrup, The Wisdom of Menopause.

16. Busby, D.M., Carroll, J.S., & Willoughby, B.J. (2010). Compatibility of restraint? The effects of sexual timing on marriage relationship. Journal of Family Psychology, 24, 766 – 774. The study looked at 2,035 married people ranging in age from 19 – 71 and in length of marriage from less than 6 months to more than 20 years. This research showed a positive correlation between time of consummation of the marriage and longevity.

17. Scientists develop new breath test for stress, March 18, 2013. Journal of Breath Research, Professor Paul Thomas, Loughborough University & Imperial College, London.

18. Effects of chewing gum on cognitive function, mood and physiology in stressed and non-stressed volunteers, A. Smith, Cardiff University, Center for Occupational and Health Psychology, School of Psychology, U.K., (Feb. 2010).

19. Buss & Shakelford, 1997, Susceptibility to infidelity in the first year of marriage. Journal of Research in Personality, 31, 193 – 221.).

20. Anderson, K.G., 2006, How well does paternity confidence match actual paternity? Evidence from worldwide nonpaternity rates. Current Anthropology 48, in press.).

21. English psychiatrist John Bowlby, psychologist Mary Ainsworth, researched primate and human bonding patterns as secure, avoidant, ambivalent, or disorganized developing from parenting styles. How we were parented as children, results in our adult patterns of attachment. Susan Johnson's book "Hold Me Tight" looks at how patterns of attach-

ment play out in our relationships in the present in a feelings approach to greater attunement.

22. Carolyn Myss, PH.D., Why People Don't Heal and How They Can, (2001).

23. Pay it Forward (2000). Movie starring Helen Hunt, Kevin Spacey, Directed by Mimi Leder. Troubled by his mother's alcohol addiction and fears of his abusive but absent father, a young boy attempts to make the world a better place after his teacher gives him that chance.

24. Message In A Bottle, 1999 romantic drama, directed by Luis Mandoki, based on novel (same name) by Nicolas Sparks.

25. Dan Goleman, Emotional Intelligence, (1995)

26. Web MD., Exercise and Depression, Dr. Joseph Goldberg, (2012).The American Journal of Psychiatry, Vol 158, No. 2, Feb. 2001. The Use of Complimentary and Alternative Therapies to Treat Anxiety and Depression.

27. Reported November 26, 2012 in the Globe & Mail, One of the authors, professor Gun Semin of Utrecht University, says the findings suggest smell plays a role in the way we communicate emotions. He explains his research may have practical applications, such as reducing anxiety in patients undergoing magnetic resonance imaging (MRI) tests by getting rid of the chemo signals of fear produced by previous patients. "If what we're saying is correct," he says, "then the odor [others] leave behind is actually going to amplify the fear they're going to have."

28. The Oxytocin Factor: Tapping the Hormone of Calm, Love, and Healing: Kerstin Uvnas Moberg, M.D., Ph.D., (2003).

29. Becks Depression Inventory, created by Aeron Beck, is a 21 question self report inventory measuring the severity of depression. There are many other depression assessment tools, but this one remains most widely used in the medical population.

30. Shumway & Kimball, (2012). Six essentials to achieve lasting recovery, Sumway & Wampler (2002). A behavioral focused measure for relationships. The couple behavior report (CBR). The American Journal of Family Therapy, 30, 311-321.

31. The Yoga-Sutra of Pantanjali: A New Translation with Commentary (Shambhala Classics) (2003).

32. Joshua K. Hartshorne, Nancy Salem-Hartshorne, Timothy S. Hartshorne, in press with Journal of Individual Psychology, Birth order effects in the formation of long-term relationships, Harvard University.

33. Dan Siegel, M.D., Mindsight: The New Science of Personal Transformation, Random House, (2010).

34. Dr. Susan Johnson, Hold Me Tight, Little Brown & Company, (2008).

35. Dr. Dan Siegal, Mindsight (above).

36. Joshua K. Hartshorne, et. Al., Birth order effects in the formation of long-term relationships, Journal of Individual Psychology, Harvard University, (2009).

37. In a Harvard Medical School report, being on your own increased the risk of early death by 24% in people 45 – 65, and by 12% in people 66 – 80 (Alice Park, Time Magazine (June 19, 2012).

38. Stress Statistics, American Psychological Association, American Institute of Stress, NY, (2013).

39. Amanda Klein, 'Text Messaging: Effects on Romantic Relations and Social Behavior,' (August 2012).

40. On Death and Dying, Kubler-Ross (1969).

41. Brian Mustanski, PhD., How Often Do Men Think of Sex, The Sexual Continuum (Dec. 6, 2011),

42. State of the Global Workplace Gallup, Employee Engagement Insights for Business Leaders Worldwide, (October 8, 2013).

43. "Secrets of the Super Young", Dr. David Weeks (Neuropsychologist) Royal Edinburgh Hospital (2012), studied 3,500 American and European volunteers between 18 – 102 and found their youthful looks were only 25% due to genetics. The rest were due to behavior, including sexual behavior.

44. David Schnarch, Passionate Marriage, Love, Sex and Marriage in an Emotinally Committed Relationship, Barnes & Noble, 2009

45. Dr. Pat Love, Hot Monogamy: Essential Steps to More Passionate, Intimate Lovemaking, (2012)

46. Sex lowers blood pressure. A Brigham Young University study (2008) Annal of Behavioral Medicine, found that happily married people had lower blood pressure than singles; and even lower blood pressure, yet than unhappily married people. The study concluded that even singles with strong social networks did not fare as well with blood pressure

than the happily married study subjects. This suggests happy close love relationships can be good for heart health.

47. Boost Immunity. Scientists at Wilkes University in Pennsylvania say sex can boost your immunity – specifically raise your levels of immunoglobulin A (IgA), an antibody that can prevent the cold or flu. The Wilkes researchers asked more than 100 undergrads how many times they had sex in the previous month. They also measured the amounts of IgA in the subjects' saliva. The results: those who had sex once or twice weekly had 30% more IgA in their saliva than those who did the deed less than once a week.

48. Reduced depression: University of Albany suggests that women who have sex without condoms are less depressed than women who use them. In the 2002 study, 300 women filled out anonymous questionnaires that determined elements of their sexual behavior. Respondents also completed the Becks depression Inventory (BDI). The women in the study who engaged in sexual intercourse without condoms had lower BDI scores, indicating they were less depressed. Scientists say semen contains mood-altering chemicals that can elevate mood when absorbed vaginally. Lead researcher Prof. Gordon Gallup, doesn't suggest not using condoms – the unwanted pregnancy & sexually transmitted diseases.

49. Lower mortality: a study of nearly 1,000 middle-aged men published in a 1997 edition of the British Medical Journal tracked the relationship between orgasms and mortality. Researchers of the 10-year study found that the mortality rate dropped by 50% in the men with "high orgasmic frequency" compared to men who had fewer orgasms.

50. Babies choose sides before they can speak, (UBC Study, as reported in the Vancouver Sun, March 13, 2013). Babies, based on an in-born developing propensity to like those who have similar features to themselves and dislike those who don't. "These tendencies are already operative in the first year of life" (Dr. Kiley Hamlin)

51. Adrian Furnham, Professor of Psychology at University College London, as reported in The Sunday Times, www.thesundaytimes.co.uk [http://www.thesundaytimes.co.uk], Feb. 12, 2012.

FastPencil

http://www.fastpencil.com